Forgive Us Our Debts

Forgive Us Our Debts

The Intergenerational Dangers of Fiscal Irresponsibility

Andrew L. Yarrow

Yale University Press

New Haven and London

Set in Adobe Garamond and Stone Sans by The Composing Room of Michigan,
Inc., Grand Rapids, Michigan.
Printed in the United States of America.

Library of Congress Cataloging-in-Publication Data

Yarrow, Andrew L.
Forgive us our debts : the intergenerational dangers of fiscal irresponsibility /
Andrew L. Yarrow.
    p.   cm.
Includes bibliographical references and index.
ISBN 978-0-300-12353-1 (alk. paper)

  1. Debts, Public—United States.   2. Budget deficits—United States.
3. Fiscal policy—United States.   I. Title.
HJ8119.Y37 2008
336.3'40973—dc22

                                                              2007038338

A catalogue record for this book is available from the British Library.

The paper in this book meets the guidelines for permanence and durability
of the Committee on Production Guidelines for Book Longevity of the
Council on Library Resources.

10 9 8 7 6 5 4 3 2 1

To my son, Richard, and to the memory of my mother, Marian Yarrow, and of my father, Leon Yarrow.

Contents

Acknowledgments

Many people are deserving of thanks for their varied contributions to this work. Mike O'Malley, my editor at Yale University Press, has provided encouragement, advice, and wise and prompt feedback. Dan Heaton, Alex Larson, and others at the Press also have provided great assistance in bringing this book to publication. Many budget scholars, political scientists, and policy makers have provided considerable input and advice. These include former Representative William Frenzel (R-Minn.) and Representative Jim Cooper (D-Tenn.); Bob Bixby at the Concord Coalition; Ron Haskins and Alice Rivlin at the Brookings Institution; Stuart Butler, Alison Acosta Fraser, and Mike Franc at the Heritage Foundation; Eugene Steuerle at the Urban Institute; former Congressional Budget Office director Douglas Holtz-Eakin; Joe Antos at the American Enterprise Institute; Maya MacGuineas at the New America Foundation and Committee for a Responsible Federal Budget; Ruth Wooden at Public Agenda; Jim Capretta at the Ethics and Public Policy Center; Jared Bernstein at the Economic Policy Institute; Richard Gross, formerly the op-ed page editor of the *Baltimore Sun;* Robert Samuelson at *Newsweek;* Rich Wolf and

George Hager at *USA Today;* Comptroller General David Walker and Susan Irving at the U.S. Government Accountability Office; Professor Hugh Heclo at George Mason University; Charles Kolb and Joe Minarik at the Committee for Economic Development; Stan Collender at Qorvis Communications; Diane Rogers and others on the staff of the House Budget Committee; Sarah Kline and Lee Price on the Senate Banking Committee; David Vandivier, Doug Steiger, Joan Huffer, Jim Hearn, and others on Senator Kent Conrad's and Senator Judd Gregg's staffs on the Senate Budget Committee; Assistant Treasury Secretary Phillip Swagel; and Peter Orszag, Congressional Budget Office director.

The View from Washington: Six Democrats and Six Republicans Talk About Debt

Kent Conrad (D-N.D.): The long-term deficit outlook is bleak, the nation's debt continues to pile up at an unsustainable rate, and the Bush administration has done nothing but make it all much worse. Despite claims that the deficit is coming down, it is still projected to explode over the long term, as the rising cost of the president's tax cuts collide with the coming retirement of the baby boom generation. (July 11, 2006)

Mike Crapo (R-Idaho): Our budget process is broken. Riddled with gimmicks and obfuscation, the current spending framework allows unfunded obligations to pile up virtually unchecked. Right now, mandatory spending grows at 8 percent annually—with no braking mechanism. All responsibility for payments is pushed forward onto the undeserving shoulders of our children and grandchildren. (June 21, 2006)

Chris Dodd (D-Conn.): Deficits act as a hidden tax on working families by driving up interest rates on loans for homes, cars, college, and small businesses. Most importantly, they are a massive debt we pass on to our children. The administration has created a government by credit card—with the bills being paid by future generations. (February 22, 2004)

Judd Gregg (R-N.H.): We cannot turn a blind eye to our long-term fiscal challenges. With the massive baby boom generation beginning to retire in 2008 and health care costs spiraling ever higher, we are facing a fiscal and demographic tsunami . . . Congress must stop looking at the next election and instead look at the next generation. (August 4, 2006)

Chuck Hagel (R-Neb.): At some point, we've got to come forward with some courage and discipline to stop this massive hemorrhaging of federal spending. . . . The American people deserve better than a U.S. Senate out of control with no fiscal discipline—further eroding the economic strength of this country, and continuing to pile up more and more debt for future generations. (May 4, 2006)

Edward Kennedy (D-Mass.): Sanity must be restored to the budget process. As was evident in the 1990s, sound fiscal discipline is central to strong economic growth. The country can be fiscally responsible while at the same time upholding its values and priorities to help those individuals most in need. (Senator Kennedy's Web site)

John McCain (R-Ariz.): We're hurting our children, our grandchildren, and who knows how many future generations of Americans. It is perhaps my greatest hope, Mr. President, that some day we'll consider tax and spending measures with no one else in mind but future generations of American taxpayers. We're tying a millstone of debt around their necks, and it is a grave mistake. (September 23, 2004)

Barack Obama (D-Ill.): We're mortgaging our future. We're taking a credit card for our children, in our children's name and our grandchildren's, and we're running up the card and being completely irresponsible. (May 6, 2005)

Ken Salazar (D-Colo.): This is recklessness at its worst, and we can do better than leveraging away this nation's fiscal future. (March 16, 2004)

Arlen Specter (R-Pa.): As the United States faces enormous deficits, discretionary spending has taken hits year after year. Congressional budgeteers and appropriators have not sufficiently recognized that education and health care are capital investments. (February 8, 2005)

John Thune (R-S.D.): Every South Dakota family must live within a budget; I don't understand why the federal government cannot do the same. (Senator Thune's Web site)

Ron Wyden (D-Ore.): It's time for a return to economic sanity. Let's overhaul the tax code and stop—for our children and our future—playing games with America. (April 14, 2006)

Chapter 1 What Are Deficits and Debt, and Why Are They Growing?

There are no representatives of future generations to protest against the burdens imposed on them as the ultimate consequence of postponement [of debt reduction], and to threaten vengeance at the polls.
T. David Zukerman, 1925

"What will you do about the deficit?"
"Nothing, Madame. It is too serious."
attributed exchange between Marie Antoinette
and Louis XVI's finance minister Jacques Necker

Everyone borrows money at one time or another. As Cole Porter might have put it, mans do it, clans do it, even Central Asian–stans do it; let's do it: let's fall in debt! We borrow to buy houses or go to college, for capital investment in new factories or highways, or to wage wars. If going into debt is for useful or necessary purposes that have a long-term payoff, and one expects to be able to pay back one's debts, borrowing can be beneficial. Responsible people and entities gauge their need and their ability to pay, and over time they pay back what they have borrowed.

If they do not, there are powerful moral, legal, economic, and psychological consequences. For much of the history of Western civilization, those who fail to repay their debts have been regarded as sinners, cheats, profligates, or even thieves. Legally, failure to pay back borrowed money under the terms of a loan can lead to foreclosure, garnishment of assets, criminal prosecution, and/or bankruptcy. And economically, sinking into unpayable debt leads to an inability to spend money on needed or desired goods or services, thus diminishing well-being, often to the point of poverty or bankruptcy. Psychologically, spending more than one earns and accumulating more and more debt can lead to stress, lowered self-image, even desperation.

The strictures against going into debt too far, or for too long, are deeply ingrained in Judeo-Christian culture. In the Book of Proverbs, the Bible warns that "the borrower is servant to the lender," and Psalms 37:21 offers the more pointed injunction that "the wicked borrow and don't pay back." Similarly, more than two thousand years ago, the Roman author Publilius Syrus declared that "debt is the slavery of the free."[1]

Such ideas, as we shall see, were fervently embraced from the beginnings of American history, when the famously frugal Benjamin Franklin warned that "he who goes a borrowing goes a sorrowing." George Washington set the moral and political tone for two hundred–plus years of public-finance discussions, saying that dangers lurked when governments did not quickly repay their debts. Indeed, throughout U.S. history, Americans and their leaders have cherished balanced budgets and been appalled by deficits (although some would say that deficits became more accepted by political elites as a result of post–World War II Keynesian economics).[2] Until the 1970s, during peacetime, and over the long haul, Americans basically succeeded at keeping deficits low.

Which brings us to today, when—despite centuries of distaste for debt—the United States will be nearly $10 trillion in debt by Election Day 2008. It has promised another $50 trillion or so in explicit and implicit benefits to be paid in the future—a number that has almost doubled during the presidency of George W. Bush; in fiscal parlance, these are "unfunded liabilities," which businesses and state and local governments are forced to report on their books—but the federal government is not.[3] To put these numbers in varying perspectives, $50 trillion is equal to nearly 100 percent of Americans' total net worth—everything that we as individuals, as businesses, and as a country own. It also adds up to a cool half a million dollars in debt for every American household. These numbers exclude an additional $2 trillion in state and local government debt and unfunded liabilities for employee pension and health care benefits.

	2000	2006	% Increase
• Explicit liabilities	$6.9	$10.4	52

• Publicly held debt
  • Military & civilian pensions & retiree health
  • Other			

• Commitments & contingencies	0.5	1.3	140
• E.g., PBGC, undelivered orders			
• Implicit exposures	13.0	38.8	197
• Future Social Security benefits	3.8	6.4	
• Future Medicare Part A benefits	2.7	11.3	
• Future Medicare Part B benefits	6.5	13.1	
• Future Medicare Part D benefits		7.9	
Total	$20.4	$50.5	147

Figure 1. Major long-term fiscal exposures, 2000–2006: national debt plus unfunded liabilities, in trillions. *Sources:* David M. Walker, "Saving Our Future Requires Tough Choices Today," presentation, Denver, Nov. 28, 2006; Government Accountability Office, 2007

They also exclude Americans' $2 trillion in consumer debt and $10 trillion in total personal debt, which rose to 130 percent of disposable income in 2007, a statistic made more haunting by the late-2007 credit crunch that may lead to at least one million home foreclosures and two million personal bankruptcy filings in 2008. While deficits have dipped somewhat toward the end of the Bush administration, they are poised to explode over the next ten to twenty years, as health care costs march upward and baby boomers retire, potentially adding tens of trillions of dollars of additional debt.[4]

To say that something is wrong with this picture, as virtually every politician and budget analyst at least *says,* is a bit of an understatement.[5] Yet Congress has repeatedly, and oh so easily, raised the national debt ceiling—the official limit on government borrowing—five times between 2001 and 2007, by nearly $4 trillion. Meanwhile, America's ratio of debt to national income, or gross domestic product (GDP), rose from 57 percent to 66 percent in the four years beginning in 2001.[6]

Anyone who has visited Disney World's Haunted Mansion remembers the ride's signature beginning: visitors enter a room, the doors close and the ceiling appears to keep rising and rising as a spooky voice intones that there is "no way out." America's national debt bears frightening similarities to this Disney attraction. The debt ceiling, like the physical ceiling of the Haunted Mansion, keeps rising and rising, and whether there is a "way out" is a matter of economic

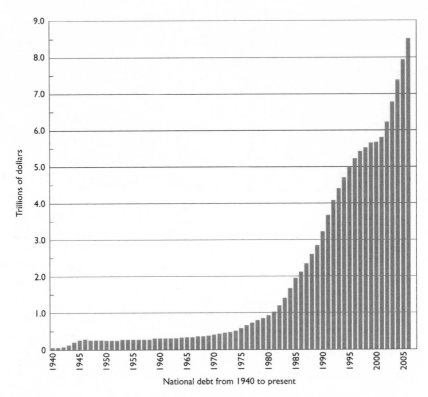

Figure 2. National debt, 1940–2006, without adjusting for inflation. *Source:* National Debt Clock, www.brillig.com/debt_clock/

and policy debate and political will. Either way, the prospect of runaway deficits and debt is a good bit scarier—and distinctly less illusory—for the American people and their nation's future than Disney's animatronic wizardry.

But the ceiling isn't rising because there is nothing we can do about it. The Congress and the president are consciously making decisions to increase spending while cutting taxes and thus decreasing revenues. The 109th Congress, which slipped into the night of history in January 2007, passed legislation that increased projected deficits through 2011 by $452 billion—more than the global sales of America's big three automakers in 2006.[7] And President Bush and the Congress pushed through six tax cuts during the Bush administration's first five years, resulting in about $1 trillion in lost revenues during those years. If the Bush tax cuts are extended beyond their nominal expiration in 2010, the losses to the U.S. Treasury are projected to be a mind-boggling $3.6 trillion between 2008 and 2017. Moreover, if the alternative minimum tax—designed to better capture revenues from upper-income taxpayers, but now plaguing some twenty-three million middle-class filers—is reformed, as most Democrats and Republicans pledge, the government would lose another $750 billion to $1.2 trillion in revenues over a decade. And Republican talk of repealing the estate tax would result in another $1 trillion in lost revenues in ten years.[8] The businessman and budget hawk Peter Peterson has said that "long-term tax cuts without long-term spending cuts are not tax cuts."[9] Essentially, it is as if you bought more and more and ran your credit card debt ever higher while your income and ability to pay it off were going down. But the mantra of many Americans and their elected leaders appears to be that of the caricatured housewives of *The Flintstones,* who emphatically said, in earlier days of consumer credit: "Charge it!"

So whether we piously read the Bible, follow Washington policy wonks' warnings, or are spooked out in Disney's Haunted Mansion, year upon year of borrowing to pay for some of the costs of the federal government is inexorably raising America's national debt to the point that some sort of economic meltdown seems increasingly likely. Ever since the presidency of Ronald Reagan, growing deficits and debt have been the subjects of much political hand-wringing, and occasional constructive action. Bill Clinton, the Congress, and a strong economy conspired to give us four years of unexpected budget surpluses between 1998 and 2001, but the turnaround from 2001's projected ten-year surpluses of $5.6 trillion to the deficits of the early 2000s represents a staggeringly rapid deterioration of America's fiscal position.

While there are many causes of deficits—and their relative importance is fiercely debated—first things first: what are deficits and debt, and do they matter?

In this and the following chapters, I will look at the nature, scope, causes, and history of America's national debt. I will explore the consequences of our fourteen-digit debt for the nation's economy and for individuals, if we continue on our current path of fiscal recklessness. I will examine the political torpor that has allowed our debt to grow like some alien life form out of a 1950s science fiction movie. And finally, I will consider what politicians have done in the past and what *could* be done to rid our nation of its potentially ruinous debt.

For governments, deficits represent the imbalance between revenues and spending, which requires borrowing money. They are a form of what economists call "negative savings." Debt is the accumulation of deficits, with a portion of the borrowed money owed to individuals, financial institutions, and other countries' investors and financial institutions in the form of U.S. Treasury securities (T-bills, notes, bonds, and so on), and a portion owed to other U.S. government entities. Yet either form of debt represents money that is not being saved, not available to be spent on other things (be it a nation's stronger defense or a household's new car), and liable to interest payments. Although medieval Christians railed against "money-lending" and "usury," modern economists of all stripes recognize that money—like any other good or service—has a cost, and that cost takes the form of interest payments. In the 2008 fiscal year the U.S. government is projected to pay $261 billion in taxpayer dollars in interest payments—half of that to foreigners—and present trends suggest that that amount will skyrocket past half a trillion dollars in a few years. The expense is projected to consume half of all government revenues by the 2030s—and all of them a decade later. In fact, interest payments, expanding by 20 percent a year, are the fastest-growing part of our budget. And the projections assume that interest rates won't go through the roof. Even $261 billion is more than the federal government currently spends on education, homeland security, justice, science, natural resources, and the Departments of State and the Treasury put together, or on the Iraq War.[10]

While I focus in this book on federal budget deficits and national debt, many commentators note that budget deficits are only one of three or four serious deficits facing our nation. America's enormous, and rising trade or the related current-account deficits more than doubled between 2001 and 2006 to $900 billion.[11] The country has amassed a personal savings deficit; beginning in 2005 Americans, on average, are for the first time since the Depression spending more than they earn, whereas they saved about 8 percent of their income in the mid-1980s. And many observers cite a "leadership deficit," suggesting that, despite all the lip service paid to reducing deficits and balancing the budget, most politicians not only are not doing anything constructive to reduce deficits but are actively doing things to make them worse.[12] They are increasing spending, including on pork-barrel "bridges to nowhere," and cutting taxes as if balance sheets need not balance. These four deficits exclude state and local governments, which are collectively in debt despite many states' legal requirement to balance their budgets, and which are being further squeezed financially by federal deficits and fiscal policy. Net national savings is the combination of government surpluses or deficits, personal savings (or debt), and business savings. With only the business sector in the black, net national savings have fallen precipitously in recent years.

But, like Chicken Little, armies of everyone from conservative Republicans to liberal Democrats histrionically have warned that the specter of deficits is haunting America and that the sky will soon fall. President George W. Bush has said that "future generations shouldn't be forced to pay back money that we have borrowed," and that the continuing excess of spending over revenues "will leave future generations with impossible choices—staggering tax increases, immense deficits, or deep cuts in every category of spending."[13] He is right, although his actions belie his noble words.

Yet, look up: the sky is still hanging in there.

Despite a stable but somewhat cloudy sky, deficits are already distorting, if not harming, both the public and private sectors of our economy. It is certainly true, as the twentieth century's most influential economist, John Maynard Keynes, argued, that governments can stimulate the economy by occasionally running deficits either through tax cuts or increased government spending. So, as John Kennedy said in 1963, proposing growth-inducing tax cuts and deficit spending, and George W. Bush said after 9/11, such short-term "countercyclical" deficits can pull America out of recession and stimulate growth. Moreover, many economists believe that deficits need not pose a significant economic threat, so long as the economy is growing at least as fast as the accumulation of debt, and deficits are relatively low—say, 1 or 1½ percent of national output, or GDP. A few economists argue that the threat of deficits is overstated, as totals of liabilities, or debt, ignore government assets and fail to correct for inflation.[14] And a growing cadre of policy types see deficits more as a symptom than as the core problem—a subject to which we will return.

However, most economists believe that long-term "structural" deficits and large deficits or debt—above a much-argued-about threshold proportion of GDP—have the potential to wreak havoc. But do they simply create a drag on the U.S. economy by slowly increasing interest rates, crowding out other spending, decreasing growth, and making living standards improve less quickly, or are they like "a category 6 hurricane," as U.S. Comptroller General David Walker, the outspoken official chief auditor of America's finances, has said?[15] Many believe that some sort of crisis will ensue if deficits continue to grow on their current trajectory—rising to levels at which entitlement programs, interest on the federal debt, and other mandatory spending programs will absorb all federal revenues at historical levels in about two decades.

Of course, these assume current trajectories—an assumption that often famously has been proven wrong. For example, the Bureau of the Census in 1946 projected that the U.S. population in 2000 would be half of what it turned out to be. Similarly, when Medicare was enacted in 1965, government actuaries projected that Part A would cost $9 billion a year in 1990, much less than it actually turned out to cost by that year.[16] So much for projections! Wise policy decisions, very strong economic growth, and unexpected demographic changes could ameliorate or eliminate deficits and bring down the debt. But to avoid the need for more draconian and painful policy changes later, we need to begin acting now. On the other hand, policies that make the problem worse—as have all too often been enacted—and weaker-than-expected economic or population growth could make deficits and their effects larger and more harmful than projected.

Yet all indicators suggest—and almost all informed observers agree, conservative and liberal alike—that in the absence of significant, if not radical, policy changes, deficits and debt will grow and could cause catastrophic damage to the United States. Former Federal Reserve Chairman Paul Volcker has predicted a 75 percent chance of "crisis" by the end of this decade. His successor, Alan Greenspan, has said that "deficits must matter" and could bring "economic devastation." Bill Clinton's Treasury secretary, Robert Rubin, has declared that "we confront a day of serious reckoning." President Reagan's chief economist, Martin Feldstein, has said that "persistent budget deficits are harmful" and "impose a burden on future generations." And these opinions are echoed by the pooh-bahs on Washington's think tank row—ranging from Urban Institute President Robert Reischauer, who has said that a deficit "tsunami" is heading toward shore, to C. Fred Bergsten, director of the Peter Peterson Institute for International Economics, who has said that if budget and trade deficits continue to grow, "things can get pretty nasty."[17]

Others have suggested that the damage wrought by deficits may be more like gradual erosion than a tsunami—or like smoking, which won't kill you overnight, but probably will in the long run. Charles Schultze, a former top economic adviser to Presidents Kennedy and Johnson, has said: "The problem is not that the wolf is at the door. It's more like termites in the woodwork."[18]

Although what that damage would look like is the subject of heated debate, the possibilities are not pretty—a depression or severe recession, falling living standards for the average American, a boarded-up U.S. government, a banana republic–style U.S. default on its debts, and a dramatic long-term loss of U.S. economic and geopolitical power and prestige. Many economists and political scientists have noted that world power generally goes hand in hand with being a creditor nation.[19] Moreover, as Feldstein and others point out, the potential damage of deficits is moral as well as economic: by amassing debt that presum-

Figure 3. February 2006 *AARP Bulletin* cover. Used with permission

ably will have to be paid at some time, current generations are passing the costs of their fiscal profligacy on to their children and grandchildren.

So why don't we—the American people and our elected leaders—act? Why don't we rise up in arms, say that this unacceptable, and work with—or push—our leaders to take constructive steps to reduce our national debt, address its causes, and prevent the potentially hazardous effects of doing nothing?

Brian Riedl of the Heritage Foundation has written: "The bipartisan consensus [is to] ignore the problem and let the next generation deal with it."[20] That attitude is somewhat akin to taking your infant granddaughter to the Mercedes dealer, buying a CL-class coupe on credit, cooing at her, and saying,

"You can pick up the tab for me in twenty-five years." Similarly, two babies, arm in arm, were pictured under the headline "$156,000 in Debt" on the cover of a magazine published by AARP (formerly the American Association of Retired Persons), belying the stereotype of greedy seniors. As Herbert Hoover once said: "Blessed are the young for they shall inherit the national debt."[21]

Waiting is not only morally wrong and politically irresponsible. It also will make any solutions more difficult. The sooner we begin to take action, the less difficult, costly, socioeconomically disruptive, and controversial it will be to dig ourselves out of our debt morass. Conversely, the more we delay, the more costly it will be—economically, politically, and psychologically—to reduce our national debt and address its causes.

GOVERNMENT SPENDING AND REVENUES

Federal government spending has grown enormously over the past few generations. President Bush's 2009 budget request is approximately $3 trillion. That is about 21–22 percent of the entire U.S. economy, and doesn't count another $2 to $3 trillion in state and local government spending, although nearly half a trillion dollars of that total comes out of federal grants to the states.[22] The federal $3 trillion also does not include as much as $800 billion a year in "tax expenditures" through tax breaks to corporations and individuals. Many liberals would say that deficits are largely a function of insufficient revenues, made worse by recent tax cuts that have decreased federal revenues from about 20 percent of GDP around 2000 to 16 percent today. Many conservatives would say that deficits are largely a function of spending, although Republican George W. Bush and a Congress under Republican control until 2007 have irked many conservatives for increasing spending by about 5 percent a year in inflation-adjusted terms, or 60 percent. That is more than two and a half times as fast as spending increased under Democrat Bill Clinton, although neither Democrats nor Republicans have been shy about spending ever more. Greenspan said: "My biggest frustration remained [Bush's] unwillingness to wield his veto against out of control spending."[23] And that rate of spending growth makes Bush the biggest of the big-time spenders since Lyndon Johnson.

Most, however, would agree with the editors of *Business Week,* who proclaimed: "The deficit morass is due as much to a revenue shortfall as to excessive spending."[24] Yet saying that the problem of—and by implication the solution to—America's fiscal woes stems from both factors, while accurate, fudges the issue. How much are spending and revenues "off," and by what standard? If revenues are too little and spending is too much, why is this so, and what do we do about it? And—because in an ever-changing society and political process, neither revenues nor spending is static—which way are both headed and why?

It is these questions that provoke often bitter debate and seem to stymie politicians, policy wonks, and the other exotic inhabitants of the Alice in Wonderland world of budgeting.

The short, simple answers are: Due to tax cuts, a disastrously complex and unfair tax system, and inadequate tax collection that misses hundreds of billions of dollars of owed taxes each year, revenues *are* too little. Due to rapid increases primarily in America's three big "mandatory" entitlement programs—Social Security, Medicare, and Medicaid—but due also to increases in defense and much other "discretionary" spending, spending *is* too high. Polls regularly show that most Americans 1) want government to do more for them and 2) want to pay less in taxes. To paraphrase Bob Dylan, you don't need an accountant to know which way this wind is blowing.

With America graying, its over-sixty-five population multiplying, and health care costs increasing annually by an average over the past half century of 2½ percentage points more than national income, the gorilla in this fiscal jungle is entitlement-program spending. "Entitlements"—a nifty term that neatly emerged with the society-owes-me-something culture of recent decades—are technically benefits for a legally specified population that are automatically funded in the budget (rather than debated and voted upon by Congress). With the first of seventy-eight million baby boomers able to claim Social Security benefits in 2008 (and up to three-quarters are expected to retire and file early, at age sixty-two), then becoming entitled to Medicare benefits in 2011, spending will really start to go haywire—unless something is done. And despite a U.S. life expectancy that has risen by thirty years during the past century, more Americans are retiring earlier, unsustainably devouring our public and private pension systems.[25]

If no reforms are made in these programs and our tax system, Medicare spending—which accounted for 1 percent of GDP in 1975 and 3.2 percent in 2006—will pass 4 percent in 2015, 7 percent in the early 2030s, and 10 percent in about fifty years, although these estimates are clouded by such factors as Americans' health, the economy's health, population, and how long people work. Similarly, Social Security is projected to rise from 4.2 percent of GDP in 2005 to 6.2 percent in 2030. And Medicaid is on target to double its share of GDP, rising from just over 2 percent in 2005 to about 4.5 percent in 2030. As a share of federal spending, Medicare and Medicaid have risen from 5 percent in

1970 to 18 percent in 2000, careening toward 25 percent by 2010. In 2007 Medicare and Social Security together passed the trillion-dollar mark for the first time.[26]

While these numbers reflect how much the three entitlements will grow as a share of America's entire economy, their effects on the federal government and its budget will be even more devastating. On our current course, Medicare's trustees say that the program will go broke in about a decade, conveniently two years after Social Security's long-running surpluses turn into deficits in 2017 (but still two decades before Social Security runs out of money). The three programs, which consumed a negligible portion of federal spending as late as the early 1970s, but 42 percent of a much bigger budgetary pie in 2006, would represent 56 percent of federal spending by 2016 and devour all of government (if it stays at its current size relative to the overall U.S. economy) by the early to mid-2040s.[27]

If we keep our current promises to pay the benefits lurking behind these numbers, federal revenues—yes, that means taxes—will have to increase by 50 percent. If the so-called "tax freedom" day—imputing the portion of the year one has to work to pay all taxes—is now in early May, that means it would then coincide with Fourth of July fireworks. What a celebration! Of course, we can all picture a politician calling for a 50 percent tax increase, and a docile population happily agreeing to it. On the other hand, it's about as hard to picture politicians stranding tens of millions of elderly Americans without the Medicare and Social Security benefits that they have been promised all their working lives.

So, what gives—or will have to give?

With the aging of America's population, most observers concede that the federal government will have to grow relative to the size of the economy, which means more spending and either more taxes or more debt. The feds already spend about $24,000 per household. Given most experts' projections for entitlement spending, the federal government would have to increase its share of the economy from about 20 percent, where it has hovered for the past fifty years, to 28 percent in little more than two decades. Just another two decades down the road, in 2050, federal spending would rise to 37 percent of GDP, with interest payments on the national debt consuming more than 20 percent of the economy.[28] And the only reason that the United States has been able to hold federal spending to 20 percent of GDP during the past fifteen to twenty years is the fortuitous fall of the Berlin Wall and a Cold War "peace dividend," as defense spending as a share of GDP declined from more than 10 percent to 3 to

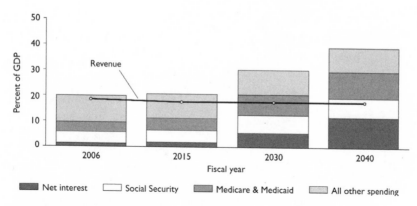

Figure 4. Composition of federal spending as a share of GDP, 2005–2040. *Source:* Government Accountability Office

4½ percent. But even a good bit of that "dividend" has disappeared, as Congress passed spending bills totaling $577 billion between 2001 and 2007 to pay for the wars in Afghanistan and Iraq, with another $472 billion forecast to be spent in coming years.[29] Likewise, the number of "earmarks"—funding for politicians' pet projects—grew eightfold from 1994 to 2006, with 15,500 earmarks costing $64 billion in 2006.[30] So looking ahead, if you add in state and local government spending, the U.S. public sector would be even larger than the largest European welfare state (not that some of them don't face similar, if not worse, prospects). And if some conservatives were carping about "creeping socialism" during the Truman and Eisenhower administrations, it is reasonable to imagine that their adjective du jour will accelerate from "creeping" to "galloping."

Even this scenario is premised on fiscally optimistic—read: foolish—assumptions. Is the rest of government going to vanish? Even if some conservatives and libertarians might like that to happen, they probably would not want to cut the 20 to 21 percent of the budget that now goes to defense, despite the fact that the Congressional Budget Office (CBO) assumes that defense spending will be cut in half as a percentage of GDP. Assuming constant interest rates, unless the United States reduces the debt itself, we can't cut the ever-rising portion of the budget that goes to paying interest to all those nice Chinese and Saudi lenders who keep our deficit binge going. (Yes, they're the ones who keep buying us another drink, but if they stop, what will a debtaholic America do?!) And without legislative change, they could not eliminate the other 12 percent of the

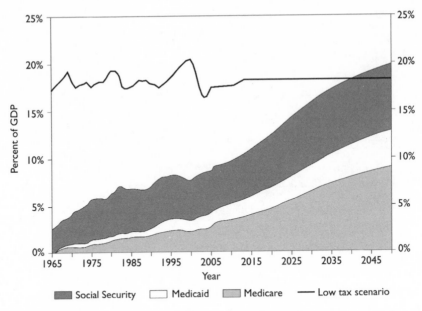

Figure 5. Entitlement spending growth as a percentage of GDP, 1962–2050. *Source:* Heritage Foundation

budget that goes to other "mandatory" programs such as unemployment insurance, veterans' benefits, agricultural aid, food stamps, and college loans.

So 42 percent of the budget goes to the big-three entitlements, 12 percent to other mandatory spending, about 9 percent to interest payment on the debt, 21 percent to defense, and 16 percent to domestic "discretionary" spending. Moreover, the United States "spends" about as much on tax breaks of myriad sorts, $800 billion, as it does on domestic discretionary spending—another fiscal trick that masks the true size of government.[31] Although under our constitutional system we elect leaders to, among other things, spend the public monies represented by our tax dollars, our elected leaders—and, by extension, voters—have control over barely one-third of federal spending. Although Congress theoretically could pass legislation to abolish Social Security or Medicare, or change the law so that benefits are drastically less, at this point at least, that is about as likely as the dream of the nineteenth-century French utopian that the seas could be turned to lemonade. Thus, for all practical purposes, the rest of federal spending (where our tax dollars go) is virtually on autopilot.

That leaves the terrain for other possible spending cuts to that 16 percent of the budget that goes to nondefense "discretionary" programs. This and de-

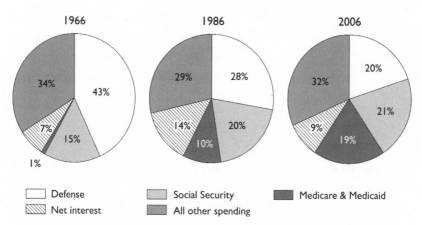

Figure 6. Composition of federal spending, 1966–2006. Because of rounding errors, some percentages do not total 100. *Source:* "Saving Our Future Requires Tough Choices Today," presentation, Denver, Nov. 28, 2006; Government Accountability Office, 2007

fense—which total a little more than a third of the budget—are the only parts of the budget that the Congress can directly control. The Senate and House vote on twelve annual appropriations bills that bundle together all defense and nondefense discretionary spending. Authority for this small slice of federal spending is vested in the Senate and House Appropriations Committees, and the Senate Finance Committee and the House Ways and Means Committee control tax legislation, among other things.

The discrepancy between fact and fiction in the federal budgeting process is another sorry tale. While one might expect the government to come up with a budget for the following fiscal year by the end of the current fiscal year, this has happened only a handful of times during the past thirty years. After the congressional committees issue budget resolutions—drawing on the president's budget, released each February, and CBO analyses—the full Congress theoretically must approve these twelve appropriations bills by the end of September for the president to either sign or veto. In recent reality, the process has been considerably more muddled. The full complement of appropriations bills has been passed by the beginning of the new fiscal year only four times since 1977, and Congress has passed ridiculous series of "continuing resolutions" (CRs, in Washington lingo), which extend current patterns of spending without forcing politicians to make tough choices. These CRs keep government from shutting down, as it did in 1995 and 1996, as well on brief occasions in 1981, 1984, and 1990. Moreover, the Congress increasingly has resorted to "emergency" spending measures that go beyond both mandated spending and the twelve appropriations bills; some have been for genuine emergencies such as Hurricane Katrina relief and Iraq War funding, although many have included billions for general Pentagon, NASA, and other agency operations, as well as additional farm subsidies that couldn't be passed as a part of the normal appropriations process.[32]

The percentage of the budget going to discretionary spending has fallen sharply since before the Vietnam War, as mandatory entitlement spending similarly has risen sharply.[33] But discretionary spending includes virtually everything else that government does. Lest one forgets, the U.S. government does quite a few things, as the roughly two thousand pages of the federal budget, with its line after line of programs, reminds one. These thousands of programs support everything from scientific research, education, federal law enforcement, and homeland security to the national parks, antipoverty programs, foreign policy, housing assistance for the middle class as well as the poor, environmental protection, job training, and hundreds of billions of dollars' worth of contracts and de facto aid programs for businesses and farmers. In fact, of the $412 billion spent on government contracts in 2006, 50 percent was awarded without competitive bidding.[34]

Think this is easy to cut? Congress went almost apoplectic in cutting the mammoth sum of 0.3 percent of discretionary and mandatory federal spending in the marvelously titled Balanced Budget Act of 2005. As in other efforts to "cut," cuts were nearly balanced by new spending. If we wanted to truly balance the budget this year without doing anything about revenues or entitlement spending, we would have to eliminate most civilian programs that Americans commonly think of as "the government." Although politicians are always out to protect their turf, as Tom DeLay may have been during his tenure as Republican whip, many conservatives would agree when the firebrand legislator conceded that there is "no fat left to cut in the federal budget."[35]

Despite all the talk of cutting, Democrats and Republicans alike, egged on by the American people, actually want to increase spending on many of these programs, not to mention adding expensive new initiatives. It may be hard to remember, or even imagine, from the vantage point of debt-besotted, early twenty-first-century America, but once—particularly from the 1930s to the early 1970s—government was an idealistic, if sometimes misbegotten, incubator of new initiatives to benefit the American people. While some may rightly disparage the mistakes of New Deal and Great Society liberalism, Democrats and Republicans both created a vast array of programs intended to make our nation a better place. And believe it or not, many of these worked! Aside from Social Security itself, or unemployment and disability insurance, think about the National Institutes of Health, the Peace Corps, Medicare, and the State Children's Health Insurance Program (SCHIP) health care program for poor children initiated under Democratic administrations, or the interstate highway system, the St. Lawrence Seaway, the Environmental Protection Agency, and the military buildup that may have hastened the end of the Cold War, all launched under Republican administrations. In fact, after twenty-five years of government bashing, a little history lesson is in order: Americans actually liked, believed in, trusted, and identified with their government before the Vietnam War, Watergate, and the post-1970s philosophical and political attacks on "big government."

Even today, despite the apparent cognitive dissonance—a fancy psychological term for having contradictory thoughts at the same time—while polls show that most Americans don't think much of government, they still want it to do more for them. One can get into fairly useless philosophical arguments about what the British once called the "nanny state"—a government that is asked to take care of almost every problem that its citizens can dream up. Yet most Americans agree that government could do a lot more than it is currently doing in quite a few realms. It could make preschool more widely available to lower-income families and college more affordable. It could fund research and development of alternative energy sources that would make us less dependent on foreign oil and the scary countries that produce it, pollute less, and reduce the threat of global warming. It could expand volunteer corps such as AmeriCorps and the Peace Corps to give young (and not-so-young) Americans a genuine opportunity to serve their country. It could help eradicate deadly diseases that kill millions in poor countries. And in our own country, it could more effectively collect health and other information that would improve the practice of medicine and help cut costs. The government could step up funding for cutting-edge technologies, given that so many technologies that have driven U.S. private-sector growth and transformed our lives—from computers and the Internet to medical technologies and jet airplanes—originated in government research labs. It could shore up our overburdened highways and airports, and support mass transit or the development of other vehicles to relieve America's traffic-choked highways. It could help make housing more affordable. It could strengthen our homeland defense and military. It could even reignite the space program, and put a woman (or a man) on Mars.

You could quibble with items on this list, or add to it. But it is easy to see that government could play a useful role in keeping America not just the wealthiest and strongest nation on earth but also a good place to live.

And this potential for *new* spending does not include responding to emergencies. These range from natural disasters and wars to epidemics and financial crises. Moreover, emergencies, by definition, are unexpected. Who's to say that some new virus won't cause significant numbers of human and/or animal deaths and illnesses, a hurricane or earthquake won't devastate an American city, millions of private borrowers or major company pension plans won't default, a civil war in Mexico won't send millions of refugees across the Rio Grande, or an unstable nuclear-armed state won't detonate a few bombs?

With entitlement spending eating up more and more of federal revenue, short of a surge in printing money or a burst of unprecedented economic growth, where are the dollars to come from? Vastly expanding the money supply is out of the question in our inflation-conscious world of central bankers who think not only of the Argentinas and Weimar Germanys of history but of the Jimmy Carter era, when fighting inflation was declared the "moral equivalent of war"—MEOW. And while financial types may salivate for the 9–10 percent economic growth that China is churning out year after year, in the United States—which is growing from a much higher baseline of wealth—most doubt that we can achieve *sustained* growth as high as the 3.3 percent real growth during the dot.com boom of the late 1990s, much less the 5 percent growth of the 1960s or the double-digit growth over seventy-five years that David Walker estimates would be necessary to close our fiscal gaps without any reforms.[36] In short, some facile rhetoric to the contrary, we cannot grow our way out of debt.

So that leads us either to reformed and increased taxes or entitlement and other spending reform—or both.

When most people think of government revenues, they think of April 15, the reviled tax day, and the hated Internal Revenue Service. As Will Rogers once said, "The income tax has made more liars out of the American people than golf has."[37] Income taxes devour three billion hours of Americans' lives every year, roughly one in every two hundred waking hours spent by the average taxpayer. This is just slightly less than the amount of time the average thirty-to-forty-nine-year-old spends having sex.[38] Tax preparation also costs the average taxpayer $200 in out-of-pocket expenses and costs the U.S. economy untold billions in lost productivity, with more paid tax preparers than doctors, high school teachers, or U.S. Army and Navy personnel combined. In addition, compliance costs are between one-tenth and one-seventh of the amount of taxes collected. Yet about $300 billion in taxes owed—more than recent, official deficits—go uncollected, as IRS enforcement resources have been cut sharply in recent years, and polls show that at least one-fifth of Americans think that it's okay to cheat on their taxes.[39]

Taxes are the major, but not the only, source of government revenues. However, the personal income tax accounts for a surprisingly small and declining fraction of federal revenues, and it is not as self-evident that taxes are simply too high, as many antitax zealots would say. Some believe that tax cuts either will pay for themselves by generating higher economic growth, and hence revenues, or will "starve the beast" of government spending. Yet only a fraction of the potentially lost revenue from tax cuts is actually recouped through stronger growth, according to such experts as President George W. Bush's former chief economist N. Gregory Mankiw and President Nixon's top economist Herb Stein. And William A. Niskanen of the conservative Cato Institute has found that tax cuts actually are associated with increased federal spending, whereas tax increases are associated with decreased spending. Niskanen's research revealed that over the past quarter-century, federal spending has risen the fastest when federal revenues have been at their lowest, as during the Bush administration.[40] In other words, tax cuts seem to provide the beast with a good, hearty meal. Despite many areas of disagreement, advocates of tax cuts and those who agree with Oliver Wendell Holmes, Jr., who said that "taxes are the price we pay for a civilized society," all probably would agree that America's tax system is horribly dysfunctional.

For most of the past half-century, tax revenues have averaged around 18.25 percent of GDP, give or take a percentage point. However, the composition of revenues has changed significantly. In 2005, as tax revenues fell to 16.3 percent of GDP in the wake of the Bush tax cuts, income tax payments had fallen to 7 percent of GDP, their lowest level in fifty-five years—while government spending became greater than ever. Perhaps surprisingly, less than half of government revenues come from personal income taxes. For all but those earning more than $100,000 a year, payroll tax payments—for Social Security and part of Medicare—are more than the sum of the federal income taxes deducted from their paychecks and submitted with their 1040s on April 15. These somewhat hidden taxes have shot up as a proportion of federal tax revenues from 8 percent after World War II to 38 percent early in the twenty-first century, while taxes paid by corporations (which, ultimately, are people) have fallen from 31 percent of federal revenues in 1946 to about 10 percent today, and excise taxes on goods such as gasoline or cigarettes have fallen from about 18 percent of revenues sixty years ago to 4 percent today. Estate taxes and customs duties bring in another 3 percent of revenues. The Byzantine federal tax code is about 17,000 pages long, with four times as many words as the Bible and a mind-boggling fourteen thousand tax-law changes in just the past twenty years—more than even the most knowledgeable accountant or tax lawyer could digest. (In fact, adding a few biblical injunctions to the tax code actually might improve this horrendous document.) In addition to tax revenues, government actually earns about a quarter-trillion dollars from some of its activities.[41] And the rest of what government spends is obtained by borrowing—that is, through deficits.

While federal income taxes—despite our annual agonies—have fallen as a proportion of how the government is funded, there are four historically significant ways in which the sources of federal revenues have changed in recent decades. The biggest is the shift of the revenue burden to payroll taxes, which are the most regressive, meaning that people earning about $95,000 a year pay the same percentage of income as those earning $30,000 a year—and a much *greater* percentage than those earning $1 million or $100 million a year. The second shift has to do with how the tax code underlying the personal income tax has changed—many, many times, as policy makers have shifted gears more often than a Le Mans racer—also becoming more regressive and favoring the wealthy. The Bush tax cuts yielded the average middle-income worker earning $56,000 in 2004 about $1,200, less than a week's tuition, room, and board at a private college, while a $1.25 million earner saved $58,000, the cost of a new Mercedes CLK coupe convertible.[42] The third long-term change has to do with the sharp decline in the taxes paid by businesses. Citizens for Tax Justice reported that 82 of America's 275 largest corporations figured out a way to pay no taxes in at least one year between 2001 and 2003.[43] One could chalk up the declining importance of corporate taxation to successful business lobbyists weaseling their way out of paying the government (all the while benefiting from federal tax subsidies, contracts, and direct payments) or to sensible tax policy that doesn't double-tax income. Both the second and third changes are matters of considerable controversy. The fourth is our old friend—funding government by borrowing money and going into debt.[44]

As noted, growing numbers of conservatives and most liberals believe that taxes will have to be increased. Many bipartisan efforts have been made either to raise taxes or broaden the tax base by getting rid of unfair and counterproductive tax breaks, and we will take a look at many proposals. Although reforming an overly complex and unfair tax system, increasing taxes, expanding the tax base, strengthening tax-collection enforcement, and/or adding new taxes will have to be part of the solution to our debt problem, the biggest contributors to America's fiscal woes are its entitlement programs.

THE BIG THREE

This brings us back to spending, but the big three entitlements—Social Security, Medicare, and Medicaid—are in a class of their own. Due to a combination of the way the programs are structured, the aging of the U.S. population, and—most important—rapidly rising health care costs, spending on these entitlements is what will send America careening toward enormous deficits in the decades ahead. (As always, the caveat must be, *unless something is done.*)

This is why many experts believe that while deficits and debt can bring catastrophic damage to the U.S. economy and Americans' living standards, the predominant root of the deficit problem is entitlement spending. That is not to say that taxes are not crying out for reform and probably need to be higher, or that other, wasteful spending cannot be cut. But the big kahuna is entitlements. And unbeknownst to most Americans, while Social Security may be the elephant in the room, Medicare, Medicaid, and health care spending more generally are like a rapidly expanding pod of blue whales in an aquarium that's barely growing. As the trustees of the Social Security and Medicare programs themselves have written: "Both Social Security and Medicare are projected to be in poor fiscal shape. . . . The fiscal problems of both programs are driven by inexorable demographics and, in the case of Medicare, inexorable health-care cost inflation, and are not likely to be ameliorated by economic growth or mere tinkering with program financing."[45]

America's health care bill has soared to about $2.25 trillion, about 17 percent of GDP—up from 13 percent of a smaller economic pie just a decade ago. (Ten percent of Americans account for more than two-thirds of our national health care costs.) Spending is rising faster than a well-baked loaf of bread, at 7 to 8 percent a year, with Medicare rising by about 13 percent in 2007 alone; overall U.S. health care costs are projected to hit $4.1 trillion by 2016, and to account for more than one-third of all the goods and services that the United States produces by 2040. Might as well trade in your flat-screen TV for a home MRI machine.[46]

Nearly half of that is paid for by the federal government, if one includes Medicare, Medicaid, and federal health spending for the military, veterans, and civilian employees and retirees, as well as up to $225 billion in lost revenues from tax breaks to corporations to subsidize employer-sponsored health plans. State and local governments pick up about one-eighth of the tab. Federal spending half a century ago was just over $20 billion—about what Americans now pay for pet health care (about $120 billion in 2000 dollars). Medicare spending will cost about $400 billion in 2008. Federal Medicaid and SCHIP spending will be in the $220 billion ballpark, and state Medicaid costs are likely to be about $160 billion—with these numbers projected to double within a decade. As we have seen, health care spending has been rising significantly faster than our nation's economic growth for half a century, and increased spending is projected to overwhelm all of our economic growth in the decades ahead.[47] To say that this is unsustainable is an understatement of the highest order.

Despite tremendous gains in health and longevity, the tragic irony of our health care saga is that while the United States spends far more per capita on health care than any other nation, huge numbers of Americans go without coverage, many face constant anxiety over costs or over loss of coverage, and Americans, on average, receive poorer health care, and are less satisfied with their care, than citizens of several dozen other nations. (Japanese life expectancy, for example, is nearly five years longer than that of Americans.) While the best of American medicine is the world's best, and while U.S. medical research remains at the forefront of innovation, it is hard to imagine a more miserably designed health care system for a rich country if one had entrusted it to the Three Stooges; even to call it a "system" dignifies a crazy-quilt of policies, players, and incentives.

Not only were forty-seven million Americans without health care coverage in 2006, but eighty-two million were without coverage at some point during a recent two-year period, and tens of millions have very limited coverage. Those without insurance are 25 percent more likely to die during any given year than those with insurance. Meanwhile, a study by the RAND Corporation found that barely half of the treatments that Americans receive are considered "best practices."[48] Few Americans are happy with their medical care, and the image of the medical profession as a selfless corps of Marcus Welbys has given way to a more prevalent belief that doctors and hospitals are greedy, insensitive, fearful, incompetent, and as honest as the proverbial used-car salesman, despite increasing discontent among medical practitioners, as physician incomes, adjusted for inflation, actually fell between 1995 and 2003.[49] While life expectancy has soared from forty-six to seventy-eight over the past century, and a minority of the population has become devotees of health foods and exercise, most Americans engage in a variety of not-very-healthy behaviors, from sedentary lifestyles to overconsumption of fatty, nonnutritious foods.

To add insult to injury, premium and out-of-pocket costs for health care rose by almost 50 percent in just five years between 2000 and 2005, from $6,200 to $9,100 per person. Unpaid medical bills, for the uninsured and the insured, are the nation's leading cause of personal bankruptcy. Part of the increase stems from excessively high and often inefficient administrative costs, with private-sector health care entities making Communist-era state-run enterprises seem like the model of market efficiency. Our country's famous litigiousness has further encouraged doctors and hospitals to practice even more defensive, and expensive, medicine, as multiple MRIs seem to be prescribed with an eye more to trial lawyers than to patient health. And the overwhelming market power of many pharmaceutical companies, hospital chains, and other health care providers has all but created a cartel in which prices for physician and hospital services and drugs are set far higher than in other rich countries. To make matters still worse, the very existence of subsidies to employers to provide insurance, and of third-party payers (whether private insurance companies, Medicare, or Medicaid), provides incentives for Americans to consume more and more health care, whether or not they really need it, because most of the real costs are hidden from them. Only 13 percent of Americans' health costs are paid for out of pocket.[50] Liposuction, the prescription for Viagra, or the race to the pediatrician every time Junior runs a ninety-nine-degree temperature have become routine in a culture that provides neither market-based nor regulatory nor moral controls on health care consumption. Virtually no patient or doctor knows what a given medical procedure costs, unless they immerse themselves in mind-numbing fine print. All because of a "system" that has eliminated a freely operating market in so many exquisitely perverse ways that it would make anyone concerned with individual health or the nation's fiscal health wish for the steely efficiency of an old Soviet apparatchik. The United States squanders more than $400 billion a year on health care paperwork, more than three times per capita what Canada spends.[51] As they should sing on the first day of medical school classes, America's health care system is "bad to the bone."

Without sinking into a wonkish recitation of numbers for public-sector health costs, suffice it to say that various projections of future Medicare expenditures resemble a fiscal sinkhole. Medicare's unfunded liability in 2007 was a staggering $38 trillion—close to the entire planet's annual output. Medicare spending is on track to triple by 2035 and quintuple by 2075. Moreover, the sources for Medicare funding are dramatically changing; whereas more than 60 percent of the program was paid for by payroll taxes and 25 percent by general government revenues in 1970, in a quarter-century, payroll taxes will fund only 20 percent of Medicare costs, with 57 percent having to come from general government revenues. If America has an Achilles' heel, it is Medicare and Medicaid and the costs that they are imposing, and will impose, on our country.[52]

If this isn't major league screwy, it's hard to know what is. Medicare and health care spending, in general, are the problem, and this is the challenge.

First, as I shall discuss further, Presidents Franklin Roosevelt and Lyndon Johnson were nothing if not well intentioned in creating the Social Security, Medicare, and Medicaid programs. These programs have been immensely successful in reducing poverty and improving health care among America's elderly and poor.[53] This is no small achievement, in either humanitarian or economic terms. In fact, the successes of these programs should make Americans proud, and polls repeatedly find almost universal support for Social Security and Medicare. (Try to find another government program with 90 percent approval ratings!)[54] Social Security provides benefits to about fifty million Americans (including three million children who are dependents of deceased or disabled workers). Medicare serves about forty-three million (including thirty-six million Americans sixty-five and older and seven million younger Americans with disabilities). Medicaid—which provides health care coverage to the indigent poor, low-income workers and their children, as well as a substantial proportion of the costs of those in nursing homes—covers about fifty-five million Americans (including many also on Medicare), and SCHIP covers another 6.6 million poor children (although millions more remain uncovered). In addition, the Veterans Health Administration and Military Health System cover sixteen million active-duty and retired members of the military and their families. And millions of federal civilian employees receive their health care from the government. In short, at any given time a huge number of Americans benefit from these entitlements, and virtually all Americans are "entitled" to benefit from them at some point in their lives.[55] While these programs have had many beneficial effects, aside from the fiscal tidal wave they may bring, they are also problematic in that the ways in which revenues are collected and benefits are paid are regressive, helping the middle class and well-to-do more than the needy, and benefiting generations born in the first two-thirds of the twentieth century much more than Americans born in the past few decades.[56]

Social Security and Medicare have radically transformed the lives and fortunes of America's elderly population. Whereas over-sixty-five Americans previously faced grievous hardship, these programs have made the elderly the age group least prone to poverty in the United States. The United States may not have the public-sector welfare state that Europeans have, but these programs— together with the private-sector welfare state of pensions and health care engendered by World War II–vintage tax policy—have provided more than half a century of old-age security that is on a par with the more generous European nations. But that "social contract" is fraying.[57]

Social Security has strengthened the income security of millions of older Americans, providing 41 percent of the income of its recipients and at least half of the income for two-thirds of its beneficiaries. Furthermore, over time, Social Security benefits have been made more generous, and have been "indexed" to increase automatically every year—something for which every retiree can be thankful. Social Security benefits are progressive, providing a higher level of benefits for those with lower average indexed monthly earnings (AIME), which is why it has been so successful in reducing poverty among the elderly.[58]

Yet it also has become America's great budgetary Ponzi scheme. Thanks to ever-increasing payroll taxes, particularly those enshrined in the reforms of 1983, Social Security near the end of the Bush administration collects about $150–170 billion more in revenues than it pays out in benefits.[59] These surpluses long have been conveniently "borrowed" against by the rest of government to pay for its operating costs and mask the true size of federal deficits. The Social Security Trust Fund, with its accumulated surpluses, currently holds more than $1.5 trillion in federal debt, but the surpluses start declining in 2008, and an aging population will turn them into deficits nine years later.[60] The so-called "unified" budget deficit, which includes the Social Security surpluses, has helped many a politician lull the populace into believing that federal deficits are not as large, or threatening, as they really are. For example, in 2005, the officially reported "on-budget" deficit was $319 billion; however, if you eliminated the "borrowed" $174 billion Social Security surplus, the deficit would have been $493 billion.[61] As Republican Senator Jim DeMint (S.C.) has said: "Congress . . . has been robbing the Social Security Trust Fund for decades to finance runaway spending. It has turned the trust fund into its personal slush fund, deceitfully spending every dollar of the $1.7 trillion Social Security surplus on other government programs."[62] But it is less than a decade until this fictitious accounting comes back to bite us. The artificially "small" deficits resulting from Social Security surpluses will then mushroom into huge deficits that include both "on-budget" nonpayroll taxes and spending and "off-budget" Social Security payroll taxes and spending on all discretionary and mandatory programs. In short, the great Social Security bailout of our government will be over, and deficits and debt suddenly will appear to spike sharply upward.

Presidents and other politicians from Franklin Roosevelt, Henry Wallace, and Harry Truman to Lyndon Johnson and Bill Clinton have dreamed of universal health insurance—something that almost every other rich country, from Canada and Japan to all of western Europe, instituted after World War II. Six times during the past century, legislative efforts were made and stymied, and it took LBJ's legendary legislative skills to achieve government-provided health care for about 25–30 percent of the population. And LBJ's achievement—aside from being a fiscal mixed blessing—has been about as simple as a Rubik's cube on steroids. Medicare was established with a Hospital Trust Fund, financed through a 2.9 percent payroll tax, with patient deductibles, and a much more problematic Supplementary Medical Insurance program that pays doctors' bills and home and outpatient care, using general government revenues and a small monthly patient premium. These are Parts A and B, while Part C provides coverage through managed-care plans. Then, in an ill-considered effort to politically trump the Democrats, the Bush administration and the Republican Congress enacted a prescription drug plan for the elderly, Medicare Part D, in 2003, in legislation that wended its way to passage by Congress long after Jay Leno had gone off the air. Sold as costing $400 billion, it is projected to cost more than $800 billion through 2017, and carries $8–9 trillion in long-term costs. Moreover, there is considerable pressure to close the "doughnut hole" in the law's coverage, which could cost tens of billions more over a decade.[63] As former Republican Senator Phil Gramm (Tex.) said, Medicare Part D was like "putting more people aboard the Titanic."[64]

Although Medicaid—a program in which the federal government provides matching funds to states—is usually thought of as a health care program for the poor, the vast majority of Medicaid dollars are spent on the elderly, with half of America's quarter-trillion-dollar nursing home tab picked up by Medicaid. These are often once-middle-class Americans who have run through all their life assets to pay for health care.[65]

One reason that Social Security, Medicare, and Medicaid face rising costs is the inexorable aging of the American population—although more expensive technology and increasing use of services by all ages are other big contributors to health care costs. With life expectancy continuing its century-long rise and birth rates relatively low, more and more Americans will be old and will spend more and more time in old age. The number of Americans over sixty-five will shoot upward from thirty-seven million in 2005 to sixty-two million in 2025.[66] Moreover, while Americans are living longer, the past few decades have seen Americans retiring ever earlier. The result is that instead of spending a handful of years in retirement before death—as was the case when Social Security was enacted in 1935—Americans now spend decades drawing retirement benefits. As C. Eugene Steuerle of the Urban Institute has said, these programs are no longer a safety net for those at the end of their lives but rather "a middle-aged retirement program."[67] Furthermore, since Social Security is a "pay-as-you-go" program, with taxes on current workers funding the benefits for current retirees, the number of workers supporting each retiree has plummeted from 16 in 1950 to 3.3 today, and is expected to fall to 2 by 2030. Only rising productivity has caused the decline in this "dependency ratio" to be less catastrophic than it might otherwise be. As President Bush's Commission on Social Security declared: "The current system is financially unsustainable."[68]

There are many reasons why Social Security—while a big problem—is an eminently solvable one, as we will see. Where the problem with Medicare and Medicaid differs is the seemingly unstoppable rise in health care costs. An aging population, sharply rising costs for public- and private-sector care, and a deeply flawed health care system make a deadly combination. And what makes the situation even worse, unlike Social Security, is that—despite many ideas being bandied about—no one really knows how to control health care cost growth.

So the expansion of government spending and deficits to pay for entitlements is where the battle lines are drawn. They are also where we, so far, have achieved a magnificent state of political stalemate. Or should one say cowardice?

Can we get out of the Haunted Mansion or escape the tsunami? We won't make it happen by sitting on our hands, while saying all the right things about the evils of deficits and health care cost explosion. Like any problem—and this is a really big one, as Ed Sullivan might have said—it takes problem-solving, hard work, and commitment. We will turn to those topics in later chapters, but first: how did we get to this state of affairs, how are we getting by with a little fiscal help from our (erstwhile) friends, and what could happen if we don't reduce deficits and their major contributor, health care costs?

Chapter 2 Balancing and Unbalancing Our Budget: A History of Government Debt in the United States

No pecuniary consideration is more urgent, than the regular redemption and discharge of the public debt.
George Washington

For most of the nation's history, other than in wartime, the United States kept its budget more or less balanced. Our Founders, perhaps steeped in a more Puritanical—or commonsensical—outlook on deficits, regularly decried public profligacy. Echoing George Washington's comments on fiscal responsibility, Thomas Jefferson said: "I place economy among the first and most important republican virtues, and public debt as the greatest of the dangers to be feared."[1] For the country's first 139 years, it ran surpluses 93 times, almost one-third of its 46 deficits were to fight wars, and its other deficits were infinitesimal. Americans and their leaders firmly believed that public debt was fiscally and morally wrong, and—until the 1960s—almost never ran significant deficits in peacetime. Wartime debts were assiduously paid off during the decades of ensuing peace.[2]

This all started to change between the 1960s and 1970s—when a combination of Keynesian economics, guns-and-butter Vietnam War–era spending, the growth of entitlement spending, and 1970s stagflation—began to wallop the nation's finances. Coincidentally, this began to happen roughly when the average American alive today was born, around 1971.

At that time, the total accumulated federal debt since the beginning of the republic was about $424 billion. In 2007 it has passed $9 trillion and is heading fast toward $10 trillion.[3] Deficits emerged as a national issue in the 1980s, culminating in the Gramm-Rudman-Hollings deficit-reduction bill, talk of a balanced-budget amendment, various budget agreements and summits, and Ross Perot's 1992 campaign. Thanks to surprisingly wise, bipartisan policy making and a strong economy, at the end of the Clinton administration, the CBO projected a ten-year, $5.6 trillion surplus, and Clinton's four consecutive budget surpluses marked the first time that that had been achieved since before the Depression. Five years later, the CBO projected that the nation would run $2.2 trillion in deficits over five years, despite President Bush's pledge to cut the deficit in half by 2009.

In short, deficits appeared at various times in American history, became a major issue in the past quarter century, and appeared to be solved by 2000, only to reemerge with a vengeance in the early twenty-first century. So how and why did the nation manage its finances so much more responsibly during the first 180 or so years of its history, and how did this long-running record of success turn into a nearly unbroken record of failure during the past three to four decades, with dramatically worse prospects looming ahead?

THE EARLY REPUBLIC, 1789–1860

The United States was born in debt. However, that debt—to the French government, Dutch bankers, and wealthy patriots—was used to finance the

---

GRAMM-RUDMAN-HOLLINGS

The Gramm-Rudman-Hollings Act, or the Deficit Control Act, included the Balanced Budget and Emergency Deficit Control Act of 1985 and the Balanced Budget and Emergency Deficit Control Reaffirmation Act of 1987. These laws were intended to control the deficit by imposing multiyear deficit caps that were to be enforced by a process called "sequestration," or across-the-board budget cuts. Gramm-Rudman-Hollings, while notable as a first salvo in the war on deficits, collapsed under political pressure and is generally seen as a failure.

colonies' successful war of independence from Great Britain. Certainly, public debt predated 1776; the colonies had issued bills of credit, and debt had led to ruin in sixteenth- and seventeenth-century Spain and helped to fuel growth in eighteenth-century Britain.[4] But post–Revolutionary War debt almost destroyed the new nation. Default on debt to foreign and domestic bondholders in 1783, which led to a massive and disastrous money-printing campaign by the Continental Congress, was one of the key crises of the 1780s that led to adoption of the U.S. Constitution and establishment of the modern nation that we know today.[5]

The debates between the Federalists and the Anti-Federalists—the former favoring a strong central government to resolve financial problems and interstate rivalries and to build a dynamic national economy, the latter holding that the philosophical rights of individuals and states were more important than the benefits of a strong nation—played out in the months and years leading up to the writing and ratification of the U.S. Constitution in 1787. In that document, by and large, the Federalists—led by James Madison and Alexander Hamilton—won, although the Anti-Federalists' concerns were addressed in the subsequent Bill of Rights.[6] So the delicate balance was established that the United States has (mostly, and brilliantly) maintained between nationhood on the one hand and individual rights and local power on the other.

Hamilton was one of America's most extraordinary political leaders. Although he played second fiddle to Madison in creating the Constitution, he was the architect of American finances and set in motion the policies that led to centuries of growing U.S. prosperity. Hamilton quickly got to work after George Washington named him the first secretary of the Treasury in 1789. He won passage of the first Tariff Act, which accounted for the bulk of federal revenues until World War I. He established excise taxes on carriages and alcohol, America's first form of taxation. He pushed for assuming the states' Revolutionary War debts of $18 million to help strengthen the power of the central government. Overall U.S. debt after the war stood at about $80 million, about 40 percent of national output, and hovered near that dollar amount until Thomas Jefferson's second term. Hamilton established the ability of the U.S. government to borrow money, overcoming Madison's opposition to paying interest to bondholders. He created America's first central bank, the precursor to the Federal Reserve Board, as a depository for federal funds, a regulator of the money supply, and a lender to local governments and banks around the country. Most important, Hamilton adopted the British philosopher David Hume's proto-Keynesian idea that public debt could be used to promote economic growth, and implemented it with steely determination. The first federal budget, under Hamilton, was about $2.8 million—one-millionth of America's current budget—with more than three-fourths of it devoted to retiring Revolutionary War debt. Within five years, America had gone from fiscal disaster to having the highest credit rating with European creditors.[7]

However, despite Hamilton's brilliance in stimulating the economy, recognizing that some debt could be useful, and paying down excess debt to improve U.S. finances, he was unique in his day—if not most of U.S. history—in *not* simply seeing debt as morally wrong. Not only did his fellow Federalists Washington and Adams decry U.S. debt, but the electoral revolution that brought Thomas Jefferson to the presidency in 1801 brought about a dramatic change in America's fiscal course. While Jefferson had artfully convinced the southern states to pay their Revolutionary debts by agreeing to locate the capital in the southern climes of what was to be Washington, D.C., and although he borrowed $15 million to purchase the Louisiana Territory with 6 percent bonds, he ardently believed that debt was an evil to be avoided. He called debt a "moral cancer" and proposed a constitutional amendment that would prohibit the federal government from borrowing money. Jefferson also repealed the hated excise taxes, which had led to revolts such as the Whiskey Rebellion; ran budget surpluses; and left office with the national debt reduced by one-third between 1804 and 1809, to $57 million.[8]

Debt reduction again was thwarted by war, as the War of 1812 increased the nation's debt from $45 million to $127 million between 1812 and 1816, despite the brief imposition of taxes. For the next twenty years, the Treasury received more than it spent, mostly from customs duties, and the nation's debt was slashed to its all-time low under Andrew Jackson in 1835, when it stood at a minuscule $33,733.05. This was just before the Panic of 1837 led many states to add clauses to their constitutions requiring that they be debt free. The only significant borrowing during this period was $5 million to buy Florida in 1824 (and think what those Palm Beach estates cost now!). The 1845 Mexican War also led to a burst of borrowing, but the 1850s were times of persistent federal surpluses. Four years before Fort Sumter ripped America apart, the national debt was a mere $28 million—barely one-third of what it had been after the Revolution![9]

THE CIVIL WAR THROUGH THE 1920s

Aside from being the bloodiest, most calamitous event in U.S. history, the Civil War imposed unprecedented strains on the nation's finances. The four-year war cost the nation a then-unimaginable sum, perhaps $6–7 billion in direct costs, with most of the Union's cost (somewhat more than half) raised through government bonds. The Lincoln administration also established a short-lived tax of 3 percent on incomes above $800, as well as a Bureau of Internal Revenue. The bureau raised about 28 percent of the North's war costs through increased excise taxes and this small income tax. In borrowing funds, however, President Lincoln expressed the then-novel idea that "men readily perceive that they can not be much oppressed by a debt which they owe to themselves"—a sentiment that has been revived in recent years by some who claim that deficits "don't matter." The war ended with the United States $2.8 billion in debt—and from 1863 to 1980, from the Emancipation Proclamation to Ronald Reagan's election, U.S. debt was to be measured in the billions.[10]

Although debt service accounted for 58 percent of the federal budget during the early years of Reconstruction—a level that would be disastrous if we returned to it—a combination of extreme fiscal prudence and a growing economy led to a generation of steady debt reduction. In fact, from 1866 to the 1890s, the government consistently ran surpluses, and paid down a significant portion of Civil War debt, reducing the overall national debt by about 45 percent before the economic crisis of 1893. However, federal spending doubled in the fifty years after the Civil War, in part to pay for Civil War veterans' pensions and in part to pay for early twentieth-century initiatives of the Progressive era. Between 1901 and 1915 the entire federal budget rose from the tiny sum of about $525 million to $746 million, with most revenues coming from tariffs. As a result, national debt doubled between 1893 and the eve of World War I, from $1.5 billion to about $3 billion.[11] This was an era during which the long-ruling Republican Party believed—like Hamilton before, and the post–World War II Keynesians—that government could be an engine of economic growth. Tariffs served the dual purpose of protecting U.S. industries and raising revenues for federal initiatives. Think of the transcontinental railroad, land to launch state universities, the creation of the first national parks, and the establishment of the Departments of Agriculture, Justice, Commerce, and Labor.

As America marched into modernity, it is worth noting that the Supreme Court in 1895 had ruled the Civil War income tax unconstitutional after Congress tried to reinstate a modest income tax to pay for the rising costs of government during the depression of the 1890s. It was one of our nation's greatest jurists, however, Oliver Wendell Holmes, Jr., beginning thirty years as a Supreme Court justice in 1902, who eloquently provided the philosophical justification for America's revenue system of the past century. As we have seen,

Holmes linked paying taxes with citizenship, and with "the price we pay" for a civilized society—for what economists call "public goods" and what politicians and the rest of us call "government." As many politicians and businessmen recognized that high tariffs were economically harmful to commerce, profits, and Americans' living standards, debates about how to raise revenues enlivened the early years of the twentieth century. Despite deep divisions between the rural West and the urban Northeast, Congress passed both a business tax and a constitutional amendment allowing the federal government to tax personal incomes regardless of state populations (a rather arcane restriction that had squashed earlier income tax plans). Thirty-six states ratified the Sixteenth Amendment, and in 1913 the Congress passed and President Wilson signed the first permanent income tax, with rates ranging from 1 percent to 7 percent on incomes above $500,000 (the equivalent of many millions today). Despite this radical step, which also created the infamous 1040 form, less than 1 percent of the population paid taxes.[12]

Once again, war plunged America deep into debt, increased the size of government, and forced new mechanisms for raising revenues. World War I, following close on the heels of the Sixteenth Amendment, led President Wilson to push for and win passage of the Revenue Act of 1916 and two subsequent war revenue acts, which lowered the tax threshold, doubled the base income tax rate to 2 percent and raised the top rate, for the very few Americans earning more than $2 million, to 15 percent; the act also created an estate tax. Yet even with wartime tax increases, only 5 percent of the population paid taxes.[13] The war caused government spending to skyrocket, rising from $713 million in 1916 to $18.5 billion in 1919, and the debt to soar from $3.6 billion to $27.4 billion.[14]

As we all know, America won the war and "returned to normalcy," albeit a corruption-riddled, financially speculative, supposedly alcohol-free, and socially unequal "normalcy" during the 1920s. Government never returned to its prewar size under the three Republican administrations of the 1920s, with budgets under Harding, Coolidge, and Hoover hovering between $3 billion and $3.5 billion—five times Wilson's last prewar budget. Yet we did run surpluses, cut taxes five times, and paid down about 40 percent of our debt before the Depression hit us like a Mike Tyson punch to the fiscal gut.[15] The 1920s also brought the formal establishment of a national budget, created by the Budget and Accounting Act of 1921. This established the Bureau of the Budget, required the president to submit an annual budget, and gave the president greater authority over fiscal matters.[16]

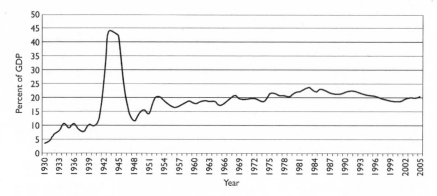

Figure 7. Outlays of the federal government as a share of GDP, 1930–2005. *Source:* Office of Management and Budget, *Budget of the United States Government, Fiscal Year 2008: Historical Tables* (Washington, D.C.: Government Printing Office, 2007), Table 1-2, Summary of Receipts, Outlays, and Surpluses (or Deficits) as Percentages of GDP: 1930–2012, 23–24

THE EMERGENCE OF MODERN GOVERNMENT:
THE DEPRESSION TO NIXON

The hardships of the Depression led government spending under Herbert Hoover and Franklin Roosevelt to grow from $3.1 billion in 1929 to $4.6 billion when Hoover left office four years later, and to $9.5 billion in 1940. Neither the hapless Hoover nor Dr. New Deal was able to "cure" the Depression, yet their initiatives did alleviate some of the suffering of America's worst economic crisis—thus far. FDR, though surrounded by Keynesians and agreeing to meet the great British economist in the White House, embraced deficit spending only reluctantly. Like all American presidents, with the possible exception of John Kennedy—whose 1962 Yale University speech explicitly espoused deficit spending—he believed in balanced budgets. Yet many would say that Roosevelt ushered in the era of intentional deficit spending to stimulate the economy—not necessarily a bad idea. Perhaps the sign of a great leader, then and now, is his or her ability to profess adherence to orthodox thinking, be flexible enough to embrace new thinking, and successfully demonstrate compassion for the American people, while fudging the ideological bases for benefits to them.[17]

Many conservatives and liberals alike date the growth of "big government" to the New Deal. As a result of a host of programs intended to assist millions of struggling Americans and pull the economy out of depression, federal spending grew from 3 percent of national output in 1929 to 10 percent in 1939. It is important to remember, however, that this "growth" in spending was as a proportion of a declining, or stagnant, economy. Government stepped in to try to create jobs, build dams and national parks, and create basic income-security programs because the private sector had failed so miserably. Business was in the doghouse, American capitalism was in crisis, and—some histrionic business rhetoric to the contrary—FDR aimed to save the American "system," not permanently transform it into a socialistic economy. The architects of the New Deal sought to introduce greater equity and progressivity in taxes—but few Americans still paid taxes, with federal revenues never going above 5 percent of GDP (and taxes above 3 percent), and government was still relatively small until World War II.

Of course, the greatest spending innovation that FDR introduced—which many have called the single most influential piece of legislation in the last century—was the 1935 Social Security Act. Social Security initially was intended to provide modest retirement security for Americans over sixty-five, at a time when the average American lived to be sixty-two.[18] Although, à la *Groundhog Day*, we will return—and return, and return—to Social Security, no one in the 1930s, or even the 1960s, foresaw that it would create the floodtides of the fiscal "tsunami" that Robert Reischauer and others now discuss. Instead, it was seen as one of Roosevelt's greatest triumphs. Social Security always has been overwhelmingly popular among the American people. It succeeded in all but eliminating what had been widespread poverty among the elderly. And Social Security was embraced by almost everyone on the political spectrum; in fact, as we will see, it was expanded repeatedly by presidents from Truman to Nixon.[19] And decades after Lyndon Johnson won authorization of Medicare and Medicaid as amendments to the Social Security Act, George W. Bush's Medicare prescription-drug bill expanded coverage again. Republicans and Democrats, for decades, tried to outdo each other in providing more generous benefits for the elderly and their ever more powerful political lobby.

The combination of a weak economy and spending on these social programs, however, led federal spending and the national debt to more than double in the first eight years of the Roosevelt administration. Nonetheless, for those who blithely criticize the New Deal for expanded government spending and debt, it is significant to note that during just the three Depression years under Herbert Hoover, federal spending and the nation's debt increased by nearly 40 percent.[20]

As Dr. New Deal evolved into Dr. Win the War, Pearl Harbor finally con-

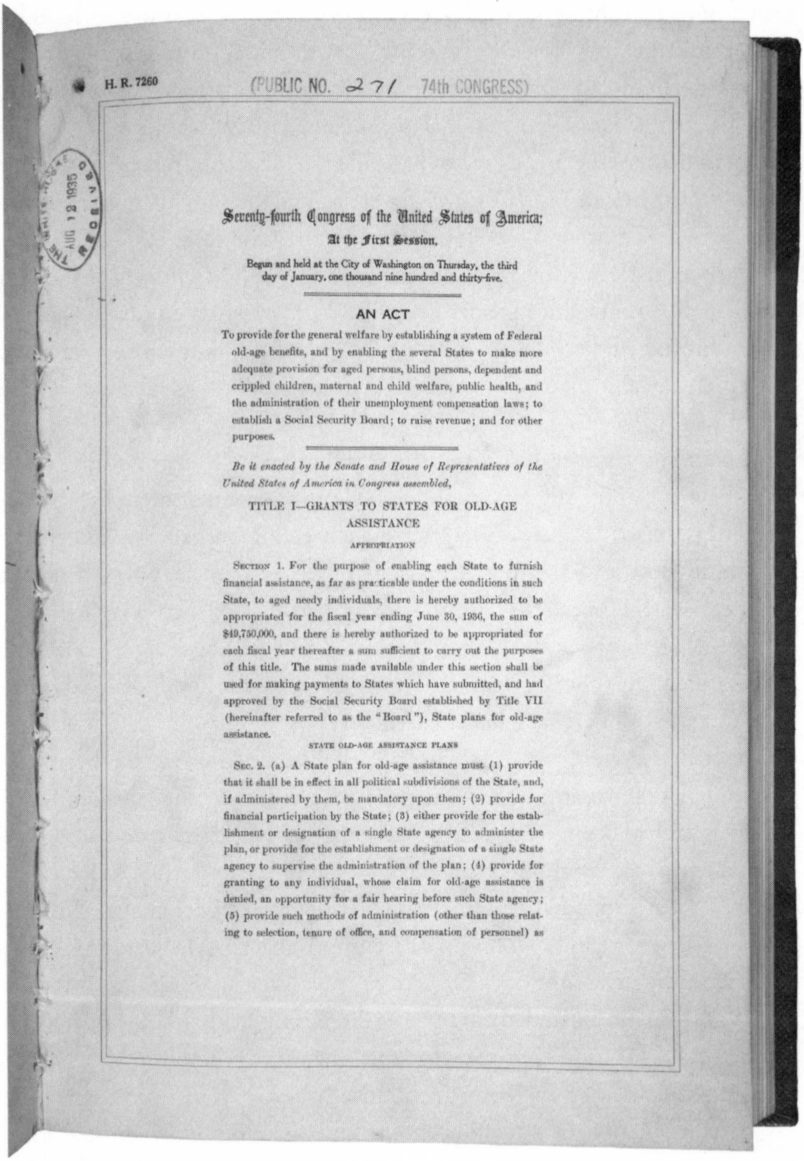

H. R. 7260 (PUBLIC NO. 271 74th CONGRESS)

Seventy-fourth Congress of the United States of America;
At the First Session,

Begun and held at the City of Washington on Thursday, the third day of January, one thousand nine hundred and thirty-five.

AN ACT

To provide for the general welfare by establishing a system of Federal old-age benefits, and by enabling the several States to make more adequate provision for aged persons, blind persons, dependent and crippled children, maternal and child welfare, public health, and the administration of their unemployment compensation laws; to establish a Social Security Board; to raise revenue; and for other purposes.

Be it enacted by the Senate and House of Representatives of the United States of America in Congress assembled,

TITLE I—GRANTS TO STATES FOR OLD-AGE ASSISTANCE

APPROPRIATION

SECTION 1. For the purpose of enabling each State to furnish financial assistance, as far as practicable under the conditions in such State, to aged needy individuals, there is hereby authorized to be appropriated for the fiscal year ending June 30, 1936, the sum of $49,750,000, and there is hereby authorized to be appropriated for each fiscal year thereafter a sum sufficient to carry out the purposes of this title. The sums made available under this section shall be used for making payments to States which have submitted, and had approved by the Social Security Board established by Title VII (hereinafter referred to as the "Board"), State plans for old-age assistance.

STATE OLD-AGE ASSISTANCE PLANS

SEC. 2. (a) A State plan for old-age assistance must (1) provide that it shall be in effect in all political subdivisions of the State, and, if administered by them, be mandatory upon them; (2) provide for financial participation by the State; (3) either provide for the establishment or designation of a single State agency to administer the plan, or provide for the establishment or designation of a single State agency to supervise the administration of the plan; (4) provide for granting to any individual, whose claim for old-age assistance is denied, an opportunity for a fair hearing before such State agency; (5) provide such methods of administration (other than those relating to selection, tenure of office, and compensation of personnel) as

Figure 8. Social Security Act, 1935

THE SOCIAL SECURITY ACT OF 1935

Drafted as part of the president's New Deal by FDR aide Edwin Witte to alleviate the hardships of the Depression in general and old-age poverty, then affecting more than 50 percent of the elderly, the Social Security Act was passed by the Congress and signed into law on August 14, 1935. Initially, it provided retirement benefits only to workers employed in businesses with ten or more workers, but it was expanded in 1937 to widows and orphans; in 1956 to include the disabled; in 1956 and 1961 to provide early retirement benefits to women and men, respectively, at age sixty-two; in 1965 to include Medicare; in 1975 to include automatic cost-of-living increases; in the late 1970s to include immigrants; and in 2003 to include prescription-drug coverage for the elderly.

Probably Americans' most cherished government program, and the world's largest government program, Social Security provides monthly benefits to fifty million retired workers, widows and orphans, and the disabled. Since Medicare was an amendment to Social Security, it has provided old-age medical benefits as well.

---

vinced Americans that the global Axis threat had to be combated and defeated. While the United States stood on the sidelines during the first years of the war, once it entered the conflict in December 1941, it created a successful military machine unprecedented in size and power. And with all but universal domestic support, America won the war in less than four years, while transforming its moribund economy into an immensely productive, prosperous "arsenal of democracy."

The war effort brought about a gargantuan mobilization of American society. The federal government took the lead not only in getting seventeen million men and women in uniform, contracting to build thousands of weapons, ships, aircraft, and the other infrastructure of total war, and deploying them to all theaters of the war, but also in choreographing private-sector industrial production, and in managing the economy and financing the war effort. Federal spending increased nearly tenfold from 1940 to 1945, growing from $9.5 billion to $92 billion.[21] The war brought the first broad-based income tax—with the number of Americans filing returns rising from four million to forty-three million almost overnight and tax revenues climbing from 8 percent of GDP to 20 percent.[22] However, most of the war was financed through the sale of bonds and other borrowing. Deficits grew to $55 billion in 1943, or a still-unequaled $486 billion in 2000 dollars, and the national debt soared from $3 billion in 1940 to $269 billion in 1946. Debt as a proportion of GDP skyrocketed to 114 percent—quite a difference from the 17 percent of a much smaller economy in

1929.[23] If the United States was ever a state-run and -planned economy, it was during World War II, when the federal government accounted for 44 percent of national output—compared with 3 percent in 1929 and about 20 percent since 1950.[24]

The war was won at huge costs in human lives, physical devastation, and expenditures. But the wartime effort had a variety of unexpected and unintended consequences for the U.S. economy, government, and federal finances.

First, the U.S. economy, unscathed by the fighting that ravaged Europe and Asia, doubled in size, bringing unheard-of prosperity to tens of millions of Americans.[25] Second, because wages were frozen during the war, employers in a tight labor market indirectly boosted workers' pay with such fringe benefits as health insurance, pensions, and paid vacations. A then-powerful union movement played a major role in locking in these benefits after the war, and thus, in effect, was born America's postwar "private welfare state." Whereas European and other countries embraced universal, publicly financed health care and more generous old-age and other government benefits, the package of private benefits put in place during and just after the war set the pattern for the hybrid, uniquely American model that worked very well for most citizens until very recent years. When one adds in spending by employers, America's mixed economy of public and private social-insurance and social-welfare benefits was every bit as generous as those established by "socialistic" states of western Europe.

A third effect of World War II—compounded by the rapid onset of the Cold War in 1946—was the creation of a permanent big government, whose cornerstone was the "military-industrial complex" that President Dwight Eisenhower so famously warned against. From World War II through the Vietnam War era, and even up to the end of the Cold War in 1989–91, defense spending gobbled up a huge share of federal revenues.

Fourth, while taxes and federal spending were cut after World War II, and a remarkable portion of wartime debt was repaid—unlike after World War I— the income tax, together with the new Social Security payroll tax, was here to stay. Federal tax collectors acquired their modern moniker, the Internal Revenue Service, only in 1953. And while federal spending fell to less than 15 percent of GDP in 1949, it never dropped to prewar or pre-Depression levels, and the outbreak of the Korean War in 1950 pushed federal spending up to 20 percent—a level around which it has magically hovered ever since, even as the economy grew.[26]

In addition, at war's end, many feared a return to depression and mass unemployment, and thought that the U.S. economy was "mature," requiring some sort of government intervention to provide jobs and stimulate "purchasing power" (to maintain, that is, if not raise, incomes).[27] The ensuing quarter-century, however, turned out to be an unparalleled period of economic growth.[28] Due to a combination of propitious factors—business-government-labor cooperation; huge government investment in wealth-generating infrastructure, technologies, and skills; pent-up and rising consumer demand and aspirations; public and private efforts that all but ensured that incomes would keep increasing; and a war-devastated world that left America without any real economic competitors—the U.S. economy, most Americans' and businesses' incomes, and federal finances grew beyond people's wildest dreams. Not only was a "rising tide lifting all boats," as John Kennedy later said, bringing prosperity to a vast middle class and sharply reducing poverty, but government coffers were also filling with tax revenues from the nation's rapidly expanding economic pie.

Yet another change—and the one that was, perhaps, most portentous for the fiscal and economic shape of the twenty-first-century United States—was that Americans between the late 1940s and 1970s came to believe that they could have it all: rising personal incomes, rising profits, and a growing government to fund both the "guns" of the Cold War and the "butter" of ever-expanding social programs.

While the military buildup for the Korean War increased federal spending from $43 billion in 1950 to $76 billion in 1953, unlike during previous postwar eras, and perhaps surprisingly for a Republican administration, government spending did not fall during the Eisenhower years that followed. In fact, by the time that Ike left office in 1961, the government was spending $96 billion a year.[29] One reason for escalating government costs was the Cold War arms race, which led the United States to build thirty-three thousand nuclear weapons by the mid-1960s and establish countless military bases around the globe. Another was Eisenhower's commitment to the New Deal initiatives that provided rising purchasing power for all Americans, along with his acceptance of Keynesian deficit spending to stimulate the economy during times of recession. Social Security benefits were doubled under Truman and Eisenhower, with four increases in the 1950s. The number of eligible families increased sevenfold during that period, thanks to Social Security Act amendments in 1950, 1952, 1954, 1956, and 1958. Disability insurance was added, self-employed and farm workers were covered, women became eligible at sixty-two, and others were drawn into the system. As Eisenhower said in 1956: "If the day ever comes when sound economic policies fail to serve the ends of social justice, our form of society will be in grave jeopardy."[30]

The miraculous part of this story is that the national debt barely increased, inching up from $266 billion to $296 billion during the Eisenhower years. The booming economy allowed the United States to pay down much of its World War II debt, reducing debt as a share of GDP from 130 percent at war's end to 58 percent in 1960.[31] Part of the reason is that, with incomes rising so fast, Americans tolerated strikingly high tax rates; the top marginal tax rate for incomes more than $200,000 under Republican President Eisenhower was 94 percent—something hard to imagine as tolerable among twenty-first-century Republicans (or Democrats).

The 1960s—despite the controversial Keynesian policies of John Kennedy and his economic Svengali, Walter Heller, or the fiscal follies that began under Lyndon Johnson—marked the end of America's fiscal glory days. *Avant le deluge!* While government spending doubled from $98 billion in 1961 to $196 billion in 1970, the economy grew at its fastest sustained pace in U.S. history, and national debt increased only by one-third, to $390 billion.[32] This was despite everything under the sun that should have increased deficits and debt astronomically.

President Kennedy, giving the American public a lesson in Keynesian deficit spending, successfully called for tax cuts in 1962 to boost economic growth—even though the economy was not in a recession.[33] Enacted after JFK's assassination, the cuts seemed to work like a miracle. Business loved them. Taxpayers loved them. And Wall Street loved them. The economy took off like a Gemini rocket, and the 1965 year-end issue of *Time* magazine proclaimed the long-dead John Maynard Keynes "man of the year." At the time, as Americans felt wealthier than ever, poverty declined to its all-time low point, and deficits—as the eighteenth-century British seemed to say—were nothing but a boon to economic prosperity.

Yet storm clouds were gathering. And they gathered under the alternately beneficent and deceitful watch of President Lyndon Johnson. Sadly, for those who would like moral clarity in life, it was the "good" things that LBJ did that caused the greatest damage, while the fiscal lies, in the long run, were to be the least of twenty-first-century America's worries. First, the deceit: LBJ, whose presidency was destroyed by the Vietnam War, cooked the books over federal spending for Vietnam, hiding the true size of federal deficits and igniting inflation. But that was small potatoes.

The big deal, as far as we're concerned, was adoption of the Social Security Amendments of 1965, which authorized the Medicare program. Medicare, signed with fanfare in the Independence, Mo., hometown of former President Harry Truman, was Johnson's and America's compromise in providing publicly subsidized health care. Universal health care, a dream from Franklin Roosevelt to the present in America, was not to be, but the master legislator LBJ won passage of federally supported in- and outpatient hospital, physician, and other medical care, and related services for those sixty-five and older. He also won passage of legislation that provided medical coverage to the poor—Medicaid. While far from universal health insurance, Medicare and Medicaid have provided health care to nearly 30 percent of Americans, significantly increasing life expectancy among the elderly and reducing health disparities between the middle class and the poor.[34] From the vantage point of the Great Society, before its warts became apparent, these were enormous triumphs. Aside from the disaster of Vietnam and the ticking fiscal time bomb in these two programs, Johnson would be an unblemished American hero for bringing health care to the elderly and the poor.

Unfortunately, history and economics are not kind.

THE DEFICIT ERA, 1970s TO THE FUTURE

In the famous world of vicious cycles, Vietnam-era inflation led President Richard Nixon and Congress to the momentous decision to index Social Security benefits to wage increases in 1972. The proverbial cat was out of the bag, as entitlement spending on Social Security, Medicare, and Medicaid—tiny in the late 1960s—started to head for the inflation-adjusted stratosphere. Federal spending under Presidents Nixon and Ford leapt from $184 billion in 1969 to $409 billion in 1977, as the national debt nearly doubled from $368 billion to $719 billion.[35] Relative defense spending actually declined with the end of the Vietnam War and Cold War détente, but nondefense spending rose by more than 9 percent a year under these big-spending Republicans. Nonetheless, 1970s inflation led to "bracket creep" and rising tax revenues. Nixon—like Presidents Ford, Carter, Reagan, and their successors—tried to impose the first price and hospital-revenue controls on Medicare, but his efforts had a modest impact at best. In fact, Nixon was the first president to declare rising health care costs a "crisis"—in 1972.[36]

Say good-bye to that poor fiscal cat. The 1970s began an era of budgetary meltdown that has haunted America ever since, although the ghoul at the door during the past thirty years is like a noisome fly compared with the monster poised to wreak fiscal havoc in the thirty years ahead. As entitlement spending started to escalate, Nixon's Watergate and Vietnam troubles led to a broad assertion of congressional powers, including over the budget. Shifting gears from the 1921 budget act, the Congress passed the Budget Control Act in 1974, which created the modern budgetary oversight committees and the Congressional Budget Office to try to impose fiscal discipline.[37] Nonetheless, the combination of economic "stagflation," suddenly declining worker productivity, and the equally sudden rise in entitlement costs led to deficits of 2.9 percent of GDP under President Jimmy Carter, after averaging less than 1 percent during the preceding quarter-century.[38]

Frustrations over the nation's economic problems, a growing grassroots tax revolt, the discrediting of Keynesian economics, and the rise of neoconservatism and supply-side economics, together with post-Vietnam and post-Watergate cynicism about the federal government all contributed to the great about face of the 1980 election. Ronald Reagan was elected on a mandate to reduce the size of government, cut taxes and deficits, and get the economy moving again. While his rhetoric to this effect was soaring, and some significant reforms were accomplished—only through bipartisan compromise—Reagan's record did not match the rhetoric. In his 1981 inaugural address he proclaimed that "government is not the solution to our problem; government is the problem," and took aim at America's deficits in language that still sounds current: "Great as our tax burden is, it has not kept pace with public spending. For decades we have piled deficit upon deficit, mortgaging our future and our children's future for the temporary convenience of the present. To continue this long trend is to guarantee tremendous social, cultural, political, and economic upheavals."[39]

Reagan did cut taxes and some government spending, while Federal Reserve Chairman Paul Volcker's war on inflation succeeded, but only at the cost in 1982 of the deepest post–World War II recession. Yet the Reagan administration vastly increased military spending as the Cold War entered a final and dangerous phase, and the president was unable to control entitlement spending growth. As a result, under anti–"big government" President Reagan, the federal government grew by 1984 to its largest size in U.S. history as a share of the overall economy—nearly 25 percent. Deficits nearly tripled during Reagan's first two years in office, to $208 billion, or an unprecedented 6 percent of GDP, and the national debt, which topped $1 trillion for the first time during his first year in office, rose to $2.8 trillion by the time he left office. The Gipper's fiscal legacy was that nearly twice as much debt accumulated during each of his two terms than had during all of prior American history.[40]

The idea that taxes could be cut to spur enough growth to actually increase federal revenues—sold to Reagan by supply-siders Jude Wanniski and Arthur Laffer—was famously ridiculed in the 1980 campaign by George H. W. Bush as "voodoo economics." Reagan's budget director David Stockman was "taken to the woodshed" for publicly declaring that the administration was "cooking the books," and that the numbers simply did not add up.[41] Despite continuing rhetoric about tax reduction and a 1984 Republican platform that promised no tax increases, taxes were raised a half dozen times as the Reagan administration wore on. While Republican Senate leader Bob Dole (Kan.) courageously pushed through tax-increase measures in 1982, 1984, and 1987, the two most successful fiscal measures of the Reagan years were the Social Security reforms proposed by the bipartisan 1983 Greenspan Commission and the Herculean 1986 tax-reform legislation.

The fifteen-member commission chaired by Alan Greenspan had dallied for two years and all but given up until some members meeting in a Georgetown apartment recognized that Social Security was on the brink of being unable to mail out benefit checks.[42] With the nation in a panic, Congress acted with un-characteristic dispatch. The commission proposed increasing Social Security and Medicare tax rates to their present 15.3 percent rate (which had risen from their original 2 percent in 1937), reducing cost-of-living increases, taxing self-employed Americans and Social Security benefits themselves, reducing benefits for those who retire between ages sixty-two and sixty-five, and increasing the full-benefit retirement age over more than three decades to sixty-seven. Now Americans born between 1943 and 1954 are able to collect full benefits at age sixty-six, with full-benefit retirement age increasing by two months a year for those born during the next five years; those born in 1960 or after will be able to draw benefits when they are sixty-seven. The 1983 Social Security Amend-ments, which passed and were signed into law, raised revenues and restored sol-vency to the system, and represented what many observers have hailed as a tri-umph of good governance.[43]

The 1986 Tax Reform Act also is often cited as a model for how Democrats and Republicans can compromise and productively craft legislation that is fis-cally responsible, while satisfying many of the goals of the conflicting parties. Democrats such as Senator Bill Bradley (N.J.) and Representative Dan Rosten-kowski (Ill.) worked with Republican Senators Dole and Bob Packwood (Ore.) to produce a bill that lowered tax rates, a Reagan goal, while providing tax benefits for poor and working Americans and introducing an earned-income tax credit (EITC), a Democratic goal. At the same time, the act broadened the tax base by making it harder to avoid paying taxes. It eliminated many tax shelters and loopholes and cut top marginal tax rates to a postwar low of 28 percent.[44]

That the mid- to late 1980s were an era of deficit consciousness raising is an understatement. While the long-term fiscal problems of the early twenty-first century make deficit politics of the mid-1980s to mid-1990s look like a romp in the playground, it is hard to exaggerate the Sturm und Drang of deficit reduction from Reagan's second term to Clinton's second term. Balanced-budget legislation and proposed constitutional amendments, first proposed by the frugal Andrew Jackson, became de rigueur, particularly in Republican circles, in the decade beginning in the late 1980s.

The first, hollow symbolic movement to balance the budget came with the passage of the Gramm-Rudman-Hollings Deficit Reduction Act of 1985. Billed as the scourge of profligate spenders, Gramm-Rudman turned out to be one of the most toothless, cynical acts of Congress in U.S. history. It set year-by-year targets to eliminate deficits in six years, supposedly requiring the president to sequester funds if these targets were not met. However, it relied heavily on budget gimmickry and rosy budget assumptions, and it finally fell victim to Gulf War spending needs; Congress formally scrapped the act in late 1990. As Phil Gramm, Warren Rudman, and Fritz Hollings all were to acknowledge, to varying degrees, Gramm-Rudman was a "bad idea whose time had come."[45]

The Gulf War, the savings-and-loan bailout, and the recession under President George H. W. Bush sent "on-budget" deficits into the uncharted territory of $290 billion in 1992, with national debt increasing by a mind-numbing $1.5 trillion during the four ill-fated years of the Bush père administration, thanks to even larger additional "off-budget" deficits reflecting borrowing from Social Security and other trust funds. In the annals of modern political rhetoric, few lines deserve more ridicule than Bush's "Read my lips: no new taxes" pledge in 1988, although Bush and his successor proved to be the most fiscally responsible presidents of the past half-century. While Bush's ill-fated broken promise contributed to his 1992 election defeat, the Omnibus Budget Reconciliation Act (OBRA) of 1990—treason to the tax cutters, but a model of bipartisan fiscal rectitude to others—included massive spending cuts, tax increases, and a Budget Enforcement Act that required that new spending or tax cuts be matched by offsetting revenue increases or spending cuts.[46]

Despite the medium-term success of OBRA 1990 in slowing the growth of America's debt, it was a screechy-voiced billionaire Texan who thrust deficits into the public limelight in 1992. H. Ross Perot, the brilliant but eccentric businessman, bought his way into presidential contention, briefly leading in three-way polls in the spring of 1992 while railing against deficits as portending a fate worse than the Great Depression. While Perot pushed Democrat Bill Clinton and President Bush to address deficits in the 1992 campaign, there also were grassroots efforts such as New York businessman Seymour Durst's creation of a National Debt Clock near Times Square in 1989 and the 1992 formation of the antideficit Concord Coalition by Senators Paul Tsongas (D-Mass.) and Warren Rudman (R-N.H.) and former Nixon Commerce Secretary Pete Peterson.[47]

Despite the modest successes of the 1986 tax deal and the 1990 budget deal, entitlement spending was already turning into a fiscal cancer. Social Security outlays in current dollars, which were $1 billion in 1950 and $17 billion in 1965, had risen to $374 billion in 2006, or from 0.3 percent of GDP to 2.9 percent. Meanwhile, Medicare spending rose from less than 1 percent of GDP in 1975 to 3 percent in 2006. And Medicaid jumped from nothing in 1965 to $181 billion in 2006, or from 0 to 1.4 percent of GDP. In short, the three entitlements' annual cost rose from about 2.5 to 8.5 percent of national income between Presidents Johnson and George W. Bush.[48]

Nonetheless, a certain political momentum—together with luck—resulted in significant deficit reduction during the late Clinton years. While cutting deficits—also known as reneging on the "no new taxes" pledge—was a big political loser for the first President Bush, President Bill Clinton pushed through a five-year deficit-reduction package in 1993 with only Democratic votes in Congress, raising taxes and cutting spending—contributing to the Democrats' electoral defeat in 1994. Whereas Bush I raised the top marginal tax rate from 28 to 31 percent and Clinton raised it to 39.6 percent, Medicare and Medicaid spending was restrained, more Social Security benefits became taxable, the "pay-as-you-go" (or PAYGO) rules of the 1990 Budget Enforcement Act were extended, and defense spending was cut.[49] In fact, one piece of America's fiscal good fortunes of the 1990s stemmed directly from the fall of the Berlin Wall, as Cold War–inspired defense spending fell from 10 percent of GDP from the 1950s to 1970s to 3 percent at the end of the 1990s—and today it remains between 4 and 5 percent. The so-called "peace dividend" was real, but it was spent on hiding entitlement-spending growth and used to borrow time against a fiscal day of reckoning.[50]

Efforts at deficit reduction were boosted in the mid-1990s by the short-lived passage of the line-item veto (quickly ruled unconstitutional by the Supreme

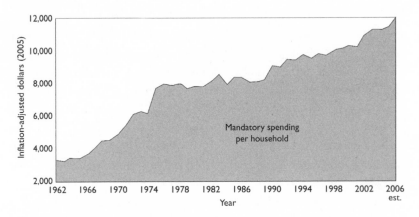

Figure 9. Mandatory spending per household, 1962–2006. *Sources:* U.S. Bureau of the Census; Heritage Foundation

Court), a booming economy, and a bipartisan 1997 budget deal. This Balanced Budget Act brought about further cuts in both discretionary and mandatory spending, with restraints imposed on Medicare prices, as well as tax relief for low-income Americans.[51] Despite the $500 billion nominal deficit reduction in both the 1990 and 1993 measures, and the further cuts in 1997, it was the high-tech-driven economic boom of the late 1990s—unprecedented since the 1960s—that caused federal revenues to soar and deficits to melt. This was compounded by the fiscal restraint exercised during the Clinton presidency and a Republican Congress, which resulted in the slowest spending growth of the past fifty years. During the Clinton administration, real government spending grew by an average of just 1.5 percent a year, compared with more than 5 percent a year under Lyndon Johnson and George W. Bush.[52] After the Clinton–Newt Gingrich showdown that shuttered the government twice in 1995 and 1996, Clinton promised to balance the budget by 2002.

Then, as if fiscal angels had descended from on high, in 1998 President Clinton announced the first budget surplus in twenty-nine years. And the good times were only to get better, Monica Lewinsky aside. The $290 billion deficit of Bush I's last year had become a $236 billion surplus by 2000, and Clinton grandly proclaimed in 1999 that the entire $5.6 trillion national debt could be paid off by 2015. Clinton and his Wunderkind, Treasury Secretary Robert Rubin, called for staying the course of deficit reduction. The president appointed two commissions—on entitlement reform, under Senators Bob Kerrey (D-Neb.) and Jack Danforth (R-Mo.), and Medicare reform, under Senator John

Breaux (D-La.), both of which produced good ideas, as we will see, but whose reports resulted in no policy changes.[53] As the national debt virtually stabilized during Clinton's second term, all looked like sunshine and roses.

Our story might have seemed to be over when George W. Bush was inaugurated in 2001. Surpluses were predicted as far as the eye could see. Budgeteers, normally a taciturn bunch, were downright giddy. But euphoria turned to gloom faster than a transplanted Yankee could clear brush on his Texas ranch. Certainly, much beyond Bush's control went wrong all at once: the dot.com boom turned into a stock-market collapse; the United States was attacked by terrorists, leading to wars in Afghanistan and Iraq; and a mild recession depressed incomes and federal revenues. Moreover, the U.S. population continued to age, as baby boomers marched inexorably from *Sesame Street* toward Medicare, and not only was Social Security once again in need of reform, but the specter of out-of-control health care costs made it clear that Medicare and Medicaid reform were essential if that fiscal tidal wave were not to inundate Washington and rest of the nation. Yet that was only part of the story. Bad geopolitical, economic, and demographic luck go only so far to explain the $10 trillion deterioration in projected federal finances during Bush's first term. A series of massive tax cuts and equally massive spending increases during the Bush administration made all but the most shameless fiscally conservative Republicans blush, at best, and scream bloody murder, at worst. The PAYGO rules were allowed to expire in 2002, only to be reinstated in somewhat weakened form in 2007 by a Democratic-controlled Congress. The old-time Republican cri de coeur against "tax-and-spend, big-government liberals" had given way to widespread Republican and Democratic broadsides against "spend-and-borrow, big-government conservatives." By 2004 deficits were back above $300 billion and were well over $200 billion in 2007, and nearly two-fifths of the debt accumulated during all of U.S. history has been piled up during the first seven years of the Bush II presidency.[54]

Whatever his other legacies, George W. Bush has left the United States with massive debt, just as demographic and economic realities suggested that much worse was yet to come during the first third of the twenty-first century. So before we get to prognosticators' proverbial hell-in-a-hand-basket fiscal scenarios, let's pause to consider just how we, the United States, can get away with owing the princely sum of $10 trillion without armies of pinstriped bankers committing hara-kiri or without a financial Moses to lead us (back) to the land of milk, honey, and fiscal rectitude.

Chapter 3 How Deficits
Are Funded

Every morning at 11:30 A.M., the Treasury Department publicly announces the size of the national debt that day, based on data from about fifty sources. This number, which rises by an average of about $10,500 per second, is also tracked by various others, from the national debt clock near Times Square in New York, a number of deficit-hawk members of Congress who have holographic "debt clocks" in their offices, and antideficit advocates such as the Concord Coalition, which produces a cheery debt-clock refrigerator magnet for those who want to check up on the nation's fiscal fortunes as they reach for their broccoli or beer.

So in 2008 the United States government was approaching $10 trillion in public and intragovernmental debt, not to mention additional trillions of unfunded promises to future generations. The $10 trillion alone would be equal to a $135,000 mortgage for each of America's 74 million homeowners, or about $110,000 in debt for every credit card holder in America (thirteen times the actual figure). If privately borrowed, that $10 trillion would provide every adult American with a lifetime of vacations, or every American household with enough money to send their children to Harvard. One could translate this total ad nauseum, into paying everybody's health care bills or creating a new aid program to fill the world's closets with Manolo Blahnik shoes.

The problem is that debt is funny money, par excellence. Debt—as the eighteenth-century Bishop Berkeley, Abraham Lincoln, and some George W. Bush administration officials have said—is ultimately a nation's, or a world's, money owed to itself. So, if it's just a multitrillion-dollar pool of sloshing liquidity, what does it matter, if *someone* actually has the cash?

At a hypothetical level, it doesn't matter. If U.S. trade deficits continue to climb annually at double-digit rates, maybe the plethora of Chinese goods sold in the United States will continue to yield ever more revenues that are ploughed back into investment in U.S. government securities. It's a devil's bargain, between Chinese communo-capitalists on the one hand and American consumers and shortsighted federal lawmakers on the other: the Chinese fund our debt; we buy goods to create jobs for their teeming hundreds of millions of workers. Think of it as a U.S. taxpayer–funded job-creation program for the Chinese.

At another level, as history and current experience show, debt instruments represent real financial obligations. While the heroin addict of yore may have stolen money to sustain his or her habit, unless we descend into a Hollywood dystopia, however crooked some members of the executive and legislative branches may be, they are not going to hold up Americans, Chinese, Japanese, Saudis, or Europeans at gunpoint and demand that they keep lending us money. (Though it could make a good screenplay.)

U.S. debt isn't as bad as some other countries' as a percentage of GDP, although the U.S. proportion has risen significantly and is on a spike trajectory. On the other hand, if you listen to those talking about unfunded obligations, accrual accounting, and the like, as Comptroller General David Walker, Representative Jim Cooper (D-Tenn.), and others do, $10 trillion is the tip of an iceberg that makes the one that downed the *Titanic* look like a Popsicle.[1]

So where and how do we get the money to finance twelve-figure federal deficits or fourteen-figure federal debt? While this is a mechanical question, it is also a philosophical question, and a question about America's and Americans' future.

Philosophically and morally, it is a question of whether we saddle future generations with the costs of our current fiscal foolhardiness. It is a moral—as well as a political and an economic—question about whether debt, per se, is bad, and whether America, or people in general, should pay for what they consume in a relatively timely fashion, as our more morally and frugally hard-nosed Founders said. Finally, it is a moral—as well as an economic—question whether it is better for a nation, or a person, to save for a rainy day or to borrow to pay for present consumption, leaving only IOUs for future needs and desires that inevitably will arise.

Practically, U.S. government debt is financed from a variety of sources. It is divided into so-called public debt and intragovernmental debt. About 60 percent of U.S. debt is held by "the public," while the remainder constitute "intragovernmental holdings." The "public" is a curiously Orwellian rubric; it includes real, individual American investors, giant institutional investors such as banks and pension funds, and foreign investors such as the communist central bank of China or the Wahhabi fundamentalist regime in Riyadh. Commonly reported deficit numbers are based on "on-budget" differences between spending and revenues, and fuel the growth in public debt. Intragovernmental debt represents government borrowing from a series of federal trust funds to help pay for current operations. When the government borrows from the Social Security Trust Fund, for example, the trust fund gets real interest-paying bonds, essentially IOUs that eventually must be paid back. These are off-budget deficits, which are rarely reported by administrations seeking to make debt numbers look lower. However, official debt includes both public and intragovernmental debt. A third, more controversial category of implicit debt includes the mercurial "unfunded liabilities" that government incurs. The federal government does not have to report the tens of trillions of dollars of future spending to which it has committed, particularly for Social Security and Medicare, for its hundreds of millions of citizens, most of whom eventually will reach retirement and benefit-eligibility age. While using unfunded liabilities as a yardstick, even over a defined period such as an average American lifespan, is controversial, the cash accounting currently used by the U.S. government does understate the problem.

THE U.S. BUDGET PROCESS AND DEBT

Deficits—on- and off-budget—which accumulate into debt, are a product of U.S. government spending exceeding revenues. Federal spending clearly is a function of an extraordinarily complicated budget process. Congress, supposedly holding the proverbial power of the purse under article 1, section 8 of the Constitution, is now constrained by the fact that more than three-fifths of federal spending is for mandatory entitlement programs and interest on the debt. The rest of the budget goes through an annual appropriations process that has gradually devolved from a well-choreographed dance among executive branch agencies, congressional committees, the entire Congress, and the president into an often stumbling, bumbling, politically motivated, fiscally dishonest, and procedurally dysfunctional ritual that is the antithesis of good management in almost every way.

Since the Budget Accounting Act of 1921, the president has submitted a budget for the following fiscal year to Congress at the beginning of each February. This massive Valentine combines a wish list of proposals and predictions of the nation's needs. Since the 1974 Budget Act, the Senate and House Budget Committees have held hearings on the president's budget. Appropriations bills for discretionary spending are to be passed by the beginning of the fiscal year, October 1, but in recent years, budgets have come in three or four months late. If a student turned in homework that late, he or she would get a big fat F. If a corporate manager turned in an assignment that late, he or she would be fired.

As part of the long budget process, Congress is supposed to deliver a budget resolution by April 15. Among other things, this resolution is accompanied by arcane-sounding documents called 302(a) allocations, which set out the amounts of money that all Senate and House committees, including the Appropriations Committee, are allowed to spend.

During the appropriations process, Congress hammers out, or stumbles to, agreement on how much of the appropriations allocation will be spent on new tanks, national parks, federal education and justice initiatives, civil service and military pay, and so on. Ultimately, all federal discretionary spending, including for defense, is shoehorned into twelve appropriations bills. These so-called spending bills, created through House-Senate conference reports, often make up a crazy quilt that includes wildly unrelated programs and many of the so-called pork projects that reflect the ability of members of Congress to "bring home the bacon" to constituents. Congress has become ever more dilatory and sloppy, unable to pass appropriations bills by the end of the fiscal year on September 30 in twenty-four of the twenty-eight years from 1977 through 2004, requiring continuing resolutions to keep the government from shutting down (as it did twice, in 1995 and 1996). Congress also has resorted to rolling all, or many, of these bills into omnibus spending bills that are monstrous grab bags of spending for countless federal programs and activities that have no functional relationship to one another; in a sane world, each would be considered separately on its merits. The sheer bizarreness of this process allows many earmarks to be slipped in by particular members without most of their colleagues realizing what has been added to these massive documents. Needless to say, while many poorly paid congressional staffers are tasked to track the budget, there is nary a member of Congress who reads appropriations acts from cover to cover. To make matters even more absurd, these measures are often passed under duress, with little debate, in the wee hours of the morning, on simple yes-or-no votes. Finally, as an example of our nation's growing profligacy, the president increasingly has requested and Congress increasingly has passed supplemental spending bills that ostensibly are for national emergencies, such as the war in Iraq or Hurricane Katrina, but typically include a huge amount of additional, unrelated, pork-barrel spending.

Once this supremely sensible process is completed, the president is given these bills to sign into law or veto. As we have seen, President Clinton briefly had a line-item veto, which enabled him to delete particular lines of spending, something that many conservatives have supported, but which was ruled unconstitutional by the Supreme Court. With the president's signature in place, and souvenir pens duly distributed, the trillion or so dollars that makes up the discretionary 36 percent of the federal budget start flowing. More than half of this goes to the Defense Department.

To get the money to pay for these discretionary and mandatory programs, the government has to dip into either the general fund of monies raised from taxing and borrowing, or funds earmarked for specific purposes and the big trust funds such as Social Security. While we have discussed the composition of federal taxes and other revenues, the nature and size of what taxes are levied are considered by the House Ways and Means Committee and the Senate Finance Committee. Like spending bills, tax legislation wends its way out of these committees to the full Senate and House for passage, and then to the president for approval or veto.[2]

And since revenues fall short—and increasingly will fall farther and farther short—of spending, the government resorts to deficit financing. As a result, it needs to borrow money to make up the difference.

THE NATURE OF DEBT

Of course, the government doesn't just hold out its hand and say to citizens, financial institutions, or foreign investors, "Can you spare a few hundred billion?"

While many ignore or downplay intragovernmental debt, because it seems like one hand of government slipping cash to the other, it is real money owed that will have to be paid back; it is enormous; and—most frightening—the giving hand of government soon will not have the resources to give that it has had in recent decades. Tsunami alert number one.

In the not-so-long run of a decade or so, the idea of intragovernmental debt as money that we owe to ourselves becomes quite problematic. The $3.7 trillion of intragovernmental holdings in 2006 were overwhelmingly monies borrowed from Social Security and other government trust funds, which, actuarially, cannot be trusted to exist a decade from now. About half of this has been borrowed from Social Security, which has been taking in more revenue than it has paid out—a circumstance that will reverse itself in 2017. In fact, the size of these surpluses begins to decrease this year, and Medicare Part A, or hospital insurance, and projected assets will be outstripped by spending in 2013. Almost two-thirds of a trillion dollars was borrowed from federal employee retirement funds, $300 billion from the federal hospital insurance trust fund, $204 billion from the federal disability trust fund, $65 billion from the unemployment insurance trust fund, and the remainder from a motley assortment of trust funds for such things as highways, airports, FDIC bank-deposit insurance, and federal employees' life insurance. All told, the government has more than two hundred trust funds, but the Social Security, Medicare, and Civil Service Retirement funds account for the lion's share of receipts and assets.[3] Ultimately, not only will these monies have to be repaid, but as some of these sources of intragovernmental borrowing dry up—especially Social Security, but also federal-employee retirement funds—the government will have to rely ever more heavily on public borrowing.

While intragovernmental borrowing is the still relatively benign gorilla in our fiscal closet, the best-known, time-worn way that the United States, or any other government, incurs debt is through public borrowing. Throughout U.S. history, the government has sold Treasury bonds, bills, notes, and other securities that many Americans—and others—have bought as a safe way of saving. Coming with "the full faith and credit of the United States," they have long been considered the world's safest investment. These securities are basically IOUs, in which the government borrows money on which it pays market-based rates of interest.

A myriad of securities exist to suit every investor's taste, from the conservative, short-term grandmother in Topeka to Wall Street financial behemoths. Aside from old favorites such as T-bills and U.S. savings bonds, there are more exotic-flavored securities such as zero-coupon bonds, inflation-indexed TIPS, and the somewhat grisly "flower bonds" payable on death to cover estate taxes. Treasury securities come in almost every denomination, with maturities ranging from three months to thirty years. Treasury notes and bills account for more than 80 percent of the total value of all public debt. Interest is paid on all of these, with rates a function of the Federal Reserve Board's federal funds rate, market demand, and the length of maturity. In eras of high interest rates, such as the late 1970s, T-bills and notes paid high, double-digit rates of return; during times of low interest rate, such as the 1950s or early 2000s, payments relative to borrowing were extremely low. The market for Treasury debt is the world's largest and most liquid, with a daily turnover of about $600 billion—more than all U.S. stock exchanges.[4]

The more than $5 trillion in public debt in early 2008 was owned by a wide variety of investors—with the lion's share *not* held by the proverbial average American small investor. About half a trillion dollars was owned by state and local governments; $300 billion was held by pension funds; and almost $600 billion was owned by U.S. financial institutions.[5]

Barely 15 percent of public debt is owned by individuals, despite long-standing efforts to encourage Americans to save money by buying Treasury securities—and most of this is owned by wealthy and upper-middle-class investors. Unfortunately, Americans' savings rate has been steadily declining to the point that, today, for the first time in history, Americans spend more than they earn. We're not saving for retirement, putting money in bank accounts or stocks, hiding it under the mattress, or—most problematically for the U.S. government—buying U.S. government debt. If Americans were buying T-bills as they once were, at least it would represent personal savings, contribute to future wealth, and bear out Honest Abe's notion that Americans owe money only to themselves.

This brings us to the second big problem. Someone has to step into the breach. And that someone has been foreigners. In September 2007, foreigners owned more than $2.2 trillion, or nearly half of American public debt. Whereas just one-seventh of public debt was owned by Japanese, European, and other non-U.S. investors in 1995, today it's 45 to 50 percent. And the percentage has been rising like a rocket headed for deep space. Since 2001 at least three-quarters of federal borrowing has been done by foreign central banks and other investors. China's holdings alone increased more than fivefold in six years, from $60 billion to $350 billion.[6] By and large, these "foreigners" are not rich women in Paris or industrialists in South Korea. They are other governments, and a handful in particular—the Chinese, the Japanese, the Europeans, and the Saudis.

As Stephen Roach of Morgan Stanley has said: "The United States—long the main engine of global growth and finance—has squandered its domestic saving and is now drawing freely on the rest of the world's saving pool. America is currently absorbing about 80 percent of the world's surplus saving in order to finance open-ended government budget deficits and the excess spending of American consumers."[7]

Much of the money for these purchases, particularly since 2002, has been amassed by foreigners through their growing trade surpluses with the United States. This gets us back to the complex and troubling relationship between America's twin deficits—budget and trade (or among its four deficits, as David Walker has highlighted). Foreign trade surpluses—or U.S. trade deficits—result from Americans buying more Chinese, Japanese, and other foreign goods than Americans sell to the rest of the world. These foreign sales to the United States result in hundreds of billions of dollars flowing into foreign hands every year, which they, then, need to invest somewhere—and U.S. Treasury securities have seemed like a pretty good place to put some of this money. All told, the United States—not long ago, the world's greatest creditor nation—owed about $3.5 trillion to foreigners in 2005, with public debt accounting for more than half of that.[8]

While the Japanese remain our friends and allies, and we certainly have deep relationships with the Chinese and Saudis, China remains a nuclear-armed Communist country that illegally detains dissidents, and Saudi Arabia is a theocratic oil producer that spawned the likes of Osama bin Laden and most of the 9/11 terrorists. If political or economic problems emerged between the United States and China, for example, China could curtail its funding of a trillion dollars of debt, sending our financial markets and economy into a tailspin. An Islamic revolution that toppled the House of Saud, for all its other effects, could have a similar fiscal impact.

Some countries already are starting to become wary of U.S. debt as a prudent investment. In the past few years, South Korea briefly balked at buying more U.S. securities; Italy announced it was shifting a substantial portion of its dollar investments into British pounds; and Russia, Sweden, and the United Arab Emirates moved to make similar shifts, explicitly citing fears about America's budget and trade deficits.[9] Some observers worry that foreign investors could shift their assets into Euros, pounds, or yen. If this shift started to occur, the United States would have to ramp up interest rates to try to attract foreign investors. Higher interest rates could plug the hole in the dike but could also have the perverse effect of dramatically slowing U.S. economic growth, leading not only to hard times for American households and businesses but also reduced federal revenues and even greater difficulty in paying for U.S. government services.

Aside from the risks of foreigners pulling the plug, foreign financing of U.S. debt may have other, more immediate consequences. What may be most rankling to taxpayers is the fact that an ever-growing share of the interest payments that the U.S. government is obliged to make is being paid to foreign lenders. About $90 billion in taxpayer money was paid in interest to foreigners in 2005—more than the federal government spent on health care for children, job training, and medical care for veterans combined—and this de facto U.S. assistance to not-so-needy foreign central banks is rising at an alarming rate.[10]

While the $10 trillion of public and intragovernmental debt—whether owned by potentially fickle foreigners, soon-to-disappear trust funds, or others—is the frequently billboarded U.S. debt number, some would say that the U.S. debt problem is many times larger. And this is the part that isn't funded by borrowing; it is simply unfunded. These are the tens of trillions of dollars of promises made to America's citizens to pay them Social Security, Medicare, and other benefits over the coming decades for which we have no revenue stream or borrowing source to cover the costs. So while federal "unfunded liabilities" technically are not debt, are not borrowed money, and have no debt instruments funding them, they are financial obligations of the U.S. government— and hence the American people—that we don't have the funds to pay for. Some may quibble with the very concept of unfunded liabilities—although they are a standard bookkeeping procedure for business—yet sometime, somehow, somewhere someone needs to cough up the money and/or reduce the size of the obligations.

So maybe those who say that driving our economy by consuming is patriotic are right, as every dollar spent on a Chinese-made tchotchke at Wal-Mart is partly funding our debt and our government's operations. But the bottom line is that the Social Security Trust Fund is going to run dry as a source for borrowing, Americans need to save much, much more and invest the money in Treasury securities, and foreigners aren't going to keep bailing us out forever.

Since printing a lot more money is out of the question in an inflation-averse world, what happens if the U.S. Treasury holds a securities auction and (almost) no one comes?

This leads us to the potential, and potentially calamitous, effects of rising debt on the nation and its citizens.

Chapter 4 How Deficits and Debt Affect America and You

Things can go wrong in such a rich variety of ways.
Laurence Ball and Gregory Mankiw

The ultimate test of a moral society is the kind of world it leaves to its children.
Dietrich Bonhoeffer

Most Americans today don't pop sleeping pills worrying about our several hundred billion–dollar budget deficits, $10 trillion debt, and $50 trillion in unfunded liabilities. Yet the fact of the matter is that deficits and debt affect every one of us, particularly in three arenas where they should hit home—the pocketbook, the fortunes of our children, and the broader quality of life in America.

Harry Truman famously, and frustratedly, said that he wished he could find a one-armed economist. Economists, like indecisive gamblers, are notorious for observing that "on the one hand," if x, y, and z happen, then all will be well with the economy, but "on the other hand," if a, b, and c happen, then disaster will strike. In other words, they marshal the same data to make opposing cases, or they hedge their bets to make highly conditional analyses and predictions, filled with lots of "ifs."

So on deficits and debt, as with other economic matters, some economists say one thing, some another, and some say "it all depends." Basically, however, there are three camps—two small and one so large, distinguished, and bipartisan that it is likely to be right. The small camps take the positions either that "deficits don't matter," as Vice President Cheney said, or that they *can* be beneficial.[1]

Since the overwhelming majority of economists, politicians, and other soothsayers say that deficits and debt *do* affect the American (or any other) economy, and not in a particularly good way, let's spend a few minutes with those contrarians who say otherwise.

DEFICITS DON'T MATTER

When President Bush's former Treasury secretary Paul O'Neill warned about rising budget deficits in late 2002, Vice President Dick Cheney famously told him, a month before O'Neill was fired: "You know Paul, Reagan proved that deficits don't matter."[2] Former congressman and professional football player Jack Kemp is among those who have noted that there is little empirical data that deficits have harmful economic effects, although most economists and politicians would counter that there is a big difference between an absence of significant effects in the short term and the near certainty of serious macroeconomic effects over a ten-to-twenty-year time horizon.[3] Cheney, never a master of tact, nonetheless expressed a view that has some intellectual pedigree, albeit a slim one. While Reagan's budget director David Stockman warned his president that tax cuts and spending increases didn't add up, and Reagan professed fealty to fiscal discipline, Reagan did not prove that deficits don't matter. Reagan's calls for a balanced-budget amendment, the post-1982 tax increases, the budget agreement of 1986, the 1985 Gramm-Rudman-Hollings Act, and the deficit worries after the 1987 stock market crash all suggested that Ronald Reagan was keenly aware that deficits mattered. (But Dick Cheney was just an obscure congressman from the wilds of Wyoming then.)

Yet let's consider the arguments that deficits and debt don't matter. Robert Eisner, one of the chief academic exponents of this view, argues that interest on the debt is unimportant because most of it goes back into American pockets (no longer, pal). Moreover, deficits don't affect interest rates, because the Federal Reserve Board sets rates, and global liquidity provides a sufficient pool of capital so that the cost of money does not rise too high. In addition, many rightly scoff at the idea that the United States is "bankrupt" or heading rapidly toward bankruptcy. As these critics correctly point out, Americans have at least $100 trillion in wealth, and the value of public assets (public lands, for example), as well as buildings and other physical plant, not to mention the incalculable value of our "human capital," adds even more to this stock of wealth. And they say that deficits and debt should be judged in relation to national wealth, not the size of the federal budget or even the GDP. Finally, some believe that reducing deficits may slow economic growth.[4] Although reality belies this, a few economists say that, theoretically, lower public savings should mean higher private savings—the same argument that federal debt goes into the pockets or bank accounts of American citizens.[5]

As for the case that deficits are (or can be) beneficial to the economy, we have already touched on the Keynesian argument that in the short term, deficits— through tax cuts or deficit spending—can provide a shot in the arm to a lackluster economy.[6] Between the 1940s and the early 1970s—and even in 2001, with the recession and 9/11—strategic tax cuts and spending increases were used successfully to revive a lagging economy. Those are largely special cases. Keynes himself, the Keynesians of the 1940s to 1970s, and more recent anti-Keynesians who still have followed Keynesian-style thinking and practices— such as George W. Bush and Ronald Reagan—all said that budgets should be balanced in the long run, and that deficits should be a short-term, counter-cyclical medicine for an economy in recession. When an economy regains its strength, it should use its surpluses to repay debt and eliminate deficits.

Nonetheless, a few have taken this argument a step further—although it has little practical bearing on today's, or tomorrow's, U.S. economy. They say, perhaps rightly, that borrowing money to pay for useful investments in the nation's future strength is good policy. If that's what we were borrowing money for—to build back a first-class education system, modernize our transportation networks, restore aging housing, water, and other infrastructure, invest in scientific research, enhance early child health or even seed promising new industries—the monies could have a strong, positive effect on economic growth and improved living standards. Moreover, there are differential effects of different kinds of spending and tax cuts. Appropriately targeted tax cuts can not only stimulate the economy in the short term but also boost the purchasing power of lower-income Americans, as the Earned Income Tax Credit has shown.

Supply-siders also believe that it is okay to run deficits by cutting taxes, because such cuts purportedly stimulate the economy more than enough to compensate for the cuts. In the 1990s, however, when taxes were raised and spending was under control, national savings rose at a healthy clip, largely stimulated by the increase in government savings, or surpluses; this, in turn, contributed to the strong economic growth of the era. Although precise revenue returns on tax cuts are debated, virtually all research—including studies by such conservative economists as William Niskanen and Gregory Mankiw—has shown that tax cuts do not pay for themselves; at best, a tax cut stimulates enough economic growth to repay only a fraction in tax revenues of every dollar in revenues lost.[7]

SO IF DEFICITS DO MATTER, WHAT'S THE STORY?

It would be nice to believe that hundreds of billions of dollars of annual deficits, $10 trillion in national debt, and trillions more in unfunded liabilities were inconsequential, the concern of politico-economic Chicken Littles. It also would be nice to believe in Santa Claus and the tooth fairy, but even my son discarded such beliefs by the time he turned eight.

In fact, as countless economists and policy makers across the political spectrum argue, deficits and debt have a wide variety of potential consequences—and none of them is particularly good. Before reaching for your Prozac, or bourbon, remember that not all of these effects are certain, their degree of severity is unknown, and wise policy in the near future to reduce deficits and debt can attenuate these problems, if not make them go away.

While deficits have many effects on the overall U.S. economy, the most important is that they deplete saving for our future and for funding investments in the economy and society of the future. National saving, which enables us not only to save for that proverbial "rainy day" but also provides capital for private and public investment, is necessary for economic growth and rising living standards.[8] National saving is made up of government, business, and personal savings. Both government and personal savings are now in negative territory, while recent high profits have allowed business to maintain a fair savings rate. But even in a global economy with as much as several hundred trillion dollars of wealth, there is a limited pool of money from which governments, businesses, and individuals can borrow.

And it matters greatly for everyone's well-being whether that public, private-sector, or personal borrowing is for productive purposes—such as building new ports or mapping the genome, constructing new factories, or paying for a college education—or for less productive purposes—such as paying interest on our national debt or funding bloated programs such as Medicare, underwriting CEOs' golden parachutes, or buying cars or clothing that one cannot afford and may not need. While private investment is vital for economic growth, productive public investments are, too. If we are spending taxpayer dollars on interest payments to foreigners instead of investing in children's and veterans' health and job training, we are enriching foreigners at the expense of investing in the present and future well-being of the American people.

Even more serious, if we were not so fiscally straitjacketed, we would have funds for the twenty-first-century equivalents of public-sector investments that helped spur late-twentieth-century American prosperity. By accumulating deficits—and devoting an ever-greater share of spending to entitlements and interest payments on the debt—we are crowding out possible spending on things that could make our lives better. We could be spending these hundreds of billions on the environment, new technologies, transportation to relieve our choked highways, public education, life-extending medical research, homeland security, national service programs, and initiatives to boost our nation's savings, private investment, and global competitiveness—among many other things. For example, $35 billion per year—peanuts compared to our interest payments, deficits, and debt—would buy America public preschool. As Pete Peterson of the Blackstone Group, Nixon's former commerce secretary and a leader of the antideficit Concord Coalition, has noted, such "future-oriented" spending has shrunk from about 32 percent of outlays in 1965 to 14 percent in 2000.[9]

But as many conservatives have come to recognize, cutting discretionary spending is not a viable way of balancing the budget. Not only are the sums far too little, but some have argued that the "starve the beast" philosophy of cutting government by cutting taxes simply does not work.[10] Likewise, deficits hinder government's flexibility to spend on unforeseen needs—whether a Hurricane Katrina or other natural disasters, a war or terrorist attack, or the outbreak of an epidemic disease. The effects of federal deficits also ripple down the governmental food chain, adding expenses for state and local authorities. On the one hand, a federal-state program such as Medicaid, which is growing like a budgetary gorilla on steroids, is already squeezing states' budgets, forcing them to either raise taxes or, more commonly, cut spending on other items such as state university systems. On the other hand, things for which the federal government no longer pays the bill—such as some consequences of poverty or natural disasters—as well as "unfunded mandates" passed onto the states by Washington lawmakers (like those required under the No Child Left Behind Act), add to states' fiscal burdens. And as has been pointed out, state finances, including unfunded liabilities for public-employee pension and health care plans, are not exactly in rosy shape either these days.

We have seen that long-term debt reduces national savings and thereby crowds out funds that might be available for productive, growth-producing investment. This is true because capital—or money to borrow—is not limitless. It is also true because of a basic principle of Econ 101: if the demand for any good, including capital, exceeds the supply of it, its cost will rise. Thus high government demand to borrow money, coupled with demand from businesses and individuals, drives up the cost of money, or interest rates. Indeed, government and business become competitors on capital markets, with government seeking money to pay for its operations and finance its ever-growing debt, and businesses seeking money to productively invest. In the process, they bid up the price of money, with negative impacts on both. The leading luminaries of the economics profession—including former Federal Reserve chairman and economic rock star Alan Greenspan, Reagan's top economic adviser Martin Feldstein, Nixon's chief economic adviser Herb Stein, Clinton's Treasury Secretary Robert Rubin, and former George W. Bush economic adviser Gregory Mankiw—*all* say that long-term debt will lead to rising interest rates, slower economic growth, and lower (or less rapidly rising) living standards for Americans.[11]

As Greenspan has said: "Long-term deficits . . . [are] likely to be consistent with rising interest rates, which would slow long-term growth." Rubin, credited in part with achieving the four Clinton-era budget surpluses, is even more blunt: "The reduction in national saving raises domestic interest rates, which dampens investment. . . . The reduction in domestic investment (which lowers productivity growth) and the increase in the current account deficit (which requires that more of the returns from the domestic capital stock accrue to foreigners) both reduce future national income, with the loss in income steadily growing over time."[12]

Efforts to calculate the exact numerical effect of deficits on interest rates are complicated by the politics of the Federal Reserve, the uncertainties of global capital markets, and the unpredictability of unforeseen events. That, of course, has not stopped economists from trying to come up with numbers (which takes us back to Harry Truman's problem with economists). For example, Pete Peterson estimates that each percentage point in long-term federal deficits increases interest rates by 25 to 50 basis points, or one-fourth to one-half of 1 percentage point. Mankiw and the Johns Hopkins economist Laurence Ball estimate that deficits at 3.5 percent of GDP raise interest rates by 100 to 200 basis points.[13]

Increased interest rates would hit the individual pocketbook by raising the cost of mortgage and other borrowing. Some estimate that a $250,000 mortgage could cost up to $2,000 more a year under realistic scenarios. Others have estimated that a 1 percentage point increase in interest rates, consistent with a 4 percentage point increase in deficits as a share of GDP, would raise the average auto loan by $168 a year, student loans by $130 a year, credit card debt by $74 a year, and small-business loans by about $1,250 a year. Including all interest that the average American pays each year, the additional costs could total at least $3,000.[14] And this is assuming that interest rates go up as economists' models project, rather than going into orbit in some crisis, which would push personal costs much higher. Higher interest rates also would depress consumption, as fewer Americans would go into debt (or deeper into debt) to buy all the goodies of life; such consumer restraint, in turn, would depress the national economy. It also would drive many small companies out of business and deter many entrepreneurs from new businesses.

Just as deficits are blamed for hiking interest rates, they are also fingered by a wide variety of economists for ultimately stoking inflation. This can happen in a number of overlapping ways. Borrowing contributes to an increased perception of wealth, thereby stimulating consumption and demand, which tends to put upward pressure on prices. If the Federal Reserve adopts an expansionary policy to accommodate deficits, it can result in too much easy credit, which drives up prices. A depreciating dollar also could spark inflation. In addition, although it is unlikely in our monetarist world, government could be tempted to increase the money supply unduly, which also would be inflationary.[15]

Beyond reduced national savings, increased interest rates, reduced investment, and perhaps inflation and reduced economic growth, sustained deficits and debt have other less than salutary effects. Economically and morally, they unjustly transfer the burden of paying for current consumption onto future generations. It's like going on a shopping spree and telling your toddler that he or she will have to foot the bill in twenty years. From the earliest days of the republic to the present, political leaders from George Washington to George W. Bush have concurred that this is morally wrong. And the immorality of it has a firm economic basis. We are reducing our children's and grandchildren's future living standards by handing them a fourteen-figure tab as they try to embark on happy, prosperous lives.

"Fiscal deficits impose a burden on future generations," as Martin Feldstein, the president of the National Bureau of Economic Research and President Reagan's chairman of the Council of Economic Advisers, has bluntly said. "Borrowing only postpones the time when taxes will have to be paid."[16]

Many sensibly argue that each generation should "pay for itself," and some economists such as Lawrence Kotlikoff of Boston University and Alan Auerbach of the University of California, Berkeley, have suggested that we should introduce some form of "generational accounting" to assess whether the costs and benefits of succeeding generations are balanced. For example, Kotlikoff has estimated that those born in the early 1960s would pay more than $300,000 each in taxes over their lifetimes, compared with just $80,000 for those born in 1921. Similarly, those born before the end of World War II will as a group have received $11.5 trillion in benefits more than they paid in, in present value, whereas most of the 90 percent of population born since then will get back slightly less than they contributed to the program. The younger you are and the higher your income is, the less you will get back of the monies that you and your employer paid into the Social Security system.[17] Conversely, some say that as America and its people get wealthier over time, it is not entirely unfair for future generations to bear a greater cost if they are paying for investments by their parents' generation that contributed to their increased wealth.

Deficits also constrain the freedom of future generations to spend their tax dollars as they, or their elected leaders, see fit. If most government spending is committed to entitlements and interest payments, adults in the 2020s and beyond will be unable to choose to spend on new, needed, and unforeseen programs, and unable to spend less on costs mandated by their forefathers (that is, us). Those born around 2000 will be unable to make political choices about how to spend their tax dollars, which our American democracy historically has promised. Furthermore, becoming financially boxed in by higher taxes and interest payments will limit their private choices as well, financially constraining their historic American freedom to the "pursuit of happiness."

Part of this burden on Americans born after, say, 1965, would result from lowered living standards due to slower economic growth. This, as we have seen, would result from lower savings and investment to develop new businesses, productivity-enhancing technologies, and jobs. If real economic growth slows from 3 percent a year to 1.5 percent (or less), it would take Americans' incomes forty-seven years or more to double instead of twenty-four years. Slower growth and higher costs—aside from Americans' historically rising aspirations—would mean that the average American would need to work longer hours to keep up. That might mean more hours at the same job, taking multiple jobs, and/or more hours worked by both members of a couple and even their children.

However, as income growth slowed, debt-related costs would rise, further nibbling away at American living standards. As Feldstein suggests, inevitably the tax man will have to be paid. If nothing is done, federal taxes would have to increase by one-third to one-half in the next twenty years. If things get worse, or we spend additional monies on either useful or not-so-useful things, that tax bill could be even higher. As conservatives rightly point out, this further distorts and harms the economy by reducing the funds available to save, invest, and consume—all drivers of economic growth.[18] While no one can honestly say, especially as income is growing, when taxes truly become "too high" and become a drag on the economy, there is no doubt that sharply increased tax rates would hurt the overall American economy as well as tax-paying Americans.

At current growth rates, taxes, in constant dollars, would have to rise for the average taxpayer by at least $7,000 over twenty years. Of course, not all Americans are "average" or equal. Since all tax cuts, as well as spending, eventually will have to be paid for, it is the 85 percent of households that today earn less than $100,000 who would be the big losers in the long run, because broad-based taxes in the future would need to compensate for recent massive tax cuts for the wealthy.[19] Moreover, Social Security and Medicare taxes would skyrocket, if those programs are not reformed. Depending on how long reform is delayed, Social Security taxes, now at 12.4 percent, could rise by 3 to 5 percentage points over the next generation, and Medicare taxes, now at 2.9 percent, could rise by anywhere from 3 to 10.5 percentage points.[20]

Yet this is only part of the story of lowered living standards, thanks to federal debt. Whether Social Security and Medicare are reformed or not, benefits will go down, even though the costs of paying for benefits (even with private accounts) will go up, at least over the next generation or two.[21] Today's young Americans, in particular, will be shortchanged because—under our "pay-as-you-go" financing structure for Social Security—the return on the payments into the FICA pot will be steadily less than for those of older cohorts. If nothing at all is done about Social Security, it will be able to pay only about three-quarters of its scheduled benefits in 2041, when the trust fund is completely ex-

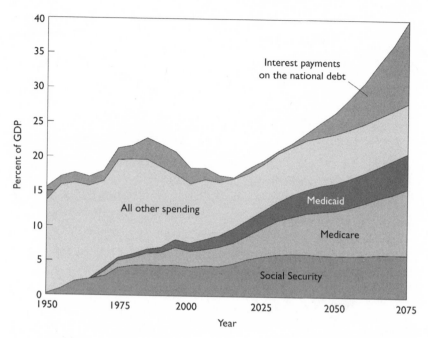

Figure 10. Federal outlays by category, 1950–2075. *Source:* Congressional Budget Office, "A 125-Year Picture of the Federal Government's Share of the Economy," 2002

hausted. Alternatively, under proposals by both liberals and conservatives to re-form Social Security, anyone who is younger than about forty-five would suffer benefit cuts ranging from 1 percent to 15 percent, with the biggest cuts affecting those under twenty-five. Middle-income Americans could be expected to suffer larger-than-average cuts if reforms were instituted that protected the poor and low-income citizens.[22]

The scary part about Social Security and Medicare (and Medicaid) benefit cuts is that many Americans rely entirely on these programs for their financial needs in old age and/or ill health. Despite an average monthly check of just $900, for two-thirds of recipients Social Security accounts for more than half of their income, and 17 percent have no other income whatsoever. More than half of U.S. workers have less than $25,000 in savings aside from their primary res-idence, about one-third of baby boomers have no retirement savings other than Social Security, another third have far too little, and one-fifth never had chil-dren who might support them in old age.[23] One-quarter of American workers earn less than $8 an hour, and average credit-card debt alone has more than tripled in fifteen years, reaching $8,500 in 2005.[24] The fact that Americans' sav-

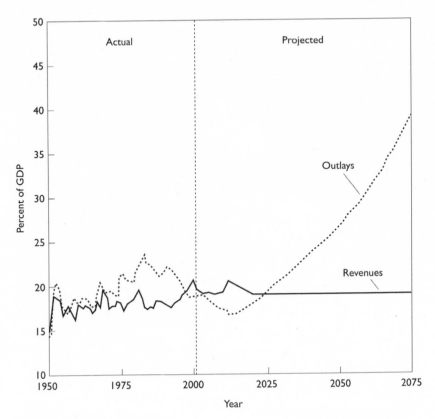

Figure 11. Federal revenues and outlays, 1950–2075. *Source:* Congressional Budget Office, "A 125-Year Picture of the Federal Government's Share of the Economy," 2002

ings rates have descended into invisible territory is a troubling and complex story. Certainly, one cause is economic, as many Americans cannot make ends meet, do not have money to save, and have to borrow to meet their needs. Yet another part of the story is cultural: Americans have long had rising aspirations to acquire more and more things. These aspirations have been stoked by advertising and "keeping up with the Joneses," or what is now called "competitive consumption." While many Americans face genuine hardship and cannot save, there is also a disturbingly short-sighted quality about a population that loves shopping malls, online shopping, bigger houses, new cars, more vacations and dinners out, yet fails to save.

The gloomy picture for Americans' old age deepens, as only about half of all workers participate in private pension or health care plans—a percentage that has been steadily falling—and most are now in "defined contribution" plans such as 401(k)s, with little money stashed away. Moreover, many of the older, traditional defined benefit plans are underfunded, and employers may not have the money to pay for them. (Thanks to federal law, the government insures these funds—which is good for beneficiaries, but bad for the country and debt, because any default would mean an additional, enormous federal expenditure, somewhat similar to the savings-and-loan bailout of the early 1990s.) Finally, it is estimated that only about one-fourth of baby boomers expect to receive an inheritance, and—despite grand stories about the intergenerational transfer of trillions of dollars of wealth—the median inheritance is expected to be less than $50,000.[25]

While all these economic costs—lower wages, higher interest payments, higher taxes, and declining benefits—add up, there is a subtler aspect to stagnant or declining living standards. Put simply, this was never what America was about. This nation was founded and has grown on the promise of better tomorrows, and, over the long haul, it has delivered. Particularly, in the era after World War II, the nation brought rapidly rising incomes to most of its citizens. If that were to end, what would that say about America, and what would it do to Americans' confidence in their country and its future? The psychological costs of a debt-induced fall in living standards are hard to calculate. People would probably become more pessimistic and depressed about their own futures and their nation's. Those who might escape these horrors—the rich—might become the object of considerable antipathy. Public cynicism—already high toward government and many other institutions—would be likely to rise, and patriotism might start to wane.

From deficits to depression to declining patriotism. It might seem a stretch. But the ingredients are there.

Chapter 5 The Potential Dangers of Doing Nothing, or Fiddling While Our Economy Goes Up in Smoke

If early and meaningful action is not taken, the U.S. economy could be seriously weakened. The longer we wait, the more severe, the more draconian, the more difficult the objectives are going to be. I think the right time to start was about ten years ago.
Federal Reserve Chairman Ben Bernanke

Herb Stein, the legendary economist and adviser to presidents, once said: "That which cannot go on forever won't."[1] In other words, something's gotta give when it comes to America's growing national debt. Essentially, there are two options: 1) muddling along for a while, not doing much, and letting the problem get worse, or much, much worse, which is ultimately unsustainable; or 2) thoughtful and courageous reforms that reestablish the nation's fiscal well-being and position the United States for strength, growth, and better lives for its citizens in the twenty-first century and beyond. While the second option, which—in theory—everyone hopes will come to pass, will be the subject of the concluding two chapters, we will address the less promising first option in this chapter.

As most deficit watchers recognize, the potential ill effects of

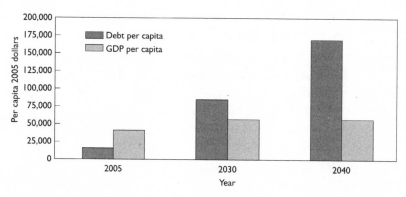

Figure 12. Debt per capita compared with GDP per capita, 2005–2040. *Source:* Government Accountability Office

deficits are not likely to happen overnight. Remember Charles Schultze's comment: "The problem is not that the wolf is at the door. It's more like termites in the woodwork."[2]

If this is the case, the danger is a slow, almost imperceptible decline in America's macroeconomic health and its people's living standards as debt continues to grow. Needing an ever more massive infusion of cash to pay for the promises our society has made, mostly to those in retirement, as well as for the rest of

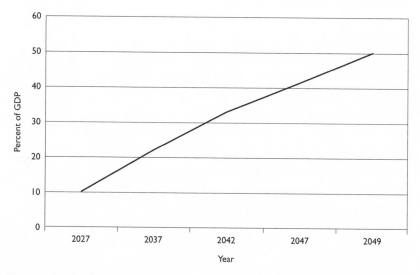

Figure 13. Projected growth of debt held by the public. *Source:* Concord Coalition

government and rising interest on the debt itself, the government either sharply raises taxes, or cuts spending so close to the bone that our then-skeletal government can barely stand, or borrows more—or does all three. To paraphrase the late, great Illinois Senator Everett Dirksen, "a trillion here and a trillion there, and pretty soon we have real money"—and serious liabilities.

In short, the potential consequences of doing nothing—or conducting business as usual—are manifold. We would have no money for needed new initiatives or emergencies. Government spending on essential public goods would be slowly crowded out. State and local governments would be squeezed. Taxes at all levels of government would go up. As the young perceive that they are paying an undue share of their nation's historical burden, resentment toward older generations could grow. If domestic savings continue to decline and foreigners reduce their lending to the U.S. Treasury, interest rates would rise; growth would slow as fewer businesses could afford to borrow the capital to invest in new buildings, equipment, and workers; and standards of living would barely increase or would start to fall. The Chinese and others would gain more power over our finances, and consequently would assume greater geopolitical weight in the world. Psychologically, the combination of failed government, broken "promises" to the elderly, stagnant or falling living standards, intergenerational resentment, and declining U.S. clout and prestige in the world would sour a historically optimistic, future-oriented nation. This is a scenario that could be characterized as analogous to the slow decline of the Roman Empire or the long twilight of Edwardian England. As Josh Blivens of the Economic Policy Institute has said: "The longer the debt is allowed to grow, the more significant is the loss of future income claims and the more intense the pressure on U.S. living standards."[3]

So once again, the question of why we don't do something *now* cries out for an answer.

Let's pause for a moment to review the numbers: nearly $10 trillion in debt, with a growing portion of it "public" (that is, owed to investors, not soon-to-dwindle government trust funds), with $50 trillion in promised benefits for future generations for which we have made no provision to pay.[4] Those numbers are currently rising by about half a trillion and two trillion dollars a year, respectively, with Medicare and Medicaid expenditures expected to double between 2006 and 2016. (Medicare alone is likely to pass defense spending in 2010 to become the single biggest item in our budget.) If nothing is done to reform our fiscal morass, annual deficits are projected to climb to more than $700 billion by 2015. Continuing the Bush administration's tax cuts would reduce revenues by 2 percent of GDP (about $250 billion a year). At the same time, Bush's Medicare Part D program will add an estimated $500 billion to our debt by 2015, and that is only if the "doughnut hole" in the program is not closed by providing even more benefits. And if nothing is done to rein in cost growth, by about 2040 the three major entitlement programs will devour the entire 18 percent of our economy that has gone to federal revenues since the 1950s. Simultaneously, interest payments on our debt could devour an additional 18–22 percent of GDP by the 2040s (and interest payments could be even higher if interest rates leap upward). All told, our national debt will be three times the size of our economy by 2040 and five times the size of our total national output by 2050, if we stumble down our current path.[5]

So all those scary "debt clocks"—there's even one on the U.S. Treasury Web site—keep ticking away like time bombs.[6] Or perhaps the seeming unreality of such enormous debt makes them appear more like those children's cartoon clocks whose hands spin wildly out of control.

If we don't control entitlement spending, coupling it with modest tax broadening, the American people will be faced with a tab that will rise so rapidly that it would be like adding endless lobster thermidors or filets mignons to a restaurant bill faster than the waiter could retally the tab. Gluttonous we may be, but the sad thing is that *we* wouldn't even consume most of that, as the payments will go to entitlements for the elderly or interest increasingly paid to foreigners. So once again, pass the lobster to grandma and the Chinese, and sock it to Junior.

One way that Americans in the coming years could feel that higher tab would be through rising federal, state, and local taxes. Noting that deficits and tax cuts eventually will have to be paid for, Alan Greenspan offered the enduring homily: "There's no free lunch."[7] As we've noted, federal taxes would have to increase from their current 17–19 percent of GDP to 24–28 percent of national income. This, on average, is about $7,000 per household more to be forked over to the good ol' IRS. States, which also have to pay a portion of Medicaid and are already cutting funds for higher education, transportation, and other initiatives to pay for Medicaid and K–12 public schools, would have to raise income, sales, and/or property taxes. Increased federal, state, and local taxes, most economists believe, would slow economic growth by making resources scarcer for businesses to invest and individuals to consume and save.[8]

Although polls, surprisingly, show that Americans are willing to pay more taxes if they feel they are getting something for their money and not passing bills on to their children and grandchildren, these taxes overwhelmingly would go to growing entitlements and interest payments, not to programs for working families or investments in education, highways, medical research, a cleaner environment, homeland security, and all the "good," "better future" things that most Americans say that they want. In short, there would be little money to invest in the future, at a time when the American Society of Civil Engineers, for example, has given failing grades to U.S. transportation, flood defense, drinking water, and other infrastructure systems, and estimated that the United States currently needs $1.2 trillion in infrastructure investments, including $400 billion for schools alone.[9]

In addition, Social Security and Medicare payroll taxes would have to rise even more steeply. Joe Antos of the American Enterprise Institute told Congress that to fully pay for all parts of Medicare, the current Medicare payroll tax would have to rise from 2.9 percent to 13.4 percent over the next quarter-century. Similarly, the Social Security payroll tax would need to climb from about 11 to 17 percent by 2030, with 3 of those percentage points coming out of workers' pockets and the other 3 from employers.[10] All told, if nothing is done, the average taxpayer would be paying 35–40 percent of his or her income in federal income and payroll taxes, in addition to state and local taxes—a level equal to some of the most tax-burdened western European welfare states, which, to their credit, at least deliver many of these and other services better than the United States currently does. But as Antos said, such a tax burden would be nothing short of "intolerable."

The one probable caveat to this potential future of much higher taxes is that American incomes also will be higher. In fact, income growth is expected to outstrip the projected dollar amount of tax growth, still leaving the average citizen with more money in his or her pocket. And some, not entirely unreasonably, argue that it's not wrong to saddle future generations with the financial burden of present-day profligacy because richer future generations will better be able to afford this fiscal burden. Some truth, some rationalization.

Yet even this stance is predicated on some shaky assumptions. First, and most troubling, is the old truism that averages are deceptive: if everyone's incomes were rising together, perhaps this premise would be legitimate, but in fact, for the past thirty years or so, upper-income Americans have seen their incomes rise rapidly, middle-class Americans have seen their incomes barely grow, and incomes of the poor and working poor have fallen. Second, these assumptions that incomes will grow faster than needed taxes are predicated on current economic growth rates—which, in turn, are based on current projections for interest rates, investment, productivity growth, and labor-force growth; they could be better or worse. Interest rates and productivity could be higher or lower. (For example, the difference between 1 and 1.5 percent average annual productivity growth over the next thirty years translates into the difference between American GDPs of $23 trillion or $34 trillion, and per capita incomes of $48,000 or $73,000.)[11] The same uncertainty applies to birth and immigration rates, as a larger workforce could contribute to greater national output. While the termites merely may nibble away at our great House of Prosperity, if the projections are wrong, the wolves might gather, and any projected income growth could vanish in the conflagration of economic crisis or depression.

If we continue to muddle along, without seriously tackling entitlement and tax reform and without attempting to bring our budget at least close to balance (much less pay down our debt), the U.S. government will have to face the prospect of draconian spending cuts. This doesn't "just" mean doing away with most of the popular programs that make up the ever-smaller sliver of the budgetary pie that is "domestic discretionary" spending and defense; it also would entail painful cuts in Medicare and Social Security benefits that most Americans have come to treat as a God-given promise. And, for a population in which huge numbers of people have no personal savings, no employer pensions, and poor health-insurance coverage or none at all, this could be felt as consigning an enormous proportion of our people to the twenty-first-century equivalent of Victorian poorhouses. (If this were to happen, who would be the American Dickens to chronicle American destitution in the age of early- to mid-twenty-first century debt?)

Furthermore, as we have seen, there would be no fiscal wiggle room to pay for—heaven forbid—needed new spending, not to mention such emergencies as wars, natural disasters, or economic calamities. It bears remembering that the war in Iraq ultimately may cost $1 trillion to $1.5 trillion.[12] It also is worth remembering that Hurricane Katrina's not terribly successful cleanup costs have run to $200 billion, or that most climatologists believe that the next generation is in for an upsurge in hurricanes. And estimates suggest that the costs of a tsunami and earthquake hitting southern California could well equal Katrina's economic toll.[13] Finally, the savings-and-loan bailout of the early 1990s cost taxpayers a half-trillion dollars then, and a similar federal bailout of the Pension Benefit Guaranty Corporation (PBGC), which insures millions of shaky, employer-provided pensions, easily could have an eleven-figure price tag, with the agency reporting $450 billion in private-sector pension obligations in 2006. (Unfunded public-sector pension obligations are estimated at another $500 billion.)[14]

If we stay the course on a trajectory in which taxes have to be raised and/or benefits cut while personal savings remain negligible and private pensions and health care coverage continue to decline, and few can bank on hefty inheritances, many Americans could face severe economic hardship in older age, not to mention lowered living standards throughout their lives. In addition, one-sixth of American adults are currently burdened with medical debt, a proportion that will only rise under current trajectories. Declining economic confidence could lead to falling stock and home prices, further depressing the wealth upon which Americans could draw.[15] They might be forced to work two or three jobs, or until they are seventy-five—if they can. Individuals might have to go even deeper in debt—taking out more home-equity loans, signing up for reverse mortgages, and ramping up their credit card balances to pay for the needs of old age. They might slide into poverty and indigence, forcing them to rely on public assistance. Homelessness could rise. But as public-assistance programs for the poor, such as Medicaid, are squeezed, more may have to rely on private charity. The "golden years" after sixty-five, enjoyed by millions of Americans during the late twentieth and early twenty-first centuries, might turn into dark decades of despair for a large proportion of the over-sixty-five population. Goodbye Florida golf course; hello Wal-Mart jobs, Medicaid, insecurity, food banks, and penury.

Beyond the economic dangers of doing nothing, there are social and psychological dangers that are rarely considered. As polls and conversations endlessly reveal, most younger Americans believe that Social Security (and Medicare, about which they think less) will not be around when they retire. For some, the result is cynicism and fear. Others, who raise the banner of "generational equity," angrily proclaim that they have been shafted. The economist Lawrence Kotlikoff calls this "fiscal child abuse."[16] While the United States hasn't seen mass youth demonstrations since the 1960s, this just might be the issue to get a seemingly apathetic and cosseted youth back to the barricades.

We are hardly likely to see the science-fiction scenarios in which the young kill off their elders. Yet many Americans born after 1970 or so may deeply resent that generations born during the first two-thirds of the twentieth century benefited so handsomely from old-age pension and medical-benefit programs, while those born later will be paying the multitrillion-dollar bill for their parents and grandparents. And these younger Americans would receive a minimal return, if any, on their lifetime investment of tax dollars in Social Security and Medicare.

Such circumstances undoubtedly would breed considerable bitterness among both young and old. Many would perceive that lifelong "promises" made to them by their country and government were being broken. Cynicism about government, already rampant, might deepen in perilous and unexpected ways. Voting might diminish, or fringe candidates might emerge and win public office.

Even such a "slow" deterioration in economic conditions may lead not only to Americans' questioning their patriotism but also to other nations increasingly devaluing the power and prestige of the United States in the world. Such perceptions, perhaps coupled with a straitened military budget, could lead to diminished U.S. geopolitical clout. As the economist Milton Friedman once said: "World power and influence have historically accrued to creditor countries. It is not coincidental that America emerged as a world power simultaneously with our transition from a debtor nation . . . to a creditor nation, supplying investment capital to the rest of the world."[17]

The superpower could seem like Clark Kent without his cape and wearing a kryptonite necktie. As power is relative, other nations might challenge the United States for global political and economic dominance. Nonstate actors such as terrorists, perceiving America to be particularly vulnerable, might see U.S. weakness as an invitation to strike. In short, growing debt becomes a national-security problem too.

But this gradual erosion of U.S. living standards and strength may be optimistic. Charles Schultze and others could be wrong. We could be in for what economists euphemistically call a "hard landing." "As countries increase their debt, they wander into unfamiliar territory in which hard landings may lurk," economists Laurence Ball and Gregory Mankiw drolly note. "If policymakers are prudent, they will not take the chance of learning what hard landings in G-7 countries are really like." The very possibility should be enough to get policy makers off their duffs and reduce the debt, they add.[18]

Forget the termites, brace for the wolves. This could be called the "*Blade Runner* scenario." If investors—domestic and foreign—begin to lose confidence in "the full faith and credit of the U.S. Government" to be able to repay its debts, they may cash in their dollar-denominated securities, moving their assets into other currencies. Standard & Poor's already has said that U.S. government debt is headed for junk bond status by 2020 and will lose its AAA rating in 2012 if nothing is done. Think euro, yen, sterling, and yuan. If that were to happen—as several foreign central-bank investors in U.S. debt have already hinted—the dollar would depreciate and/or interest rates would have to rise even more sharply to continue to lure investors. Even America's most successful investor, Warren Buffett, said in 2003 that although he never had invested in foreign securities during his first seventy-two years of life, he would diversify into foreign-denominated securities because of the "risk" of dollar-denominated Treasury securities.[19]

The Fed might be forced to respond with an unprecedented interest-rate increase, or it and the Treasury could embark on a binge of printing money. Or a health care crisis such as an avian flu pandemic that hits the poor or elderly disproportionately could cause an even greater spiking in Medicaid or Medicare expenditures. The United States could be attacked in five or ten years, after worried budgeteers had started to slash the defense budget. A global warming–induced series of hurricanes could put Florida and the Gulf Coast under water. Without the resources to respond adequately to any of these crises, stock and bond markets could be spooked enough to send share prices tumbling. If this happened, on top of stagnant incomes, negative savings (in the context of growing socioeconomic inequality), and a protracted bursting of the housing bubble, Americans could suddenly see their net worth plummet. In short, as we have seen, continued rising debt can have myriad negative effects on Americans' future socioeconomic well-being.

From an economic perspective, it's then that the scary games would begin. Employers in both the private and public sectors would lay off workers and/or cut wages and benefits. Consumer spending would crash. This would further depress business revenues, probably leading to major corporate or financial-institution bankruptcies, unloading further liabilities on federal agencies such as the PBGC or the Federal Deposit Insurance Corporation, or putting pressure on the government to bail out strategic industries, as it did for Chrysler in the late 1970s. And the spiral would proceed downward.[20]

Unlike the last time a depression hit the United States, the nation would be unable to turn to deficit spending—especially, we would hope, not to war-driven deficit spending, such as occurred during World War II—to restore the economy to its global strength and preeminence. Instead, in a most draconian scenario, the U.S. government might be forced to default on its debt, as third-world countries have done in recent decades. The magnitude of a U.S. default, however, is probably not something the global economy, much less the International Monetary Fund, could handle, as it did defaults in Argentina, Mexico, or sub-Saharan Africa. Like a boulder tied to a drowning swimmer, an insolvent

U.S. economy could pull the entire world economy under. So the riptides of an American debt-induced crisis could cause unemployment, hardship, and social unrest on much of the planet.[21]

And this is only the economic side of the story. In true dystopian fashion, angry Americans could take to the streets and mob violence could break out. Revolution, anarchy, modern-day Whiskey Rebellions or Wacos, wealthy communities seceding from the country, even class warfare—not exactly common occurrences in U.S. history—cannot be ruled out. Demagogues could come to power, and nuclear- or bio-weapons-armed terrorists could hold key global resources hostage or see an American economic crisis as prime time for major attacks.

Or maybe the Chinese or Indians would be so economically strong by the time of such a crisis in, say, 2030, that they would help to bail us out. They might do so out of their own economic and geopolitical interests so that they could keep selling to the U.S. market—much as the United States bailed out failing nations in the twentieth century. But like those countries that America once assisted, we would become essentially a client state of our benefactors. And in a most curious twist of post-Marxian, post–Cold War fate, Americans might become reliant on hypercapitalist dictators paying homage to Chairman Mao.

Looking at such possible futures, former Congressional Budget Office Director Douglas Holtz-Eakin has said: These are "the good old days."[22] Comptroller General David Walker has said much the same thing: "We have the elements of the perfect storm—a potent mix of ignorance, apathy, and inaction in all sectors of American society. If we continue on our present course, a fiscal crisis is not a matter of 'if' but 'when.'"[23]

But none of this will really happen, will it? As many budget experts hope, a lesser crisis will be the catalyst to get U.S. political leaders off their lobbyist-comforted rear ends and force them to address our deficit and debt problems.[24] But even that, we should hope, will come soon. Thanks to the wonders of compound interest, every year that we dawdle, failing to implement serious fiscal reforms, adds an astounding $1 trillion to the price tag for reform, Brian Riedl of the Heritage Foundation estimates.[25] Yet what would constitute a "crisis" sufficient to make U.S. political leaders act, yet not so draconian as to inflict great pain on millions of Americans and others around the world? A "minor" stock-market crash such as the one that occurred in 1987, which did inspire some fiscal reforms?

Alternately, could wise, far-sighted leaders act before a crisis hits—or is the very idea of "far-sighted" politicians an oxymoron, as that group typically focuses no farther ahead than the next election cycle? How we might prevent either the termites from destroying our home or the wolves from eating us, and the difficulties of doing so, are the subjects to which we will turn in the next two chapters.

Chapter 6 The Politics
of Deficits and Debt

Politics is the art of looking for trouble, finding it everywhere, diagnosing it incorrectly, and applying the wrong remedies.
Groucho Marx

At some point, we've got to come forward with some courage and discipline to stop this massive hemorrhaging of federal spending. . . . The American people deserve better than a U.S. Senate out of control with no fiscal discipline.
Senator Chuck Hagel

When it comes to squarely confronting our nation's mounting fiscal problems, the oft-used phrase "political leaders" requires a careful parsing. Politicians across the spectrum for several decades have decried America's growing debt and looming crisis in the wake of the baby boomers' retirement (see The View from Washington), but there have been few leaders with the courage and clout actually to lead the nation in addressing the issue.

While recent history has shown that some successful efforts have been made—from the 1983 Greenspan Commission and the 1986 tax reform to the 1990 Budget Enforcement Act and budget deals of 1990 and 1997—a raft of commissions under Presidents Clinton and George W. Bush have led to no substantive reforms whatsoever. Zippo. If anything, recent policies—the Bush tax cuts, the enactment of Medicare Part D, and the Bush administration's wild spending spree—have only made matters worse. It is not that President Bush and most Republicans and Democrats do not recognize the dangers of growing debt, as Bush's words and ill-starred effort to reform Social Security indicate. It is simply that they are largely fiddling while Rome-on-the-Potomac burns.

But why?!

In this chapter, we will explore the many reasons that politicians have done little to tackle the interrelated problems of the national debt, entitlement reform, tax reform, and governmental reform. In addition, we will consider what factors, or sets of circumstances, could goad our elected leaders to act before the problems become immeasurably worse and even more difficult to solve. And finally, we will examine the role of public opinion as both an impediment to, and a catalyst for, reform.

The "short" answer for why our leaders have not stepped forward to lead on this critical issue includes denial of the problem, bitter partisanship and unwillingness to seek compromise, the complex politics of spending and taxes, a perceived lack of public concern, the short-term focus of politicians who are geared only to the next election cycle, theoretical rationalizations for deficits, the power of interest groups, and a lack of leadership and accountability on the part of the president and Congress.

Denying that a problem is a problem is an all but universal human way of coping with difficulties, as Freud and a host of psychologists and philosophers have recognized. Without sinking too deeply into the miasma of Washington psychology, let's just say that its "say it ain't so" approach is a form of magical thinking that George Orwell satirized so well, and so wickedly, in *1984*.

It is all too easy to just proclaim and pretend that deficits are being cut in half by 2009 or 2012, or that they "don't matter," or that America can grow its way out of them through a tax cut–inspired economic boom, and all will be hunky-dory—despite overwhelming evidence to the contrary. Many members of Congress and the administration, as well as informed staffers of both branches of government, recognize that most politicians have a penchant for denial rather than solving problems in ways that may cause short-term pain to the public (read: electorate), who may then vote those politicians out of their jobs. Congress is not required to publicly debate and vote on raising the national debt ceiling, as they do repeatedly (most recently in the fall of 2007), and the budgetary watchdogs of the Concord Coalition have noted that congresspersons find such public acknowledgment of surging debt "embarrassing or distasteful."[1] And as Pete Peterson has acidly commented, President Bush called for "sacrifice" for the Iraq War, but instead of requiring sacrifice in the form of increased taxes to pay for a trillion-dollar war, his administration cut taxes and has shifted the bill to future generations.[2]

If denial is one element of the current deficit gridlock, partisanship and an almost petulant aversion to compromise are another huge part of the problem. Many commentators have noted that Congress, particularly the House of Representatives, has become much more polarized along hardened ideological lines during the past few decades. A recent political assessment characterized just 3 percent of Republican members of the House as "moderate" in 2005, compared with 27 percent in 1989 and 49 percent in 1977, and similar trends can be seen among Democrats.[3] With Republican congressmen and -women all but swearing an oath not to raise taxes, and many Democrats committed to not cutting spending, a bipartisan agreement that would satisfy both seems like pie in the sky. "The Democrats want to avoid offending their constituencies and so have mostly sidestepped initiatives on trimming big entitlement programs," former CBO director Douglas Holtz-Eakin has said. Meanwhile, "the Republicans have chosen to stand by low taxes and big security spending and even introduced a new Medicare prescription drug benefit." One survey of Washington insiders found that only one in twenty thinks that spending could be cut by even 5 percent, and just three in twenty believe that Republicans would agree to any tax rise in the near future.[4]

Sadly, as former Republican Congressman Bill Frenzel (R-Minn.) said, comparing the gridlock to a game of chicken: "Both sides are guilty. The longer they can defend their positions, the less they'll have to concede."[5]

The polarization and partisanship—which would make George Washington, an opponent of "factions" and parties, apoplectic—largely can be attributed to a significant flaw in our political system, the gerrymandering of House districts. While the term—named for James Madison's Vice President Elbridge Gerry, who drew a salamander-shaped electoral district to ensure his opponent's defeat—dates to the early republic, manipulation of district borders has become an especially acute problem during the past fifteen to twenty years.

Every ten years, after House seats are reapportioned in the wake of the latest census (and sometimes more often), legislators in almost every state vote on how to redraw congressional district lines. (Iowa is the only state with more than one representative in the House that has an independent commission draw districts, although many states have begun to consider similar reforms.) Not surprisingly, the party controlling the state legislature concocts salamander- and other bizarre-shaped districts designed to maximize their party's number of congressional seats.

As a result of increasingly refined political and demographic analysis, these districts are created to ensure safe seats for Democrats and Republicans. Infamously, after Republicans won control of the Texas legislature in 2002, they redrew district lines with the help of then–Republican leader Tom DeLay to pick up five seats. Gerrymandering, together with the power of incumbents to raise considerably more money than challengers, has led to 90 to 95 percent reelection rates in the House of Representatives. Consequently, candidates play to their activist bases, so that conservative Republicans and liberal Democrats have been much more likely to win safe seats than have more moderate, compromise-inclined members of either party. In addition, safe seats and the recent power of incumbency lead to a tyranny of the majority, which discourages citizens opposing the incumbent from voting.[6]

Although the winds may be beginning to blow against gerrymandering and intense partisanship, these are among the problems that contribute to deficits, as an increasingly conservative Republican House has refused to countenance revenue increases, and Democrats (and, during the Bush years, Republicans) rarely have been able to say no to spending public dollars. Moreover, as the National Taxpayers Union has pointed out, not only has no member of Congress had a voting record that would balance spending increases with cuts during the first five years of the twenty-first century, but Democrats and Republicans alike, on average, voted for spending increases in the ballpark of $168 billion to $217 billion in 2005.[7]

Indeed, spending increases and tax cuts are extremely seductive to most politicians—even if they provide no clear way of paying for them. Every member of Congress wants to be credited with bringing home the proverbial bacon for his or her constituents—contracts for companies in the home state or district, money to improve local highways, federal money for a new veterans' hospital, farm subsidies, and the list goes on ad infinitum. Come campaign season, which is almost every season these days, politicians are anything but shy about touting the benefits that they have brought voters. The number of "earmarks"—special spending requests slyly appended to broader appropriations bills, which Senator John McCain has called the process of "leave no lobbyist behind"—has grown exponentially in recent years.[8]

Yet even if earmarks are made more transparent by requiring members to attach their names to them, this is only a small part of the ever-increasing spending dynamic. Few politicians want to cut programs, and most are willingly pressed by lobbyists, interest groups, and constituents to raise spending. And this applies only to the minority of the budget that does not consist of entitlements and interest payments, which are on a high-speed cruise control to increase due to inflation-adjusting formulas, increasing numbers of beneficiaries, and growing debt. Despite vague, post–Reagan era public assent for smaller government, poll after poll finds that there are few specific programs that the American people want to cut and many for which they want increased funding. And as we have seen, during six years of a Republican president and Congress, from 2001 to 2007, spending increased faster than inflation and faster than it had in forty years. As the conservative Cato Institute said before the Democrats won control of Congress in 2006: "Each year, Congress and the Administration up the ante on each other's spending plans."[9]

If the politics of spending is analogous to a Santa Claus–style desire to deliver goodies to every American under the ever-grander Appropriations Tree, the politics of taxes are, in many ways, the mirror image. If politicians perceive, generally correctly, that most Americans want government to spend more on them, they also perceive that most Americans are pleased to receive tax cuts. Although many recent tax cuts disproportionately have benefited the wealthy, providing pocket change for the middle class and tens of thousands of dollars a year for multimillionaires, many Americans are oblivious to the injustice of such arrangements and are happy to hear that their tax burden is being reduced and to take what they can get.

Tax increases—although there were many of them during the Reagan, Bush I, and Clinton years—generally have to be sugarcoated, and often elected officials see them as the third rail of politics. With few exceptions, no politician hoping to gain popularity is going to call loudly for a major tax increase. Conversely, politicians seem congenitally all too ready to curry favor by claiming to cut this or that tax.

President George H. W. Bush's "read my lips—no new taxes" promise, which was broken (wisely, from a fiscal standpoint) during the 1990 budget agreement, is widely seen as having contributed to his 1992 election loss to Bill Clinton. Similarly, President Clinton's 1993 tax increases are seen as a major factor in the Democrats' losing control of Congress the next year. In short, tax increases are perceived as political losers. As Alice Rivlin, former director of the Office of Management and Budget and first director of the Congressional Budget Office, has said, both raising taxes and cutting spending—as Republican House leader Newt Gingrich also found out in 1995–96—tend to be prescriptions for electoral defeat.[10]

On top of the usually gridlocked politics of spending and taxes, politicians have often sought, and dispensed, intellectual and rhetorical rationalizations for why increased spending or tax cuts actually constitute good policy. In the decades since World War II politicians have trotted out the liberal Keynesian notion that deficit spending is beneficial in stimulating a flagging economy. Even if this may be true in the short run, the "short run" often has a way of bleeding into the permanent run in Washington. It's a bit like the musical *Cats:* it may have been fun a quarter-century ago, but does it really need to keep on playing "now and forever," as its ads once proclaimed? Similarly, conservative supply-siders have spent the past thirty years saying that tax cuts more than pay for themselves, although endless research has discredited this claim. Finally, many have resorted to facile and intellectually contorted declamations about why "deficits don't matter." Perhaps new positions need to be created for congressional and presidential psychotherapists to provide a little reality-testing for many of our nation's leaders. In the meantime, it's much easier, as the *Newsweek* columnist Robert Samuelson has said, for politicians to "talk out of all three sides of their mouths—abhor deficits, cut taxes, and increase spending."[11]

While politicians and the public appear to be in cozily symbiotic agreement to increase spending, cut taxes, and wink at the deficit, other forces and factors play significant roles in enabling our debt to grow like a hothouse plant. One easily fingered batch of targets is made up of the villains of K Street—America's thousands of lobbyists and interest groups. Eugene Steuerle of the Urban Institute and a former adviser to President Reagan, has observed that "bills today are introduced, and often enacted, through a process of almost random reactions to pressures from interest groups and lobbyists."[12]

Powerful interest groups such as AARP, the American Hospital Association, the American Medical Association (AMA), and the Pharmaceutical Research and Manufacturers Association of America employ extraordinarily well-financed and well-connected lobbyists and lawyers to guard zealously against most efforts to control health care costs. While the AMA has since the early days of the Cold War railed against universal health care as "creeping socialism," the 1994 "Harry and Louise" ads by the Health Insurance Association of America went a long way to kill the Clinton administration's proposed health care reforms. Physicians regularly have screamed bloody murder at repeated efforts to trim Medicare and Medicaid reimbursement rates.

But the medical-industrial complex is far from the only budget-busting set of interest groups. If, as Alexis de Tocqueville famously observed in the 1840s, Americans love to form associations and groups, Washingtonians (or those who migrate to our nation's capital) love to form interest groups. Every significant industry under the sun lobbies for federal contracts or tax breaks, worth hundreds of billions of dollars a year. One thing that ultraconservatives and ultraliberals, and many in between, can agree upon is that avowedly free-enterprise America spends a fortune in taxpayer dollars on "corporate welfare." The transportation, defense, and agricultural industries are especially notorious. As Stuart Butler of the Heritage Foundation has said, "It's difficult, if not impossible, to work for the public interest because of rent-seeking by interest groups."[13]

The problem is not so much that health care and income security for the elderly are not needed, or that weapons systems or roads may not need to be built. Nor is it that interest groups, in and of themselves, are bad; in fact, they can be a sign of a vital democracy representing groups whose members' individual voices otherwise would not be heard in the corridors of power. Rather, it's that most interest groups and lobbyists not only seek what is narrowly best for their company or constituency, instead of the common good, but also tend to be extremely averse to reforms that would shake up the current, free-spending business as usual. As George Bernard Shaw famously said: "The government that robs Peter to pay Paul can always depend upon the support of Paul." And with the 10 most expensive Senate races costing an average of $34 million and the average House race costing $2 million in 2006, most politicians listen to those who put cash in their coffers.[14]

Another aspect of politics that makes fundamental debt-reducing reform so difficult stems from the short-term focus of most politicians. Despite the periodic rhetoric about America's "long-term good," most political leaders in Washington have time horizons that extend to the next election and no farther. If a House member, especially, always has his or her eyes on the next even-numbered year, the natural instinct is how best to please constituents and interest groups quickly—with an earmark or other spending here, a tax cut there. Major reforms, which require the perspective and patience to think over decades-long cycles, particularly in the case of entitlement spending, simply are not worth the political capital. Rare is the politician who behaves according to oft-professed wisdom expressed by Senator George Voinovich (R-Ohio): "When I make spending decisions, I think not only about the short-term benefits, but also the long-term costs."[15]

A series of presidents since Ronald Reagan have appointed entitlement-reform commissions and gone out on the hustings calling for new ways to rein in the torrent of dollars going to Social Security, Medicare, and Medicaid. However, with the exceptions of the several budget deals mentioned and the 1983 Greenspan Commission, which was forced to act by the dire straits of soon-to-be-unmailed Social Security checks, commission reports get filed away, and presidents are either listened to politely or loudly denounced by constituencies not wanting to lose benefits or pay more in taxes. President George W. Bush—whatever one may think of how he raised the issue or the substance of his proposals—at least attempted to spur debate over Social Security reform in 2006, only to fail.

But this increasingly short-term focus in American politics and policy making itself stems from factors beyond the perceived need to continuously run for reelection. For one, many political leaders and analysts would say that if there were significant public and business outcry over the nation's fiscal problems, politicians not only would listen but would be motivated to act. While much of the business and financial communities were in the forefront of calling for deficit reduction in the early 1990s, as Comptroller General David Walker has said, recently, they "largely [have] been missing in action."[16] Likewise, while polls and focus groups find widespread public concern about deficits, few Americans seem alarmed about our fiscal state of affairs (although there is conflicting evidence about popular worries about deficits, as we will see).[17] Some think that deficits and debt are simply too abstract and abstruse to get people riled up. So without public, business, or interest-group clamor over debt, the Washington mantra might be the old *Mad* magazine slogan, "What, me worry?"

At some level, the current, unsatisfying political stasis boils down to a lack of leadership and courage. As Harry Truman, who made many a tough decision, once said, true leadership is "getting people to do what they don't want to do and getting them to like it."[18] Even President Bush said of his ill-fated effort to put Social Security reform on the table: "In an issue like this, unless the President tries, nothing is going to happen."[19] The dearth of leadership is nothing short of staggering. Perhaps, with rare exceptions, we should jettison the very phrase "political leaders" and instead use a more appropriate locution such as "political placeholders."

At many levels, this is a function of lack of accountability. Politicians are all too ready to dispense with computer-generated phone calls and attack ads at election time, but who advertises where they stand on any budget-busting tax or spending measure? Votes—on those measures not decided by acclamation—are buried in the *Congressional Record*. As the National Taxpayers Union points out, no legislator has to own up to the vast spending increases that Congress authorizes without finding a way to pay for it. The Medicare Modernization Act of 2003, which created the prescription-drug plan of Medicare Part D, ranks as one of the great shames of democratic accountability in the history of this or any other country. A dead-of-the-night vote without debate on one of the most expensive spending sprees in U.S. history—while it may benefit senior drug consumers—makes the British taxes leading up to the Boston Tea Party look like reasonable, trivial, and procedurally just consumption levies. Democratic House Speaker Nancy Pelosi's efforts to shine light on who is behind legislative earmarks, while financially insignificant in a $3 trillion federal budget, at least puts porcine pols on notice that taxpayer dollars are not Monopoly money to be passed to local causes du jour every time ones passes Go. In brief, politicians should be held accountable for votes to increase spending or cut taxes, and, if nothing else, should be tarred and feathered on the Internet and in the media if they do not also find ways to pay for their fiscal largesse.

As the former Clinton chief of staff Leon Panetta said: "We govern by leadership or crisis." And, as we have seen, the likelihood of either a "termite"- or a "wolf"-induced crisis is high. Most political observers, including "optimists," believe that reform will come about due to some sort of crisis, because the leadership simply isn't forthcoming.[20]

It would be nice to imagine a man or woman on a white horse riding up to the O.K. Corral on Pennsylvania Avenue, guns blazing, to save us from our fiscal demons. No one expected Ross Perot in 1992, and neither did anyone expect Richard Nixon to go to China in 1972. But maybe the sort of heroes we need exist only on celluloid. Or perhaps most knights on steed arrive only in times of crisis or public clamor.

If so—and if we don't want to wait for a blade runner or a superhero exterminator to go after the plague of the termites—is part of the answer to arouse public opinion? Since various politicians, advocacy groups such as the Concord Coalition, and well-meaning Washington wonks—as well as the Seymour Durst debt clock near Times Square—have tried this, to limited effect, are the American people simply in a torpor of television, credit card, and shopping mall denial? Why are Americans not more aroused, angry, and clamoring for action on debt reduction? And if political leaders are to be galvanized to act by their constituents, how do we get more Americans to care about our debt problems and demand action?

While many elitists, foreigners, and other commentators have harped on Americans' slim knowledge of significant political, economic, and social issues, the American people are *not* ignorant of, or oblivious to, the dangers of rising national debt. Perhaps it's those in the cowardly covens of Capitol Hill who are really behind the curve. Despite the apparent softness of concern about debt among the American people, according to many pollsters, most Americans "get it," and are profoundly worried and willing to do something to get their children's nation out of hock when given even a little information about their itinerary on the *Titanic*.[21]

Research conducted by Public Agenda and Viewpoint Learning in 2006 and 2007 has found that 75 to 80 percent of Americans believe that Social Security and Medicare will be "in crisis" or have "major problems" by the late 2010s. Ninety-four percent say that "it is our responsibility to reduce the deficit so that future generations will not be burdened with the cost of our heavy debts." Surprisingly, up to two-thirds of those polled believe not only that tax cuts have been a mistake but also that higher taxes would be acceptable in order not to burden their children and grandchildren with the costs of fiscal madness.[22]

Whereas Americans during the halcyon days of Dwight Eisenhower and John Kennedy all but universally believed that the United States was on a blessed economic track to utopian abundance for all, only 10 percent of George W. Bush–era Americans reported being "very satisfied" with their families' financial situation, only 7 percent rated U.S. economic conditions "excellent," and 74 percent thought that things in the United States are on the "wrong track."[23] While such numbers are volatile, trend data since the 1970s have shown that Americans have become less happy, and more worried, about personal and national economic conditions.

These personal economic worries dovetail with concerns about the national economy—job outsourcing and insecurity; rising inequality; increasingly unaffordable housing, college, and medical costs; declining or insufficient government spending on genuine national needs; trade deficits; and even public debt. As one middle-aged white woman in a Public Agenda/Viewpoint Learning focus group said: "If we ran our household like our country is running the budget, how could we go on?" Similarly, a young African American man said: "If we continue on our current course, we're heading on the road to disaster."

Young people—worried and cynical about the likelihood of receiving the Social Security and Medicare benefits that they have been "promised"—likewise see the fiscal future through a glass darkly. "This is definitely cause for alarm," one eastern college student said. And, quite presciently, another twenty-something student succinctly, if somewhat simplistically, analyzed the budgetary and political problem: "Deficits are the unhappy combined result of conservative low taxes and liberal involved federal government. This is one of the issues which will shape the politics of the near future."[24]

Given that the public is aware of, but not panicky over, the looming effects of national debt and deficits, and given that politicians have been aware but inactive on debt issues, how do we raise public concern and pressure for action? A national consciousness-raising dialogue seems to be called for. The public opinion expert Daniel Yankelovich has identified four stages of developing public support for an issue or policy: 1) focusing on the issues, 2) acquiring a sense of urgency, 3) weighing choices and trade-offs, and 4) making decisions. If more courageous politicians can step up to the plate and try to educate their constituents, and if many more of the American people can be drawn into public dialogues, perhaps the momentum for reform can be initiated. As Alice Rivlin has said: "Exhortation doesn't work as well as discussion and engagement. People can talk about deficits civilly and intelligently."[25]

Discussing options in a rational way based on knowledge of the issues, choices, and consequences is a far more effective way to make progress on addressing any issue than trying to sell, or impose, top-down solutions on an ill-informed, frightened public, as Charles Kolb, president of the Committee for Economic Development, a national business organization, has said.[26]

Maybe the leaders need to be bipartisan, out-of-office politicians or fiscal pooh-bahs tag-teaming, such as Bill Clinton and George H. W. Bush, or Clinton Treasury Secretary Robert Rubin and George W. Bush's Treasury Secretary Henry Paulson (after he leaves office). More high-level commissions on entitlement, tax, and general budgetary reform, appointed jointly by the president and congressional leaders and including interest groups, business, and citizens, may be called for. So that such commissions do not turn into wasteful parades of testimony, press conferences, and reports, they should be given the kind of mandate that the military base-closing commission had: Congress essentially must vote up or down on their recommendations, without shelving them or cherry-picking the easier solutions.

Similarly, as Rivlin suggests, maybe politicians, civic associations, foundations, television or other media organizations, and/or Web sites need to organize highly visible "town meetings" that engage citizens, rather than relegating discussion and decisions to untrusted, inside-the-Beltway types. Perhaps rather than dragooning the usual Washington suspects into Budget and Finance Committee hearings to testify, committee members should reach out to their constituents and hold long televised hearings about public attitudes toward the debt and all the attendant issues of our public finances and how government should spend and raise money.

In sum, the current state of politics, leadership, and public opinion in the United States makes deficit reduction extremely difficult, if not impossible. Partisanship (reinforced by gerrymandered electoral districts and the influence of activist constituencies and money), denial and rationalization, short-term thinking, and the lack of political leadership and public outcry all suggest the unlikelihood of our lawmakers' addressing something so complex and fraught with political minefields as budgetary, tax, entitlement, and other spending reform.

Yet it is important to remember Herb Stein's old maxim that that which cannot be sustained won't be. Growing debt is nothing if not unsustainable. The consequence is that one way or another, it will not be. Whether it will require a crisis, unexpected leadership, or public outrage, the congeries of fiscal-related issues that plague us—from debt itself to broken tax, health care, and political systems—will force themselves into the public mind and the laps of Congress and the White House. As Samuel Johnson famously said, nothing focuses the mind quite like the prospect of hanging. We run the risk of hanging ourselves if we do nothing, and, as one congressman told me, if we're not optimistic about America and about solving this problem, we might as well plan on becoming Chinese citizens.

It should be abundantly clear that what makes the national debt such a difficult problem to tackle is that it is not a single problem amenable to a simple fix. It is a large and complex set of interrelated and mutually reinforcing problems. Aside from courage, they require deft, creative, and coordinated handling if we are not to botch any potential solutions. Politically and practically, we can tackle these problems individually, but with our eyes always on the big picture and on how one set of actions may affect other pieces of the puzzle, or we can attempt some measure of comprehensive reform that involves rethinking the role of modern government. But whichever course we choose, we must begin. How we could dig ourselves out from an avalanche of debt is the subject of the next chapter, and it must be a subject near the top of our nation's political agenda today and in the years immediately ahead.

Chapter 7 What Can and Should Be Done to Reduce America's Deficits and Debt?

Washington continues to fund tax cuts for millionaires by running up the debt burden on our children. . . . This is recklessness at its worst, and we can do better than leveraging away this nation's fiscal future.
Senator Ken Salazar

Who are we hurting by our continued spending, Mr. President? We're hurting our children, our grandchildren, and who knows how many future generations of Americans. It is perhaps my greatest hope, Mr. President, that some day we'll consider tax and spending measures with no one else in mind but future generations of American taxpayers. We're tying a millstone of debt around their necks, and it is a grave mistake.
Senator John McCain

The national debt and America's fiscal straits are much like a Rube Goldberg contraption. They are complex to the point of mind-paralyzing absurdity. They are an assemblage of myriad, moving, interacting parts. And they are conducive to neither simple policy fixes nor politically popular solutions.

However, as the Civil War, World War II, and the Cold War demonstrate, the United States knows how to overcome threats to its national survival. Even if we may be fractious, averse to radical and painful change, and prone to procrastination, Americans generally get the job done. The same can—and must—be true of bringing down our debt and reforming all the factors that contribute to it.

The glimmer of good news is that the story of fiscal and national meltdown is not inevitable. It's like the future shown in Charles Dickens's *Christmas Carol*—what might be, if Scrooge, or America, doesn't shape up. With political leadership and public outcry, a can-do country like the United States can reform its entitlement programs, cut wasteful spending, and find ways of raising new—but not onerous—revenues. However, we need open minds to all plausible solutions, a willingness to make tough choices, and a commitment to compromise. We can't solve the problem just with discretionary spending cuts, given that the scale of domestic discretionary spending pales in comparison with mandatory spending and interest payments on the debt. We can't solve the problem by pledging "no new taxes" or by promising additional tax cuts. And we surely cannot solve the problem without reining in the growth of health care costs and changing the nature of Social Security or, more broadly, security against the risks of ill health, old age, disability, poverty, job loss, or other unforeseen emergencies—although solving the health care cost explosion alone could go a long way toward resolving our overall debt problems. The old social contract, built around the pillars of Social Security, Medicare, and waning private-sector insurance and private savings, is not sustainable. But neither do we want what the economist Jared Bernstein cleverly has called a "you're on your own" (YOYO) economy.[1]

I am not going to offer in this chapter a foolproof roadmap to get from the "here" of fiscal irresponsibility and looming dangers to our national well-being to the "there" of fiscal rectitude and a more secure, rational future of solvency, greater prosperity, and national survival. It would be foolish to say that anyone knows all the answers, or the best answers. There is always more than one route to a destination, and the issues are so big and manifold that in many ways, the task of serious debt reduction is uncharted territory. It may well require an outside-the-box reconsideration of basic principles of government that rarely, if ever, has been done since Madison and Hamilton (and John Jay) created our Constitution and system of governance. Furthermore, there are some issues about which even experts who have spent years examining a topic—particularly in the health care arena—simply do not have good answers. And finally, there are honest differences of opinion, and those differing viewpoints offer valuable, if seemingly contradictory, insights and prescriptions.

Therefore this chapter will be less cure-all prescription than tour d'horizon of ideas to bring down our debt by reforming entitlements and other spending, taxes and federal revenues, the budgeting process, and the political process. It is something like a long menu, perhaps for a five- or six-course meal, in which we have to order at least one item for each course—in some cases, a number of items. But it is not just a menu of liver, pickled beets, or gefilte fish. There are some tastier treats—including redirection of some spending to new and needed causes; restoration of public trust and pride in government; simplification and reform of our tax system, with an eye to making it more fair; and, best of all, the likelihood that—after this large and sometimes difficult-to-digest repast—we, our children, and our grandchildren will be able to look forward to a more secure and prosperous future. As Hillary Clinton has said, reforms do not mean that we "give up on our obligations, but rather [that we] reinvent how we fulfill them."[2]

And there are at least three further big caveats: First, this is *not* going to be an easy, quick, or linear process. It may take years, even decades, to address. Second, there is ample potential to get some, or many, things wrong, either making the problems worse or creating new problems. As Joe Antos of the American Enterprise Institute told Congress: "It is incorrect to assume that if government takes direct action on a problem that it will deliver the desired result."[3] On this score, remember the politics, the complexities, and the curse of unintended consequences. Finally, for all but those professional soothsayers, the future is infinitely unpredictable. The United States suddenly could embark on truly unprecedented economic growth, which could make many fiscal problems diminish. A war, terrorist attack, major natural disaster, severe economic crisis, or political crisis could throw the prospects for reform to the winds. Or we could get distracted by other public issues—in recent history, just think about the Iraq War or the Clinton impeachment scandal—that could push serious domestic-policy and fiscal-reform issues to the sidelines.

But in a most unlikely similarity between the words of Harry Truman and those of Zen masters, we must think, as both said, that the optimist sees opportunity in uncertainty, whereas the pessimist sees danger. We cannot afford not to be optimists.

So where might a reform agenda begin? Whether one bundles some of the ideas suggested below into a "comprehensive" strategy or seeks a series of small victories, we must begin somewhere. Given the magnitude and complexity of our fiscal problems, we probably should not aim for one, grand comprehensive solution. Since any such—almost, by definition, revolutionary—solution is unlikely to come to pass, we must not use inability to solve everything as an excuse for failing to do anything to dig us out of our deepening fiscal hole.

POLITICAL REFORM

Although reforming the political process will not, by itself—at least not necessarily—lead to budgetary reform, it is likely to help, and would have only salutary effects on American democracy. In many ways, the goals are threefold, and proceed backward from one another: First, America needs to create more competitive House districts and a more economically level playing field for candidates at all levels of government so that extreme candidates beholden to a narrow, activist political base are less likely to be elected. As a result, we can expect fewer citizens to be cynical about, and more to engage in, public affairs, confident that their votes and opinions count. Second, while "moderation" may not be exactly the right word, since radical fiscal and governmental reforms are needed, such reforms would encourage more moderate, or big-tent, candidates in both parties who are responsive to the majority of their constituents—not just to activists or interest groups. Third, this, in turn, would encourage compromise and comity—rather than the trench warfare of recent years—in Congress and between Congress and the White House. If politicians truly were elected to further the common good, rather than posturing for hard-core supporters or cash-dispensing lobbies, they might hammer out agreements that represent give and take, and at least move the nation forward. Moreover, as many polls suggest, the American people agree on a broader array of issues than their elected representatives do.[4]

Founding father George Mason once said that the House of Representatives should be "the grand repository of the democratic principles of government."[5] Instead, with 90 to 98 percent reelection rates in recent years, it has looked a lot more like the Supreme Soviet. A host of experts finger the unintended consequences of the 1965 Voting Rights Act, which was intended in part to increase African American representation by creating "majority minority" districts through gerrymandering. They also blame the historic tradition of letting politicians in most state legislatures redraw House districts, generally after each census. Thus the "fixes" most often proposed are to have independent, bipartisan commissions draw district lines or to elect at-large House members representing entire states. Appointing independent commissions is not a new idea. Various states have dabbled with taking redistricting out of the legislature's hands—Iowa most successfully—and several states recently have held referenda on such reforms, with decidedly mixed results. In addition, the Constitution does not specify how House members are to be elected once they are apportioned to particular states—whether by geographically defined districts, at large, or in multimember districts—despite the long-standing practice of districts drawn by geography and balanced by population.[6] To reduce the power of incumbency, others have called for public financing of elections, further limits on campaign contributions, and term limits.[7]

Another approach is simply to get elected officials of different parties talking across the aisle, instead of letting them or their proxies scream at each other on talk shows or in the Capitol. Democratic Representative Steve Israel (D-N.Y.) and Republican Representative Timothy Johnson (R-Ill.) have tried to foster such comity by founding the Center Aisle Caucus, a group of about fifty House members that is supported by former Democratic House Speaker Tom Foley and former Republican Leader Robert Michel. As Israel said: "Democrats and Republicans may disagree on 75 percent of the issues. But if we agree and implement the remaining 25 percent, the country is 100 percent better off than before." Similarly, two former Democratic leaders, George Mitchell and Tom Daschle, and two former Republican leaders, Bob Dole and Howard Baker, have launched a Bipartisan Policy Center. And the 110th Congress began with some tantalizing intimations of new bipartisanship, as the Baldwin-Price and Voinovich-Bingaman health care reform bills and Rangel-McCreary tax reform bills suggest. Similar hints of bipartisanship have come from the pledged agreement on the need for universal health care involving the Business Roundtable, AARP, and the Service Employees Union International, and from proposals for entitlement-reform commissions suggested by Senators Kent Conrad (D-N.D.) and Judd Gregg (R-N.H.), and by Senators Dianne Feinstein (D-Calif.) and Pete Domenici (R-N.M.). Others take this idea farther, suggesting that a third party is needed—in particular, one that reaches across the political divide, such as the Unity08 initiative launched in 2007 to offer a presidential ticket with one Democrat and one Republican.[8] And within Congress, the forty-four-member Blue Dog Democratic caucus has become a voice of moderation and fiscal restraint, with each member sporting a debt clock outside his or her office. Bipartisanship and moderation are laudable, but they must be built upon and transformed into political action.

Even more fundamentally, some congressional old-timers (and newer members) lament the lost tradition of simple friendships between congressmen and -women of opposing parties. Many recall the days when Democrats and Republicans would go out for a beer or dinner together—a custom that largely has disappeared as a result of both partisanship and the abbreviated congressional work schedules aimed to allow members to fly back to their districts every Thursday, largely to raise money. It's almost as if we need to hold a Capitol Hill prom, in which a Republican is required to ask a Democrat out, and a Democrat is forced to ask a Republican for the first dance.

Friendship and dialogue go a long way toward helping to solve problems. Partisan, demonizing attacks and intransigence go a long way toward making things worse.

BUDGET PROCESS REFORM

"Our budget process is broken," Senator Mike Crapo (R-Idaho) has said. "Riddled with gimmicks and obfuscation, the current spending framework allows unfunded obligations to pile up virtually unchecked."[9]

If our elected leaders, as friends, foes, or Americans, are to deal with our budgetary morass, one of the easier fixes is to reform *how* the federal government budgets its resources. One of the favorite budget-process reforms of fiscal hawks, wonks, and other strange fauna unique to Washington is what is known in Beltway language as PAYGO. While it may suggest the carry-out cups for soft (or harder) drinks available at some southern restaurants, PAYGO, as we have seen, means that tax cuts and spending increases must be offset to avoid increasing the deficit. First instituted under the Budget Enforcement Act of 1990, under President Bush I, it was purposely allowed to expire under his son in 2002, and reinstated in watered-down form by the Democratic Congress in 2007. PAYGO, under the 1990 rules, applied to mandatory spending and was coupled with yearly caps imposed on discretionary spending. Such caps could either be indexed to inflation; established at a set level of across-the-board annual increases of, say, 1 percent; or even require freezing certain spending such as entitlement benefits. However, the 2007 rules are more easily waived, much as if an umpire called strike three and winked at the batter, telling him to take a couple more swings. Many believe that existing budgetary rules are paper tigers, made to be broken. Similarly, the once-in-fashion idea of a balanced budget amendment is more like a paper kitten than a paper tiger, a cheapening of the Constitution that is not worth the paper on which it might be printed.

Rules should have teeth, with specific triggers and defaults built into the budgeting process, so that if revenues and spending do not match, taxes are automatically raised and/or spending is automatically cut.[10] Senator Judd Gregg's (R-N.H.) Stop Over Spending (SOS) proposal has similarly mandatory elements. Likewise, Senator Russ Feingold (D-Wis.) has said: "Without spending limits and the pay-as-you-go rule, the remaining budgetary rules are close to meaningless."[11] Rules also should require paying for known future funding increases. Another proposed rule goes by the equally wonkish acronym of TABOR, or Taxpayer Bill of Rights, a Colorado-pioneered idea that limits spending and tax growth to population growth plus inflation. An additional possibility is to limit budget growth to GDP growth. But such policy castor oil is not a prescription for political popularity.

Moreover, many believe that the budget process should be much more transparent, not hiding behind the myriad gimmicks that make presidents and Congresses look slipperier than the slickest Las Vegas cardsharp: no more borrowing from Social Security and other trust funds, no more pushing current spending into future years for accounting purposes, no more ignoring long-term legal and fiscal liabilities. Because the near-term budgetary outlook does not look so bad—while the longer-term outlook looks horrendous—spending and tax policies should be carefully evaluated and explicitly presented in terms of their long-term implications for federal finances and Americans' well-being.

Likewise, politicians and lobbyists should have to publicly own up to all spending and taxes for which they lobbied or voted. If members of Congress and the K Street crowd are identified by name with each piece of spending and tax legislation that they have actively supported, with the intended beneficiaries specified, the American people and media could shame members and their well-heeled handmaidens who don't know how—or don't care—to balance the U.S. government's checkbook.[12]

In addition, the Office of Management and Budget (OMB) and congressional budget and finance committees not only should be given greater latitude to enforce such rules and transparency but also should be able to mandate "sunset" provisions that require that programs, spending, and taxes periodically be reviewed for their efficacy and costs. Performance-based budgeting is already the law in countries such as Canada, the Netherlands, Australia, and New Zealand: such provisions make it possible to ax needless programs and reprioritize what government does and how it does it. The 1993 Government Performance and Responsibility Act (GPRA) and OMB's rarely used Program Assessment Rating Tool (PART) offer means for gauging the effectiveness of government programs. Additional funds should be provided for more comprehensive performance evaluation, and when programs are found to be ineffective, consequences should ensue—perhaps a provision to "shape up or ship out" of government. While the line-item veto, a darling of Republicans that existed briefly under

President Clinton, died when the Supreme Court declared it unconstitutional, many believe that presidents should be given enhanced "rescission" power to slice items out of the budget, which could be overridden only by Congress.

As we have seen, longer-term budgeting than the historic yearly period also has been mentioned as a way both to more realistically assess revenues and spending over multiyear and even generational time horizons, and to get Congress away from its current endless haggling over the relatively tiny sums of money that are within its "discretionary" control each year. Other proposals include capital budgets that distinguish between long-term investments in America and other spending (although these specifics may sometimes be difficult to tease out), joint presidential-congressional budget resolutions, and a requirement that the president submit a balanced-budget option with his or her budget. Another idea is to make budgetary changes—increases or decreases—more transparent, by clearly indicating how much every program's funding has changed from the previous year.

A further process reform—relevant to the three major entitlement programs—is to take the radical step of simply doing away with the concept of "mandatory" spending and forcing Congress to vote every year, or every several years, on all spending (and necessarily taxes), including Social Security, Medicare, and Medicaid. Many on both the left and right argue for a "unified" budget that does not hide borrowing from Social Security and other trust funds, as well as other hidden spending done through a myriad of tax breaks that disguise the true size of government.[13]

Such process reforms and rules are horribly abstract, about as engaging as the telephone book, and as informative to the average American as highway signs that tell a stopped rush-hour driver: "congestion ahead." They are useful in bringing our finances into greater balance, but they are no magic bullet and all too easily could be ignored in a country that otherwise urges the "rule of law" for the rest of the world.

SOCIAL SECURITY REFORM

Sexier, more controversial, and with many more mind-boggling zeroes dangling behind the dollar sign is reforming Social Security and America's entire retirement-security system. Despite endless presidential efforts, congressional proposals, independent commissions, blue-ribbon reports, and popular fear and cynicism about Social Security, *this is the easy one.* If we aim for "small" victories, this is the one to go for, since there are workable solutions, and we are talking about *only* a few trillion dollars.[14]

Social Security, which many young and middle-aged Americans fear will disappear into the land of broken promises, can be reformed in a number of ways that can preserve the program—and certainly its premise of providing retirement security—without a lot of heavy lifting. First, we need to take into account how dramatically demographic realities have changed since Franklin Roosevelt signed the Social Security Act in 1935. Five simple facts lead to not-too-earth-shattering policy conclusions: 1) in 1935 life expectancy was about sixty-three, while today it is seventy-eight and rising; 2) in 1935, and into the Truman era, there were about sixteen workers for every retiree, while there are about three today and, in a generation, just over two; 3) even though Americans are living longer, they are retiring earlier; 4) no one can survive well on Social Security checks alone, but ever more Americans lack private savings and pensions, as cash-strapped and failing companies jettison their plans; and 5) Bill Gates doesn't need a Social Security check quite as much as Joe Sixpack or Sally Soccer Mom.[15]

Since the Social Security surpluses that government currently pilfers for other purposes soon will disappear, the challenge is how to have sufficient revenues to pay fair benefits while creatively devising other ways of shoring up the economic security of Americans in their nonworking old age. Social Security, or payroll, taxes have been raised many times since 1935, and might need to be raised slightly, but that is not the fundamental answer. The real solutions have to do with how and when revenues are collected and benefits are disbursed, and with how Social Security can be supplemented.

The 1983 Social Security reform raised the retirement age for full benefits oh, so gradually from sixty-five to sixty-six by 2009, set to inch up to sixty-seven in 2027. With the exceptions of those in physically onerous jobs and Americans with disabilities or other serious medical conditions, there is no good reason—and many bad reasons—why Americans should not work longer. As noted, more and more Americans have been retiring at sixty-two, when they are eligible for partial Social Security benefits, or earlier. Three-fourths of Americans already start drawing Social Security benefits at sixty-two. Well, as Eugene Steuerle of the Urban Institute has said, Social Security should not be—and was not intended to be—a "middle-aged retirement program."[16] Despite the program trust fund's formal name—the Old Age and Survivors Insurance Trust Fund—most of these sixty-two-year-old Social Security recipients would blanch at the idea of being called "old." As Stuart Butler of the Heritage Foundation and Marc Friedman of Civic Ventures have estimated, Americans today could spend one-third of their lives in retirement; currently, life expectancy at ages sixty-two to sixty-five is about eighteen to twenty additional years.[17]

While it may be nice to hang out on that Palm Springs golf course or sip piña coladas on that Caribbean cruise, most Americans truly are not "old" at sixty-two or sixty-five, and would be better off in many ways if they at least worked part-time through their sixties and even into their seventies. If Americans worked longer, they would earn extra income. One year of additional work could add $46,000 in savings for the average couple. In many jobs, older Americans probably would find greater meaning and camaraderie in work than in sitting in front of the television at home or in a retirement community. And these "seasoned citizens," as David Walker has called them, would contribute to overall American economic output and growth by reducing our nation's projected labor shortages, and would give back to society in needed "encore" careers such as teaching.[18] They could be encouraged to work longer by eliminating, or reducing, the Social Security tax on workers over sixty-five, raising the normal retirement age, and facilitating part-time employment at later ages.

So with the exceptions noted, why not raise the eligibility age for full Social Security benefits to seventy, and phase in the change over a relatively short ten-to-twenty-year period? Indeed, the age at which Americans become eligible for benefits could be indexed to rising life expectancy. This alone would resolve between one-third and two-thirds of Social Security's financing problems. Likewise, the formula for calculating Social Security benefits—the primary insurance amount (PIA)—easily could be raised from thirty-five to forty years of work to reflect Americans' greater life expectancy, and increasing the related formula for average indexed monthly earnings (AIME) could eliminate most of Social Security's long-run fiscal imbalance.[19]

Other, smaller ways of raising Social Security's revenues would be to include the nation's millions of state and local government workers, who are currently exempt from paying Social Security taxes. Another revenue raiser would be to increase taxes on the Social Security benefits of high-income retirees. An additional, and perhaps appropriate, way to add funds to the kitty would be to set aside all revenues from the estate tax—about $1 trillion over a decade, assuming that it is preserved in some form—for Social Security benefits.[20]

On the revenue side, the payroll tax that provides funds for Social Security is just about the most regressive—read: unfair—tax in America. Many Americans pay more in Social Security taxes than in income tax. Social Security taxes took a flat 6.2 percent of your income in 2007 whether you made $15,000 (or less) or $97,500. (Employers match this, and both parties currently pay another 1.45 percent in Medicare payroll taxes.) And because of the so-called payroll-tax cap, the richest 6 percent of Americans, including those making millions a year, pay no more in absolute dollars than those making $97,500, so that one-sixth of aggregate American earnings (those above the threshold) are not taxed at all. Therefore many have proposed the sensible step of raising the threshold to at least the first $150,000 in annual income, if not abolishing the cap altogether.[21] While these reforms would pump billions into the Social Security pot, many believe that the aging of the American population will require that the payroll tax rate be raised slightly—although that could wait until the late 2010s or beyond, when the system needs the money more. Yet even a 2 percentage point increase by itself could eliminate much of the program's long-term imbalance, suggesting that a smaller increase could be possible absent other funding reforms.[22]

Just as the payroll tax for Social Security hits lower- and middle-income earners harder than those making a lot of money, many believe that not just the tax but the benefit structure of the program should be made more progressive. Since most federal benefits, somewhat surprisingly, do not go to the needy and are thus not, in Washington-speak, "means tested," Social Security could be restructured to reduce benefits paid to the highest-earning 15 percent or so of retirees.[23] Lower- and middle-income retirees would retain their full benefits, with lower-income Americans possibly receiving greater benefits under other proposed reforms, while those most able to pay their own way would see a benefit reduction.

Another favorite Social Security reform proposal often associated with means testing is indexing increases in benefit payments to average inflation in prices rather than in wages, which tend to rise faster. Many estimate that this reform alone also would eliminate much of Social Security's long-term imbalance, although overall benefit payments would be reduced by anywhere from one-quarter to two-fifths.[24] That is why many, ranging from President Bush to CBO Director Peter Orszag call for "progressive price indexing." Such a system would index benefits for high-income retirees to prices, while keeping wage-indexing for most retirees. In addition, freezing benefits for a few years would save surprisingly large sums of money.[25]

Although most Social Security reform aims to cut spending, some suggest that Supplemental Security Income for the truly old, those over eighty, be increased by 50 percent to $10,000 a year. Similarly, others suggest that benefits to widows and widowers have been unduly stingy, and should be increased somewhat.[26]

One way or the other, how benefits are paid will have to be reformed. Maya MacGuineas, president of the Committee for a Responsible Federal Budget, has calculated that if the payroll tax is not raised, the retirement age is not increased, or the PIA benefit formula is not changed, retirees, on average, face a draconian 43 percent cut in benefits.[27] That need not occur. And as we will see, older Americans actually can have more income in retirement if these and other reforms are implemented. But unless we do something, like Scrooge with the ghoulish ghost of the future, we will be staring into our own financial graves.

However, one of the most often talked-about Social Security reforms, and one of the most controversial, is to create private, personal retirement accounts (PRAS) either in place of some portion of the current public system or as a supplement to it. From the Business Roundtable and the conservative Cato Institute to liberal Democrats, most of the political spectrum agrees that it is a good idea to increase retirement savings, and personal savings more generally, by establishing a two-part system of conventional Social Security and private savings.[28] Private accounts have many benefits—including raising individual and national savings, and increasing personal responsibility for one's own retirement. These personal savings could contribute to national savings, raising our capital stock for investment in our nation's future.

But they also have downsides. If wrongly structured, they could increase the risk for many individuals; they, too, could be regressive, benefiting the high-income elderly much more than others; and they could provide a windfall to the financial-services industry, which suddenly could have trillions of dollars to invest and on which to reap commissions. Moreover, the transition costs to creating such a system are likely to involve decades of increased borrowing and deficits, before actually helping to reduce our nation's overall debt.[29]

As Bob Bixby, president of the Concord Coalition, has said: "Private accounts are controversial. But there is a potential compromise out there. Add mandated savings accounts to the Social Security system, and pay for them with an increase in the payroll tax or other sort of dedicated revenue."[30]

Properly devised, personal retirement accounts, a sort of Social Security Part B—much like those in place in countries such as Australia, Chile, and Singapore—need to be in our future, not only to reduce the nation's debt and the likelihood of Social Security going belly up but also to genuinely improve the living standards of tens of millions of older Americans. So how can this be done?

Although the idea—broached by some conservatives—of fully privatizing Social Security is a political nonstarter, creating personal retirement accounts either as a "carve-out" of existing Social Security funds or as an "add-on" has broad, bipartisan appeal. Of course, the devil is in the details. Given Americans' savings crisis, the notion of requiring that people save a certain percentage of their income—say, 2 to 3 percent—for retirement hardly seems like a bad idea. It would make individuals more secure and better off. If put in higher-yielding investments than Social Security funds currently are, it could yield more wealth at retirement. Given the miracle of compound interest—which is our kiss of death when it comes to mounting debt—$2,000 a year saved beginning at age twenty-five, with a generous 10 percent annual return, turns into nearly $1 million by age sixty-five, whereas if one begins saving at thirty-five, it would be a mere $360,000.[31] And as noted, a sizable proportion have not begun to save at any age.

Seem like a win-win-win proposition? The problems, although manageable, quickly pop out of the woodwork. People don't want to be forced to do anything, including saving for the future, when spending now either is necessary or more alluring. Indeed, how would the many Americans who can't make ends meet today, and who are personally in debt, be able to save? As an add-on, would this just seem like an additional tax on individuals and employers, even though the funds would be presumably wealth-creating investments in the future for both? As a carve-out, or even an add-on, would PRA funds invested in higher-yield stocks and other financial instruments simply seem too risky for those accustomed to the seemingly rock-solid security of investments in U.S. government–denominated securities? Who would choose and manage the investments?

The Organization for Economic Cooperation and Development, John Podesta of the Democratic Center for American Progress, and others have suggested creating an initial multitrillion-dollar kitty to fund PRAs out of the Social Security trust fund surpluses that will continue to exist until 2017.[32] Maya MacGuineas and the business-led Committee for Economic Development have suggested that workers and employers each be required to contribute 1.5 percent of earnings to PRAS. They would have tax-preferred status like 401(k) accounts. Withdrawals would be prohibited before retirement, and would be allowed only gradually during retirement so that individuals could not blow their savings at once on a big retirement gift to themselves.[33] A variation on this idea is to essentially require individual retirement accounts (IRAS) or 401(k)s through payroll deductions that would be matched annually by the government, perhaps via refundable tax credits, up to a certain level, such as $2,000.[34] These could be either mandatory or a default option, like the thrift-savings accounts offered by many public- and private-sector employers, in which individuals actively would have to choose not to participate. So that such accounts did not disproportionately benefit the rich and shortchange lower-income Americans, some have proposed fully subsidizing "USA," "PLUS," or even "American Stakeholder" accounts for newborn babies born to those earning below a certain threshold, the grants funded perhaps with a dedicated tax on pension-fund earnings or by eliminating various tax breaks for the wealthy.[35]

Finally, there is the issue of minimizing the risk of individuals making poor investment decisions or being too subject to the vagaries of financial markets. Therefore, many have proposed that PRAs either be structured like federal employees' retirement plans, in which individuals have the choice of a high-, medium-, or low-risk investment, or be invested by an independent board that is not constituted fully by either government bureaucrats or self-interested private institutional investors.[36]

DEFENSE SPENDING REFORM

Once upon a time, in the memory of most baby boomers and their elders, defense spending was the biggest component of federal spending. Aside from the huge World War II buildup, the nearly forty-five-year Cold War cost U.S. taxpayers trillions of dollars in present-day dollars. At the height of the Vietnam War, more than two-fifths of federal spending was going to the Department of Defense (DOD). After the Korean War, defense spending consumed a remarkable 14 percent of the nation's total national output, and it remained at about 8 to 10 percent of GDP until the fall of communism. It also consumed about 57 percent of the federal budget—roughly, three times its present share.[37] No wonder that Dwight Eisenhower spoke of a "military-industrial complex."

However, the post–Cold War "peace dividend" that many heralded in the early 1990s has been enormous and real. Defense spending as a share of GDP fell under the first President Bush and, even more, under President Clinton to just 1 in 33 dollars in our national economy. Despite the fact that the dollar amount of military spending, including for the wars in Iraq and Afghanistan, has doubled between 2001 and 2008, because the economy has grown, it is still only about 1 in 20 to 1 in 25 dollars today, much less than during the Cold War.[38] Certainly, aside from the dubious geopolitical, military, and humanitarian merits of the war in Iraq and the global war on terror, if the United States were not spending hundreds of billions of dollars (perhaps, ultimately, $1 trillion or more) on those efforts and George W. Bush had not increased defense spending, our deficits and debt would be lower. The Pentagon still gets a hefty $600 billion or so a year—one-fifth of federal spending (and almost half of global military spending), which excludes many costs of the Iraq War.

Yet nobody would argue that ours is not a dangerous world or that the United States, as the sole superpower, with wide-ranging global interests, does not need a defense capability to deal with any number of possible threats. Given that the types of threats, conflicts, and potential enemies are changing, strategies for force size and deployment and technological development constantly need to evolve. And, of course, the 2.3 million active-duty, Reserve, and National Guard troops, and 700,000 civilian Defense Department employees need to be adequately compensated. Whatever one thinks of the relative wisdom or foolishness of many aspects of contemporary defense strategy, wars, terrorism, and hostile threats are not going away.

Nonetheless, when it comes to defense spending, an awful lot of people get quite emotional—and it's the generals and "chicken hawks" as much as the pacifists and deficit hawks. Many firmly believe that the United States needs a robust defense, and some conservatives believe that defense is one of the few legitimate functions of the federal government. Likewise, a long history of interservice rivalry has pitted army, air force, and navy (and the Marine Corps, within the navy) against one another, in vying for the most advanced weapons systems. To all of these constituencies, billions spent on defense is money well spent.

On the other hand, beyond the pacifist argument that most wars, and hence the money spent on them, are immoral, many liberals and conservatives question the size, nature, and efficacy of U.S. defense policy and spending. The unfortunate ethos of speaking softly and carrying a big stick has gotten the United States into much human tragedy, many political disasters, and vast sums of money poured down the drain from Saigon to Baghdad. Many internationalists, including conservatives who are no fans of the United Nations, believe that other nations should share more of the burdens of preserving peace and making the world safe. Whether that means reforming and beefing up the capabilities of the United Nations' peacekeeping and military roles or pushing our allies to supply troops, weapons, and money to more genuinely multilateral "coalitions of the willing," there is much to be said for the argument that the United States does not have to be the world's one policeman, bearing disproportionate global costs. Similarly, more robust and sophisticated multilateral diplomacy—

whether through a reinvigorated United Nations process or in concert with allies whom we treat with respect—could help prevent wars and the attendant
human and financial costs.

To deficit hawks, the cozy bidding processes and seemingly limitless cost
overruns on defense contracts—which Ike recognized nearly sixty years ago—
together with the long-remembered embarrassment of the Defense Department spending $640 per toilet seat, suggests that no profit-making business
would manage its financial affairs the way that the Pentagon and its accom-
plices in congressional appropriations committees do. For example, DOD could
have saved taxpayers $600 million if it had not procured eight additional C-
130J aircraft that the department's own inspector general called "unsatisfac-
tory"; another $1 billion was spent on 144 pork-barrel military construction
projects, $50 million on a new defense travel system, and $92 million in ques-
tionable facility repairs and other spending in Alaska, including such vital defense needs as the Arctic Winter Games. The GAO has estimated that it is not
uncommon for weapons programs to run 20 to 50 percent over budget.[39]

Many weapons systems, moreover, simply do not meet basic standards of
effectiveness and safety. The V22 Osprey aircraft, which has caused thirty acci-
dental deaths, is a good example. The joint strike fighter, while a potentially
useful tactical aircraft, was procured at huge cost without testing many of its essential components. The Coast Guard's $24 billion Deepwater modernization
program is rife with cost overruns. And the Zumwalt class destroyer simply fails
the history test: we are buying the type of warship that has not been used in any
military operation in more than half a century and is unlikely to be used in the
future, unless we somehow turn the clock back to mid-twentieth-century warfare. Cutting these and other unnecessary weapons could save the country at
least $35 billion a year.[40]

A 2003 Defense Department inspector general report found that the department could not account for $1 trillion in spending over the years, including
fifty-six jets and thirty-six missile launchers that the army somehow misplaced.
Former Defense Secretary Donald Rumsfeld acknowledged in 2002, "We cannot track $2.3 trillion in transactions," and retired Vice Admiral Jack Shanahan
said, "With good financial oversight, we could find $48 billion in loose change
in that building without hitting taxpayers."[41] With defense contracts nearly
doubling between 2000 and 2005 to $270 billion, the Government Account-
ability Office has criticized the Defense Department for facing "vulnerabilities
to contracting fraud, waste, and abuse due to weaknesses in five key areas: sustained senior leadership, capable acquisition workforce, adequate pricing, ap-

propriate contracting approaches and techniques and sufficient contract surveillance."[42]

In particular, many talk about imposing greater outside scrutiny on how defense dollars are spent, with more competition in bidding for contracts, much less duplication of weapons systems, increased international burden sharing, and more reliance on human know-how and fighting capability, as well as technology, rather than on expensive and unnecessary weapons systems that mostly provide corporate welfare to the aerospace giants of the military-industrial complex.[43] From the GAO to Congress to the general public, there is a widespread and well-founded belief that the defense budget is bloated and grossly mismanaged, and that it could be cut without compromising U.S. security.[44]

DOMESTIC DISCRETIONARY
SPENDING REFORM

Even though nondefense domestic discretionary spending accounts for only 16 percent of the federal budget, and that number has been steadily falling—many would say that it's been cut to the bone—that does not mean that savings cannot be found among the roughly one thousand programs on which the federal government spends its money. While the hoary old saw about "waste, fraud, and abuse" may be no more true of the federal government than of corporate America, there certainly is "waste" in the federal budget, and fraud and abuse come with the territory—in the public and private sectors—whenever people and money are involved. Short of getting our collective moral compasses to work better and inspiring people to believe that public service does not mean sitting on your rear end collecting a paycheck, fraud and abuse are probably better addressed by clergy, parents, and kindergarten teachers than by policy makers.

Waste in domestic discretionary spending, as in defense spending, is much more complex and ripe for pruning. Some of the budget-process rules discussed above would help—such as subjecting programs to better analyses of their effectiveness, requiring sunset provisions so that programs are not immortal and have to be reauthorized periodically, and establishing specific spending caps.

Sadly, much of the cutting in recent years has been at the expense of programs designed either to help the needy or to invest in America's future through research and support for higher education and science. President Bush's proposed 16 percent cut in domestic discretionary spending between 2006 and

2010, billed as saving $214 billion, includes cuts that could end food stamps, education support, WIC nutrition support, housing vouchers, and home-energy assistance to several million low-income Americans.[45]

Instead, the ripest plums for picking from the budgetary tree are what everyone from Ralph Nader, who coined the term, to the libertarian Cato Institute calls "corporate welfare." Estimates of taxpayer subsidies to private businesses range from $125 billion to $175 billion a year, more than the taxes paid by sixty million filers. For example, Citizens for Tax Justice estimates that between 1996 and 2000 Microsoft received more than $12 billion in tax breaks, Ford got more than $9 billion, and the dear, departed Enron paid no taxes in all but one year. While Nader has called these subsidies to the rich or those who should sink or swim in the free market "aid for dependent corporations," Cato denounces them as "taxpayer rip-offs."[46]

Among these subsidies, there are favorite targets for spending cuts, where at least the left and right (more than the center) tend to agree. Farm subsidies are mostly corporate welfare to big agribusinesses, defy free-market principles, and hinder crucial international agreements on free trade that would benefit not only the United States but many poor nations and their people. America's Market Access Program, which funds U.S. food exporters; the federal dairy support program whose perverse acronym is MILC; our sugar price-support program; and other agricultural subsidies, if eliminated, could trim at least $20 billion from the budget over five years.[47] Other oft-mentioned programs that could be slashed are the business subsidies embedded in the Small Business Administration, the Export-Import Bank, the Overseas Private Investment Corporation, the Advanced Technology Program, the FreedomCAR Partnership, and the Maritime Administration. Others have proposed cutting the subsidy to Amtrak, slashing subsidies for flood insurance (if you choose to live in hurricane country, should all taxpayers help you foot the bill?), and requiring defined-benefit pension plans to pay the $28 billion spent over five years on Pension Benefit Guaranty Corporation insurance.

The ever-popular subject of "pork," or earmarks, has become de rigueur for ridicule and potential budget cutting ever since Alaska Representative Don Young earmarked nearly $1 billion in 2005 for the infamous "bridge to nowhere," connecting an Alaskan island with fifty residents to the sparsely populated mainland. Pork, a line item in an appropriations bill for a specific purpose inserted by a particular member of Congress to curry favor with his or her constituents, has grown about twentyfold since 1991 to about $66 billion in 2006. While the term's political meaning dates back a century, its metaphorical origins derive from the colonial practice of handing out salt pork to slaves. The Citizens Against Government Waste's aptly titled annual *Pig Book* recently included funding for such nationally valuable projects as the Sparta Teapot Museum in North Carolina, the World Toilet Summit, the National Wild Turkey Federation in Virginia, hanging flower baskets to beautify Illinois, the Richard Steele Boxing Club in Las Vegas, a parking lot for a private art museum in Omaha, and Iowa's National Cattle Congress. A full listing would be laughable if it weren't equivalent to more than 1 percent of the federal budget, or the combined incomes of roughly one million Americans.[48]

While transportation investments are critical to our nation's future prosperity, many believe that the federal government squanders too much money on highways, does not spend enough on mass transit, and maintains many highways that should either be privatized or paid for with tolls or other user fees, as they are in many other nations. Transportation bills, almost as notoriously as defense appropriations, are often larded with pork, governed by little accountability and a mentality of no-holds-barred spending. Scaling highway spending back to 1997 levels, for example, could save $52 billion a year.[49]

Another popular approach to cutting domestic discretionary spending, especially among conservatives, is to privatize various functions of government and sell off assorted government assets—sort of like holding a national yard sale. In addition to fully or partially turning Amtrak over to the private sector, other favorite targets include the Postal Service, the Tennessee Valley Authority and three other federally owned power authorities, and perhaps even the National Park Service.[50] More radical is the idea of selling federal lands, mineral rights, buildings, and other inventory to the private sector, which Chris Edwards of the Cato Institute has estimated could yield a one-time cash infusion of $2.8 trillion to the Treasury.[51] This draconian proposal is unlikely to be implemented, unless we are willing—on the model of sports organizations—to allow sponsors to rename our Capitol the Coca-Cola U.S. Capitol Building and embrace the Microsoft-Yellowstone National Park, the Toyota Interstate Highway System, or the Boeing Andrews Air Force Base. While some assets could be sold and might be more efficiently managed by the private sector, this would be a risky, partial approach to reducing the national debt, available one time only. And the private sector does not always manage things better—as examples from Enron and MCI to Ford and U.S. Steel attest.

However, two other approaches to cutting spending, if done right, offer some promise. These would target federal grants to organizations and federal grants and other funds to states. The General Services Administration estimates that the federal government provided about $400 billion in grants to some thirty thousand organizations in 2006, nearly double the dollars awarded in 2000. While many of these are worthy programs, benefiting youth and helping to increase public safety, these could be scrutinized much more carefully to determine which are effective, which could be funded by private or nonprofit entities, and which could be discarded.[52]

In addition, Washington provides more than $400 billion to the fifty states in seven hundred–plus grant programs. This, too, opens much more philosophical debates about the nature of federalism in America, and the appropriate responsibilities of federal, state, and local governments. And curbing the grants would be something of a fiscal Ponzi scheme—as most cuts in federal allocations to states and localities would have to be made up for by new spending, and taxes, by lower levels of government. Nonetheless, many moderates believe that federal grants for highways and education, in particular, could be scaled back, saving tens of billions of federal budget dollars. The problem with too much devolution to the states stems from the fact that some states simply are much richer than others and can better afford health and education programs, which is why the federal government has helped play the role of the great equalizer. As Stuart Butler of the Heritage Foundation has said: "I'm less concerned about roads in Mississippi being worse than elsewhere than a child in Mississippi getting worse health care."[53]

Thus federal domestic spending cannot simply be a chopping block. From Alexander Hamilton and Henry Clay to Teddy Roosevelt and John Kennedy, federal policies and spending have boosted the well-being of the American people. And even in a book about cutting deficits and debt, we need to recognize that our nation and its needs change, and that the federal government is best equipped and most efficient at designing policies and spending money to meet some needs.

THIS IS THE BIG DEAL: CONTROLLING MEDICARE, MEDICAID, AND HEALTH CARE SPENDING

Throughout this book, and lurking behind any discussion of reducing our nation's long-term debt, is the enormous, and enormously complex, problem of controlling health care costs. Whereas better health care has enhanced and lengthened the lives of most Americans, and also contributed greatly to the nation's productivity and wealth, it has done so at a huge public and private cost.

And our current system is horribly inefficient and inequitable in its delivery of care. With health care costs swallowing ever more of our economy—like a mouse eating cheese faster than new replacement cheese can be produced—these costs threaten to overwhelm individuals, private companies, and federal, state, and local governments. Annual household spending on health care averages about $16,000, more than one-third of household median income, although most of that cost is now picked up by third-party payers such as insurance companies, Medicare, and Medicaid. Employers, who provide health care coverage to about 60 percent of Americans, have reeled under the relentless annual 7 to 8 percent cost inflation, cutting benefits, shifting costs to employees, and still suffering diminished profitability. At the same time, Americans' monthly premiums nearly doubled between 1999 and 2006, from $129 to $248.[54] However, from the standpoint of government finances, since the federal government pays nearly half of our $2 trillion–plus annual medical bill, the old, 1992 Clinton campaign slogan about the economy should be recycled: "It's health care, stupid."

As I outlined in the first chapter, other than providing a relatively healthy population, the U.S. health care system is severely dysfunctional from a wide variety of perspectives. Reforming it so that it consumes less public and private resources, while providing better, more efficient, and equitable care for all Americans is the gargantuan domestic policy challenge of the coming years. The range of issues and needed reforms is so vast, complex, and contentious that this is the fiscal problem—and national problem, more generally—that it is hardest to find a viable solution.

But on that road we must embark. For with each new MRI, hospital stay, physician visit, and prescription—multiplied by America's vast population—our nation's very future as a vital economic, and geopolitical, power depends. And while health is extraordinarily important to almost anyone's conception of what human well-being is, and philosophically cannot be measured in dollars, the trade-offs that we are making in spending so much on health care inevitably will compromise many other aspects of our national and personal well-being—from our incomes and ability to generate rising prosperity to our environment, safety, and educational capabilities.

The two issues on which there is growing, general agreement are that the United States must provide basic health care coverage to all of its people, protecting the most vulnerable, and that it must slow cost growth.[55] Where disagreement begins is on what mix of governmental and private-sector mechanisms can best accomplish these goals. Moreover, many disagree about whether we should focus solely on the problems of government health care spending, or—because public and private health care are so inextricably intertwined— need to address all health care, with government taking the lead.

Some staunchly believe that a government-provided, single-payer, universal health care system such as those in Britain, Canada, and other countries is the only way to guarantee that tens of millions of Americans are not without insurance. Many also argue that government, because of its economies of scale, is actually more effective at controlling costs than the private sector, as federal employees' and veterans' health care has slower cost growth and fewer overhead costs than private insurance.[56] Others believe that mandating private insurance for all, with government subsidies and tax incentives to ensure that all can afford basic coverage, combined with a variety of market and regulatory mechanisms to control costs, is the way to go. Yet growing numbers of conservatives—as well as the usual liberal suspects—believe that universal care is not only morally just but fiscally prudent, as millions of uninsured Americans end up in high-cost hospital emergency rooms for their care, leaching public funds.

Under a single-payer system—a political loser for the past sixty years in the United States—the government would pay for everyone's health care, using a public entity such as Britain's National Health Service to compensate doctors, hospitals, pharmacists, and other health care providers for their services. Single-payer systems implicitly ration care—a subject to which we will return—as budgeted health care dollars are finite, leading to health care wonk jokes about not getting sick in Canada in December when the money has run out. Some left-leaning Democrats and labor unions continue to advocate for a single-payer system, and many states have introduced legislation to create single-payer systems, but—while more surprising political changes have been known to occur—a national single-payer system is not likely to be in the cards.[57]

Instead, some sort of hybrid, private-public universal health care system seems to be in our future. A base of universal insurance, with government premium support, would be modified by some or all of these popular menu items: "managed competition" among insurance providers, greater cost sharing (that is, individuals paying more out of pocket), increased regulation of health care providers and their costs, greater emphasis on public health, medical malpractice reform, some rationing of care, and the use of information technology to disseminate best and most cost-effective practices, as well as to maintain a national medical records database. Whether this can be done, given the constituencies strongly arrayed against many of these ideas, is another matter. While we will get to the nitty-gritty of each of these far-from-easy, highly controversial reforms, we also must confront the fiscal elephants of Medicare, Medicaid, and other federal health care spending.

Efforts to cut Medicare and Medicaid spending are necessarily linked with more fundamental reforms and undoubtedly will require fairly radical changes in private *and* public delivery of, and attitudes toward, health care. However, many have tried the finger-in-the-dike approach of trying to patch up the existing system, even as the floodwaters rise to overwhelm not only publicly provided care for the elderly and poor, and for all Americans. There have been many such piecemeal, often politically motivated, proposals that may represent small steps in the right direction. These include legislative efforts to require the government to negotiate lower prescription drug prices, and use medical-care commissions to force Medicare and Medicaid to stay within annual budgets. Another often-tried proposal—usually batted down by medical providers—is to cut reimbursement rates to doctors and other providers. In 2007 President Bush proposed offering a standard deduction for families to buy health insurance. The White House said that the plan would save money for one hundred million Americans, and might result in lower-cost insurance, although some say that many without insurance would not benefit because they already pay no taxes. The growing fiscal hole in Medicare financing could be plugged in part by raising the 2.9 percent Medicare Part A payroll tax for hospital insurance, or by increasing the premiums that either high-income or all individuals pay on Medicare Part B for physician and home health care. But increasing Medicare beneficiaries' Part B premiums from 25 percent to 35 percent would save just $85 billion over a decade—pennies, in the scheme of America's $38 trillion in unfunded liabilities.[58]

Some also have proposed raising the Medicare eligibility age to sixty-seven or seventy. However, since health care spending tends to be at higher ages, especially in the year before death, number crunchers estimate that unlike the potential Social Security savings, raising the age for Medicare eligibility would yield only about two-tenths of 1 percent in savings. Better efforts to root out Medicare fraud, estimated to cost $60 billion a year, also would help.[59]

Likewise, those who look for cost-cutting approaches to Medicaid, without taking a comprehensive approach to health care reform, have suggested many possibilities. Among the changes proposed, in addition to cutting reimbursement rates, are elimination of federal administrative funding for Medicaid, conversion of federal Medicaid payments into fixed grants to states, a shift of Medicaid dollars to insurance premium assistance, expansion of managed care, classification of beneficiaries into different need categories based on age and health, and even off-loading Medicaid costs—57 percent of which are now borne by Washington—to the states.[60]

Yet if we truly are to tackle costs and coverage for all, these are mere palliatives. Bigger ideas, and actions, are necessary.

One of the most widely touted ideas—predating Bush's tax-breaks-for-insurance idea, adopted by several states—is that government should pay for people's health insurance, not for their health care.[61] Thus Medicare, Medicaid, SCHIP, and other federal health programs that currently pay doctors and hospitals for whatever treatments patients get would be eliminated, replaced by partial public financing of health insurance policies for everyone.

Although some disagree with the notion of forcing everyone to have health insurance, or to do anything else, most agree that—because medical well-being affects all (just think of an uninsured virus carrier infecting countless insured Americans), health insurance has to be *required* for all. Just as one must have insurance to drive, health insurance should be mandated if one is to live in America.

Many also believe that the employer-based system is outdated, as people change jobs often and employers increasingly are shedding traditional health benefits. Instead, health insurance should be individually based and "portable," following one from job to job and throughout one's life.[62]

As under the Federal Employees Health Benefit Program (FEHBP), which provides insurance to nine million civilian federal workers and their families, or the military TRICARE system, government would pay for most, but not all, of the cost of health insurance, yet offer potential beneficiaries a choice among several plans. For higher-cost plans, which provide more extensive coverage, individuals would have to foot more of the bill, while lower-cost plans, such as health-maintenance organizations (HMOs) or "consumer-driven" plans, would be less expensive to the individual. As Leif Haase has written, people would still have choice—between "Cadillac, Buick, and Chevrolet" plans—but they would be required to buy at least a minimum insurance package. The FEHBP offers five types of plans—managed, fee-for-service plans that allow one to choose one's physician; HMOs that limit care to particular provider centers or clusters; "point of service" plans that blend elements of the first two options; high-deductible plans that cover only very expensive medical bills; and consumer-driven plans that establish health savings accounts from which individuals can draw to pay their medical bills. TRICARE, when it was adopted in the 1990s, offered the choice of "standard" insurance, PPO/Extra, and HMO Prime. As any federal worker knows, the personal premiums deducted from one's paycheck are higher for higher-option plans, and lower for less-inclusive ones. At the lower end, individuals pay only about one-quarter of the cost.

Moreover, like Medicare, FEHBP not only is able to bargain for better prices than private plans but also has lower administrative costs than private-sector insurance companies.[63] Although FEHBP is far from perfect, a nationwide version also would have the advantage of creating enormous risk pools based, for example, on age, which would create considerable efficiencies to push down premium costs.[64] However, many advocates of paying for insurance rather than care believe that government should add the sweetener of subsidizing premium costs for lower-income and higher-risk Americans. Public funding for health care, whether providing premium support for insurance policies or tinkering with Medicare, should be means tested, like Medicaid, the Earned Income Tax Credit, housing credits, and other social-welfare programs intended to help Americans who are not affluent: the lower one's income or wealth, the higher the support from government should be; conversely, wealthier Americans would receive no support.[65]

Universal coverage, bundled with means testing, premium support, and consumer choice entail at least three other major assumptions—one philosophical, one programmatic, and one a little bit of both. Philosophically, because such a system still would allow higher-income Americans to purchase more expensive health care, either through high-end insurance policies or by paying out of pocket, it would create a two-tier system. To some, the inherent unfairness of such an approach may seem distasteful, but it is important to compare this to what we now have: our current health care system is horribly unfair; this would at least provide basic coverage for all, with minimum but universal standards of care. So despite reasonable qualms, with this—or any other—reform we need to be careful not to let the perfect become the enemy of the good.

The second underlying assumption for such a reform package is that, to hold down health care consumption and costs, individuals would need to bear more of the cost of care. Currently, individuals' out-of-pocket costs account for only about one-eighth of the total that America spends on health care. The fact that insurance companies, Medicare, Medicaid, and other third-party payers pick up so much of the tab creates what economists call "moral hazard." Not bearing—or, often, even knowing—the true costs of their care, Americans are prone to consume whatever medical test, procedure, prescription, operation, or second medical opinion presented as options. If we paid for only 13 percent of the cost of our houses, cars, clothing, or children's toys, undoubtedly most of us would have bigger houses, more expensive cars, an extra closet of clothing, and a playroom bursting with toys. In many ways, that *is* what we have with health care. Even though health is a different kind of public good—more obviously essential and less prone to informed consumer choice than cars or toys—and we are generally healthier than ever, Americans of all ages consume ever more health care per person each year.

Economics and common sense dictate that if a person had to bear a greater share of his health costs, he would be more selective about taking his child to the pediatrician for every case of the sniffles or going to the dermatologist to get every mole removed. This idea of burden shifting, or greater cost sharing, is widely touted as a way at least to attenuate exploding health care spending. The vehicle of choice to do this is the high-deductible health plan (HDHPs); most basic insurance policies would carry, say, $2,000 yearly deductibles. As a result, individuals would have to pay for much more of their routine care, and maybe would decide that some wasn't really necessary, while they still would be fully covered for catastrophic care and chronic conditions that run up five- and six-figure medical bills. The major problem with HDHPs in terms of saving money and digging us out of debt is that most health care spending is precisely for those expensive hospital stays and for care well beyond any reasonable deductible.[66]

This approach of paying for insurance, not care, together with increased cost sharing, has features that could appeal to those across the political spectrum. Liberals would appreciate the provision of universal coverage, with government providing the bulk of support and additional assistance to those least able to afford insurance. Conservatives would approve the preservation of consumer choice, the increased personal responsibility for health care choices and costs, and the guarantee of at least limited market competition among health plans, which would presumably drive down costs. And to all concerned about rising health care costs and debt, this approach could be expected to temper spending, as Americans become more aware of, and sensitive to, the true costs of care.

Given that many states have become more successful policy innovators than the federal government has been in recent years, there is much to be said for testing mandatory insurance, FEHBP-like programs, premium support, and other ways of reining in medical costs at the state level. Massachusetts made it mandatory for all residents to buy health insurance, giving them choices of different policies with different costs and options with subsidies for those with low incomes. However, the initial average cost per policy suggested by Governor Mitt Romney—$2,450—quickly almost doubled to a level that would be hard for many citizens or the state to afford. Maine and Vermont have similar new programs, and California Governor Arnold Schwarzenegger proposed a Massachusetts-like plan that included a mandate to buy insurance, coupled with state support for those who cannot afford it. In addition, a premium-support demonstration project based on the federal employees' plan is to be tried in six states in 2010.[67]

Moreover, since Medicaid is a federal-state initiative, and a few states such as Florida and North Carolina have experimented with giving beneficiaries money to buy insurance instead of paying for care or requiring agreements that beneficiaries follow their doctors' orders, states could be encouraged to let fifty flowers, if not a thousand, bloom. Health economists and deficit hawks have talked about restructuring the program so that the federal government would provide fixed Medicaid block grants to states, allowing them to explore different ways of providing good health care, and would no longer provide matching grants for administration. Senators Bingaman (D-N.M.), Voinovich (R-Ohio), and Feingold (D-Wis.) and Representatives Baldwin (D-Wis.), Price (R-Ga.), Tierney (D-Mass.), and Beauprez (R-Colo.) have proposed federal incentives for more states to experiment with expanded coverage.[68]

Another way in which individuals could be encouraged to bear more of their costs is the often-mentioned idea of mandating universal health savings accounts. Like personal retirement accounts, they would be required of all Americans; they would bump up our personal and national savings (a good thing); and lower-income Americans could be subsidized. The CBO has proposed a dedicated tax or payroll deduction that would force Americans to contribute $1,000 or $2,000 a year to such accounts. Employers could be required to match these, and government could institute a sliding scale of subsidies, providing most of the total for lower-income citizens, some for the middle class, and none for upper-income Americans. A less drastic approach, but also a less effective one, than mandating such accounts would be to provide incentives through the tax system, such as making contributions fully tax deductible. About three million of the two hundred million Americans in private-insurance plans have high-deductible policies coupled with health savings accounts.[69]

However, if this sort of "consumer-directed" health care may give pause to many Americans, accustomed to generous health benefits, the third, partly philosophical, partly programmatic assumption is likely to send many heading for the hills. This is the scary concept of "rationing" health care. No one wants to be told by a doctor, much less a government bureaucracy, that she cannot get certain care simply because it is not cost-effective (read: it's a waste of money). Indeed, this treads upon profound moral issues of how we value life and health. For example, is it okay to keep a healthy ninety-year-old alive with expensive procedures, but not okay to keep him alive if we know he stands a high chance of dying in six months?

Rationing, which is practiced in other rich countries, can be accomplished in several ways. As a society, we could simply set a dollar limit on how much the government will spend on health care. Or we could limit benefits, using some scientifically based criteria for what is effective and what isn't, allowing people to appeal decisions. During the 1990s Oregon's steps along this route were roundly rejected by voters. Yet the Brookings Institution health care economist Henry Aaron has said: "Unless we ration, even cost-effective care will become unaffordable. . . . Failure to ration will mean that the cost of caring for the aged, disabled and poor will require astronomical tax increases—and that working Americans will have less money to spend on anything other than health care. Employers will find it increasingly unattractive to sponsor coverage for workers, and workers will refuse increasingly costly coverage."[70]

Nonetheless, rationing—or any sort of cost control—also requires that we think about the real prices paid for different types of care, and whether they are cost-effective and reasonable. This is yet another area that intrudes on the sacred ground of Americans' and health care providers' "freedom" to choose what care to consume and what prices to charge. Do we need government, or some sort of "objective" entity outside the health care system, to decide on the efficacy and dollar value of the thousands upon thousands of medical interventions in our society? Some conservatives may scream bloody murder, but oligopolies of health care providers, insurance companies, and others already make those decisions for us—and they are self-interested, profit-driven decisions that are not necessarily in either the aggregate public interest or the interest of the individual patient.

Nonetheless, there are multiple approaches to rationing care, and to the moral—as well as economic—issues that it entails. As Stuart Butler of the Heritage Foundation rightly points out, the value of a certain health care procedure or outcome may be greater to one person than another, so that "objective" criteria about "value" may be squishy. Thus he proposes that individuals be given health care vouchers to spend as they choose.[71]

However, Butler, Alice Rivlin, and others recognize that better attempts to specify what is medically effective and cost-effective care are needed to guide patients', doctors', and other providers' decision making, since few patients and surprisingly few doctors know either the relative prices of care or data on their clinical effectiveness. Many have proposed funding an institute that would carefully study what are the best, and best-value, health care practices, and make the information available through a national, Web-based database for physicians, hospitals, patients, and others. Such an institute of clinical studies, or panels of experts, not only could determine whether one procedure or pill that costs half as much as another is just as effective, but also could determine why health care costs vary so widely in different communities and parts of the nation. This sort of "evidence-based medicine" also could improve many patients' health outcomes. Many studies and much anecdotal evidence have shown that much of the care dispensed by doctors and physicians is not considered "best practice," and many Americans suffer for it, as the one hundred thousand or so who die each year from medical errors illustrate. The use of information technology can help cut costs not only by disseminating best practices and making all Americans' medical records readily available, as the Veterans Administration already does, but can furnish a sort of report card on providers, giving patients information on providers' performance, presumably forcing doctors and hospitals to compete more on both quality and cost of care.[72]

Yet even defining cost-effectiveness is fraught with moral, technical, and economic complexities. For instance, it is clearly "cost-effective" to immunize at low cost children, who have long, productive lives ahead of them. But by that measure, is it "cost-effective" to do expensive heart surgery on a seventy-year-old man to prolong his life, even though the economic returns to society are minimal? Most of us would say, "Forget economics (it isn't called the 'dismal science' for nothing), and do the right thing: keep him alive." Other examples of economics colliding with ethics involve generic versus brand-name drugs and the costs of physician care. Everyone knows that you save money on generics, but our patent system protects pharmaceutical companies' right to profit for a certain period for drugs that they develop. Similarly, U.S. doctors charge considerably more for the same care and outcomes as doctors in wealthy, generally healthy countries in western Europe and Japan. If true competition and good information existed, classical economics would say that the market is properly setting prices. However, a million corners of U.S. life are regulated by government—from food and auto safety to patents themselves. Therefore why not regulate the cost of drugs and physician care—saying to hell with the market, we need to cut costs, so Big Pharma, our corps of doctors, and our battery of hospitals must accept less money for their products and services?

Aside from the loud screams that would rise from these extremely powerful medical constituencies, such an approach would destroy the freedom of free markets and ignore other factors that push U.S. medical costs higher than those in other countries. Two of the most noteworthy factors are the disproportionate share of research costs borne by American pharmaceutical companies and the unparalleled direct and indirect costs of our litigiousness over medical malpractice. While some say that U.S. pharmaceutical research costs should be passed on in part to other nations' consumers, such costs may be impossible to calculate for global companies operating in a global economy.

There is a growing consensus that Americans' penchant for lawsuits, abetted by hungry trial lawyers seeking their huge share of malpractice payouts, needs to be drastically curbed. Many physicians, especially surgeons, pay six-figure malpractice-insurance premiums, whose costs they pass on to patients, and most American doctors practice unduly defensive medicine, ordering redundant tests, to avoid the threat of possible lawsuits. Clearly, the nation could follow California in capping malpractice awards, eliminating astronomical "settlements"; almost all states—which control malpractice tort law—have passed or introduced bills to reform medical liability. However, despite some conservatives' fixation on tort reform, malpractice premiums account for less than 2 percent of America's health care costs, so the savings here also may be minimal.[73]

Yet another frequently discussed way of cutting America's public and private health costs is to increase public health and preventive efforts so that Americans don't require so much care in the first place. In our nation of TV-watching, beer-swilling couch potatoes, one study estimated that increased exercise would cut U.S. health costs by nearly $80 billion, or about 4 percent. As Americans' girth continues to expand, and the numbers of overweight and morbidly obese citizens increase, it has been estimated that as much as half of 1 percent of our gross domestic product is spent on the medical consequences of obesity. Certainly, people could be given tax or other financial incentives for healthy behaviors, and penalties for unhealthy ones. Moreover, government and the private sector can be more aggressive about promoting good health—as it successfully has done with curbing smoking. Yet it is notoriously hard to change behavior. People who like to run, swim, and play tennis will do so; people who like munching chips in front of the TV are also unlikely to change how they live.[74]

While armies of health care economists, consultants, policy wonks, and others agonize—rightly—about how America could control its health care spending while providing better, fairer care for all, the preceding pages suggest the difficulties involved. As we have seen, the projected future, unfunded, costs of Medicare and Medicaid dwarf everything else in our looming fiscal crisis. We can cut other spending and even reform Social Security, but if we don't succeed with health care, we are sunk. The good news is that many ideas have been proposed, and a consensus is emerging around some of them. The problems are several: These are major reforms, not the tinkering on the margins that has become typical of our timid, partisan political process. Every reform has at least one entrenched interest opposed to it, and many reforms are not the sort that Americans happily would embrace. And finally, time is not on our side. It may sound like hyperbole, but if we don't start resolving American health care problems very soon, they could pose a far bigger threat to our nation's future than a rising China, terrorism, off-shore outsourcing of jobs, global warming, or anything else.

**TAXES AND REVENUES: IT'S NOT
ALL ABOUT CUTTING**

Before we can get to any vision of a fiscally sustainable, economically prosperous future in which our debt diminishes and the United States has the resources to invest in the next "American century," as Time Inc. founder Henry Luce called the twentieth, we need to consider the other big component of returning our nation to a deficit-free and declining-debt existence: taxes, or other revenues.

Almost no one likes to pay taxes, despite Justice Holmes's injunction that they are the price for a civilized society. More to the point, almost no taxpayer, budget expert, or politician likes the current U.S. tax system, which is insanely complex, grossly unfair, and horribly inefficient. Even with many filers relying on TurboTax, perhaps the only people who like America's current system of raising revenues are accountants. Between the actual costs of preparing taxes and the lost income from time that could be spent producing goods and services—or just having fun—paying taxes in the United States cost our country between $240 billion and $600 billion in 2005, according to the Government Accountability Office, all to raise about $2 trillion.[75]

While I have discussed the nature and history of raising revenues—primarily through taxes—to pay for government, it is now time to explore how the revenue side of the budgetary equation might be reformed to reduce our deficits and debt (not to mention make life easier for tens of millions of suffering taxpayers).

Any thinking about tax reform has to be guided by the basic principles of raising sufficient revenues to pay for government in a way that is more efficient, fair, and simple. When forced to confront entitlement-spending and demographic realities, most conservatives and liberals recognize that tax revenues as a proportion of our economy will have to rise from the roughly 18.5 percent level of the past half century. However, except for hardened tax-and-spend liberals, most believe that to avoid damage to our economy, they should not rise by more than a few percentage points of our GDP. An increase of 22 percent versus one of 28 percent makes an enormous difference, as 1 percent of the U.S. economy is $130 billion. And, as has become painfully obvious, without spending restraint, even devoting 28 percent of our economy to taxes—a roughly 50 percent tax increase—still would leave our nation with enormous deficits and debt in the decades ahead.

Most ideas about increasing revenues fall into a few bundles: 1) eliminate the Bush tax cuts and raise income tax rates; 2) broaden the tax base by eliminating hundreds of billions of dollars of tax breaks and subsidies, and requiring all Americans to pay taxes; 3) introduce new taxes that either supplement or replace existing taxes, including consumption (or sales) taxes, environmental taxes, "sin" taxes, and user fees; 4) step up tax enforcement; and 5) simplify the entire tax system, reforming the income tax and payroll taxes, eliminating or revising the corporate income tax, and reforming the alternative minimum tax. In addition, since borrowing has been a part of public finance since the Revolutionary War, reforming how the Treasury borrows money, and what it borrows it for, also should be on the table.

President Bush's series of tax cuts has been widely criticized for reducing federal revenues to between 16 and 17 percent of national income, saddling the government with a shortfall of hundreds of billions of dollars that will only grow larger over time. As former Treasury Secretary Robert Rubin has said, simply repealing the Bush cuts for those earning more than $200,000 a year would reduce deficits by $1.1 trillion over a decade, although other estimates are somewhat lower. The International Monetary Fund, similarly, has estimated that letting the tax cuts expire would yield about 2 percent of GDP—a quarter of a trillion dollars—for the federal government. Moreover, the cuts have been denounced for being highly regressive, benefiting the rich far more than the middle class.[76]

Raising taxes may have become an American heresy ever since Proposition 13 in 1978, Ronald Reagan, and variations on the "read my lips: no new taxes" pledges of many Republicans, but Republicans and Democrats alike—including Presidents Reagan and George H. W. Bush—have raised taxes. And the sky hasn't fallen. Consequently, proposals to let the Bush tax cuts expire, returning income tax rates at least to the levels of the prosperous Clinton years certainly should be entertained; such measures could raise hundreds of billions of dollars.[77]

When policy types talk about "broadening the tax base," they don't generally mean requiring your third-grader to file a 1040 for his allowance (or taxing more people) so much as getting rid of much of the $800 billion or so per year in tax deductions, exemptions, loopholes, exclusions, and credits that allow individuals and corporations to pay less. Some of these are tax subsidies to businesses—a form of corporate welfare, and a hidden form of tax "spending"—ranging from the farm subsidies for our mythic family farmers (read: giant agribusinesses) to the granddaddy of them all: the $225 billion a year exclusion for employer-based health care. This "exclusion" basically exempts corporations and individuals from paying taxes on the value of the health insurance that employers provide or subsidize. As Representative Jim Cooper has said, this is a "Niagara Falls of money every year" that not only distorts and encourages health care spending, but makes it cheaper for employers to "pay" workers with health insurance instead of wages or other benefits.[78] For individuals, tax breaks range from two enormously revenue-depleting deductions—for mortgage interest and for state and local income taxes—to a host of "credits" designed to further "good" policy goals, such as the child care tax credit and the poverty-reducing earned income tax credit (EITC).

While many of these tax breaks were courageously closed with the 1986 bipartisan tax reform, politicians—being who they are—love to dole out new tax breaks to their constituents and contributors like candy on Halloween night. As Maya MacGuineas has said: "Most tax expenditures are really spending programs designed to look like tax cuts."[79]

The employer health care exclusion is a prime candidate for elimination or curtailment, but much more controversial are the deductions that millions of individual Americans love—to the extent that they "love" anything about taxes. Some have proposed eliminating or capping the mortgage interest deduction at, say $250,000, so that it continues to benefit middle-class and lower-income home-owners but doesn't subsidize Park Avenue apartments and California mansions. Capping the mortgage interest deduction and other breaks for wealthy individual taxpayers could yield $75 billion in additional revenues. Others have proposed eliminating all itemized deductions aside from a capped mortgage-interest deduction, and ones for state and local taxes, charitable contributions, and medical expenses. As simple math suggests, getting rid of many of the corporate and individual tax breaks—which overwhelmingly benefit the wealthy, who don't exactly need them—could bring a few hundred billion dollars into federal coffers, substantially helping to reduce deficits and our national debt.[80]

While many lower-income Americans do not have to pay income taxes or receive tax credits such as the EITC to boost living standards, it does not help revenues that approximately one-third of adult Americans pay no income tax whatsoever—up from about one-fifth in the mid-twentieth century. Five-sixths of income taxes are collected from just one-sixth of the population. Requiring all Americans to pay taxes may not be a big revenue raiser, and it may be controversial, but there are good citizenship reasons that every American should pay some taxes. (Remember our friend Holmes.) Such a basic reform—even if coupled with tax simplification that did away with the income tax, or consolidated it with other taxes—not only would bring billions into the Treasury's needy paws but also would reduce the growing divide, and resentment, between the two-thirds who pay taxes and the one-third who do not.[81]

Few people instinctively leap at the idea of paying new taxes, but many, on both the left and right, believe that some kind(s) of new taxes will be in our future if we are to raise sufficient revenues even for a government that drastically cuts its spending. Where conservatives and liberals generally differ is on whether "new" taxes should be in addition to existing taxes or in place of them.

The most commonly talked-about "new" tax is a consumption tax. Like state and local sales taxes, and like the consumption or "value-added taxes" (VATs) in up to one hundred other countries, this would be a federal tax on what individuals and businesses buy. Although, without modifications, a consumption tax also could be regressive, disproportionately affecting lower- and middle-income Americans, the arguments are compelling for a consumption tax as either an add-on to or replacement for the income tax.

Some of the strongest arguments for a consumption tax are that it is much more efficient to collect and difficult to shirk than the income tax; that it would encourage savings, providing incentives for people to consume less and put more into their bank and retirement accounts; and that it would better reflect people's lifetime ability to pay, rather than their current income. The idea of

coupling a consumption tax with deductions for savings and for loan repay-
ments also adds to the appeal from the standpoint of boosting savings. Others
see a targeted consumption tax as appealing in that it could dedicate funds for
specific purposes—whether to help government fund the personal retirement
accounts or health savings accounts discussed, to replace the Social Security
payroll tax, or to invest in America's future.

Purely as a way to raise revenues to pay for government and balance our budgets, the potential of a consumption tax is enormous. Whereas the income tax
today raises barely a trillion dollars a year (and FICA raises about the same
amount), a 10 percent consumption tax could raise three-quarters of a trillion
dollars, with far fewer administrative and compliance costs than the income
tax. A national sales tax of 15 to 23 percent could pay for government and enable
us to eliminate both income and payroll taxes, although some say that the rate
would have to be double that to accommodate even restrained government
spending. The tax expert Michael Graetz has suggested that a consumption tax
could exempt American families earning below a certain inflation-indexed
amount, such as $100,000, from paying income tax, eliminating 90 percent of
tax returns, with the wealthy still paying an income tax on top of a consumption tax. To address the criticism that a sales tax falls disproportionately on the
poor—as rich and poor alike have to buy the same basket of basic goods—the
plan would either exempt certain goods, such as grocery store foods, education,
and basic health care, or provide a refundable low-income tax credit. Indeed,
even President Bush's 2006 Advisory Panel on Federal Tax Reform suggested
introducing a consumption tax to replace the income tax in part.[82]

Despite all that a consumption tax has to recommend it, and the growing interest in such a tax, it faces the enormous hurdle of political and popular resis-
tance. Manufacturers, stores, and service providers are likely to bristle at the
idea of a tax that undoubtedly would have the effect of reducing their sales.
Even if the American public—and employers—could be sold on the idea that
a consumption tax might replace the current 15.3 percent payroll tax, reducing
payroll costs for employers and instantly increasing Americans' wages by 7.65
percent, many would find a 15 or 20 percent federal sales tax, on top of state
sales taxes, extremely distasteful. Perhaps it could be combined with state sales
taxes or raised to a level to eliminate them, with the federal government dis-
bursing a set portion of revenues to the states. (Indeed, federalist arguments to
the contrary, any consolidation of federal and state tax collection could eliminate the inefficiencies of multiple tax-collecting bureaucracies.) While Europeans and others have adjusted to consumption taxes, which have had the de-

sired effects of enhancing savings and raising revenues more efficiently than income taxes, many Americans simply might see a national sales tax as somehow
"foreign" and contrary to American traditions (despite the mishmash of "traditions" in our history of taxation).

Beyond a consumption tax, other potential new taxes have been batted
around by economists, politicians, and assorted advocates and experts. Many
free-market economists favor the idea of increasing "user fees" such as tolls on
highways, fees to pay for air-traffic control and our air transportation system,
and higher admission fees for national parks and charges for use of national
lands. Environmentalists, among others, favor the introduction of a carbon tax
or higher energy taxes that would have the purportedly win-win effects of reducing greenhouse gases and other pollution, fuel consumption, and depen-
dence on foreign oil, while raising new revenues. A tax on the carbon content of
fuels that could achieve the emissions reductions specified not only under the
Kyoto Protocols but by a number of U.S. state governments could raise as
much as $90 billion a year in revenues. Similarly, although Americans have
balked at gasoline tax increases far short of existing fuel pump taxes in many
other countries, even a twenty-five-cent increase in the federal gas tax could
raise at least $30 billion a year. Observers have pointed out that the portion of
fuel prices that we pay at the pump going to taxes has fallen in recent years from
about 18 percent to 6 percent, suggesting that we certainly could afford more.[83]

"Sin" taxes, despite their relatively limited potential to raise revenues—unless we broaden our definition of "sin"—are perennially popular. Most Americans have few problems with taxes on tobacco and alcohol, both as a form of social policy to reduce consumption and to raise revenues. But what if we used
the same standard of trying to use the tax system to get Americans to behave
"better" in other ways, raising billions along the way? At a time of endemic obesity—which, as noted, also adds tens of billions of dollars to our national
health care costs—some have suggested additional taxes on junk foods and soft
drinks. Reinstating the luxury tax, which was repealed in 1993, also could be
seen as a form of revenue-raising, behavior-reforming sin tax. While some lo-
calities have imposed surcharges on expensive McMansions, the old luxury tax
applied to expensive cars, private airplanes, boats, fur coats, and expensive jew-
elry, although it backfired by hurting American industries and workers.[84] Once
again, the problems are political. However much we may hate "sin," individuals seem to hate taxes and businesses seem to hate lost sales even more. The idea
of adding even a tiny federal tax to McDonald's meals, Coca-Colas, Jaguars, big
houses, or engagement rings would raise loud protest from—you guessed it—

McDonald's (and other fast-food corporations), the Coca-Cola Company (and other soft-drink manufacturers), BMW (and other luxury car makers), the high-end real estate industry, and jewelers. Nonetheless, polls reliably find the public in favor of sin taxes, which they think can go much farther than they actually can in reducing deficits and debt.[85]

A further tax option is either to preserve the estate tax, which affects only a few thousand American each year but yields $1 trillion in revenues over a decade, or replace it with an inheritance tax, under which inheritances would be taxed as income. Despite Dan Quayle's line that the estate tax is "taxation without respiration" and ideologues' characterizations of it as a ghoulish "death tax," most Americans favor it for estates worth more than several million dollars.[86]

In addition, as the discussion of entitlement reform suggests, taxing the Social Security and Medicare benefits of higher-income Americans makes sense from the perspectives of both fairness and revenue. Others have proposed taxing the overseas earnings of U.S. multinationals and going after the estimated $100 billion a year lost because of overseas tax havens—assuming that a corporate tax remains on the books.[87] Remember, the idea is to cut federal spending and raise sufficient revenues to balance our books, and this strategy helps a little bit with both.

The fourth major way to increase federal revenues is "simply" to do a much better job of collecting the taxes that people owe the government. It has been estimated that a staggering $345 billion owed to the IRS was not collected in 2001, although about $50 billion was later recovered. This means that Americans illegally avoid paying an enormous portion of the money that they owe to Uncle Sam. While some of this may be due to mistakes stemming from our overly complex system, much results from what in common parlance bluntly would be called "cheating." Cheating on taxes is hardly the sole province of any socioeconomic group, although we all have heard tales of multimillionaire executives paying no taxes. Even more ethically scary, in our land of supposed fair play and patriotism, polls have found that high percentages of Americans think that it's perfectly okay to cheat on taxes.[88]

Taxpayer "noncompliance" is hardly unique to the United States, and it is widely conceded to be impossible to collect all taxes that are owed. Nonetheless, the IRS and many independent experts believe that if enforcement were beefed up, at a relatively modest cost of a few billion dollars, the IRS could collect $100 billion more than it does. The sad fact is that in some of our misbegotten efforts to trim government spending, the United States cut IRS staffing from twenty-two thousand to fourteen thousand between 1996 and 2005, with the number of audits falling off sharply.[89] Penny wise, pound foolish.

Although each of these four broad approaches to increasing revenues could go a long way toward alleviating our long-run deficit and debt problems, even those not concerned about the national debt agree that America's overall tax system is a broken agglomeration of confusing, contradictory, infuriating, unfair measures crying out for comprehensive reform. While our ultimate goal is to raise sufficient and reasonable revenues to support reasonable public spending, reforming our tax system is likely to involve a mixture of reducing some revenue sources and increasing others.

So, given the monster known as the U.S. Tax Code, how do we either slay it or, preferably, turn it into a nice little kitty cat that uses its litter box, doesn't scratch the furniture or otherwise annoy us, and actually becomes a valued companion in our national household?

With Americans spending an estimated 3.4 billion hours, or about 25 hours per filer, doing their taxes, using many of the nine hundred or so forms that the IRS uses, the one goal that everyone agrees upon is that taxes need to be simplified.[90] Although replacing the income tax, payroll tax, and corporate tax with a consumption tax for all but the highest earners—as suggested above—may accomplish the twin goals of simplification and reducing the time and money that Americans spend on filing taxes, a pure, sufficiently high consumption tax is unlikely to happen.

Conservatives are particularly keen on eliminating the "double taxation" of the corporate income tax, suggesting that it be rolled into the income tax. The corporate tax has declined significantly over the past fifty years, but calls to reduce or eliminate it are widely heard—not surprisingly, from the business community, which argues that such a move would make U.S. companies more competitive with companies in countries with lower corporate taxes. Many also have argued for a "flat tax." The Cato Institute and Hoover Institution, for example, have advocated the so-called Hall-Rabushka tax, which calls for a single tax rate of 19 percent for all workers. Daniel Mitchell, another flat-tax booster, suggests that such a tax would require just two postcard-sized forms—one for labor income and one for capital income. And Grover Norquist, a star in the conservative antitax firmament, has called for return-free filing, putting the onus of calculating and collecting taxes on the government. The tax expert David Bradford's X-tax would be a semiflat tax: it still would tax higher wages at a higher rate, but would eliminate taxation on capital income and interest. Others suggest that a flat tax could be made more progressive and fair to lower-income Americans by expanding the EITC. However, just to replace existing revenues, William Gale of the Brookings Institution and other tax experts have estimated that a flat tax would have to set be set at between 21 and 30 percent.[91]

Many have argued that however taxes are structured, most taxpayers should be able to file without having to endure the agony of the strange numerical and alphabetical zoo full of tax forms. Leonard Burman, another tax expert at the Urban Institute, would create a Simplified Income Tax in which there would be a single family credit, a refundable work credit, a 15 percent mortgage credit, no state or local tax deduction, and a built-in 401(k) into which taxpayers would have to actively choose *not* to contribute. Simplified, or return-free, filing is also thought to reduce Americans' anger about taxes and government, and to increase taxpayer morale and compliance.[92]

Whether or not tax simplification would be "revenue neutral," or would increase or reduce revenues, it is clear that some major league simplification of how America collects taxes is necessary. But we cannot lose sight of the fact that simplification must go hand in hand with increasing overall revenues, and making the tax system more fair.

A different sort of debt-reduction measure, on the revenue side, would be to modify how the U.S. Treasury borrows money. Just as during the brief Clinton era of surpluses—when the Treasury suspended some of its auctions of federal securities—we could delay auctions or curtail the reinvestment of government securities in Social Security and other trust funds that currently just help to mask the true size of our deficits.[93] Others have proposed issuing special long-term Treasury securities to fund capital investments in America. Together with the already mentioned elimination of stealth increases in our debt limit, limiting the issuance of new debt just might restrain our proclivity for borrowing and force us to figure out ways to pay for spending with the money that we have.

This, unfortunately, brings us to the fact that two pieces of widely agreed-upon tax reforms would reduce federal revenues and need to be offset by some combination of higher taxes, base-broadening, new taxes, and greater tax compliance. Reforming the alternative minimum tax (AMT) is the most notable change that must be implemented soon—if we are to avoid an army of taxpayers with pitchforks, to paraphrase Pat Buchanan. The AMT, which initially was designed to capture revenues from high-income taxpayers, has increased its reach from a few million taxpayers to an estimated thirty-three million by 2010 and forty-two million by 2015 due to bracket creep. Reforms should increase the threshold below which taxpayers would be exempt from the AMT and reduce its rate yet retain its intent to close tax shelters. Nonetheless, such reforms—in the name of equity—would reduce government revenues by between $600 billion and $1.2 trillion.[94] You don't need a crystal ball to see AMT reform in our future, but it's not going to help us out of our morass of debt.

The other, albeit smaller, tax reform that liberals and conservatives generally support in the name of equity is expanding the EITC. The EITC, which was introduced by President Ford and vastly expanded by President Clinton, was designed—fairly well, given that it came out of Washington—as a way to both encourage work and provide greater resources to low-income Americans. Liberals like it because it works to reduce poverty and improve the well-being of the working poor, and conservatives like it because it encourages work, isn't a welfare "hand-out," and is a way of making their cherished flat tax more progressive. While its cost to federal revenues is relatively small, it has grown from a $1.25 billion program in the 1970s to $36 billion at the end of the Clinton administration. Moreover, many are champing at the bit to significantly increase this program to cover families earning more than $35,000 a year and to provide increased benefits beyond the 2005 average of only $1,872 for all recipients, even though the price tag could be $30 billion or more.[95]

Even if we somehow are able to "prune" federal spending and radically reform entitlement programs, most liberals and many conservatives recognize that federal spending as a share of GDP will have to grow—if for no other reasons than that reducing deficits and debt will require political compromises on the issues of spending cuts, tax increases, and the inevitable needs of our aging population. Whether government claims 21–22 percent of our national income, as some conservatives suggest, or takes a 24–25 percent bite out of our wallets, as some liberals advocate, a larger government is all but certain to be in our future.[96]

When thinking about this daunting array of potential reforms to help bring America's fiscal house into order, it's important to go back to the "menu" metaphor. We cannot, practically or politically, accomplish all of the above-mentioned policy changes. Like items on a menu, they need to be selected both for what is most appealing (read: fiscally effective and politically possible) and most complementary; just as one cannot order a satisfying, balanced meal consisting of chocolate cake, pecan pie, and a dollop of ice cream, we cannot just order tax cuts or spending increases. But if we are to survive, we must order something. We can't order just one thing. We need to think very carefully about what we order. And we must start ordering very soon.

Chapter 8 Concluding Thoughts: A Nation That Balances Its Books and a Government That Invests in America's Future

As the United States faces enormous deficits, discretionary spending has taken hits year after year. Congressional budgeters and appropriators have not sufficiently recognized that education and health care are capital investments.
Senator Arlen Specter

We cannot afford a plan that does nothing to stimulate economic growth, benefits only a small minority of Americans, and promises a return to the deep deficits of the past.
Senator Maria Cantwell

This or any other discussion of debt is filled with myriad economic issues, potential consequences, and paths out of the woods, but there is also a host of ethical and philosophical concerns. These go beyond the sheer propriety of borrowing trillions and passing the buck to our grandchildren for our present-day consumption. They also get to the question of what kind of nation we want to be, and what role government should have in shaping America in the twenty-first century. Spending and revenues constitute a good way of measuring, or at least inferring, what our priorities as a people and a culture are.

Clearly, almost no one thinks that we should spend one-tenth or much more of our public monies on interest payments, increasingly going to foreigners. Similarly, few think that we should be spending the majority of our huge national budget on three entitlement programs designed in the past century, which are inefficient and on course to consume more and more of our national wealth. Others would argue with the size of tax breaks and corporate welfare, some defense programs, and a number of domestic programs. Yet for all the endless lip service paid to ensuring a good future for our children and developing the skilled, productive workforce of tomorrow, our saddling them with debt rather than investing in their America speaks volumes.

But small-government advocates from Thomas Jefferson to today's conservatives agree that we do need a government, and that there are *public* services that only government can provide. Moreover, from Alexander Hamilton and Abraham Lincoln to the Progressives, Dwight Eisenhower, and John F. Kennedy, Americans and their leaders have believed that government could, and should, be a positive force not only in ensuring our defense, safety, and rights but also in promoting our national and individual economic and social well-being. We don't need the history lessons to know the huge value of Hamilton's or Eisenhower's investments in our transportation infrastructure. Nor do we need lessons in Abraham Lincoln's and others' policies to promote education or Teddy or Franklin Roosevelt's investments in our environment or people's economic security. In short, despite a generation of largely justifiable antigovernment cynicism, government has contributed enormously, and in an enormous number of ways, to making life better for hundreds of millions of Americans.

Although providing insurance against the risks of ill health and old age is a reasonable, and humane, function of a society and government, it is a gross skewing of our national priorities to spend half or most of our public resources on Medicare and Social Security. The flip from 50–60 percent discretionary spending in the 1960s to 50–60 percent mandatory spending today is ominous for many reasons. Aside from increasing our debt and constraining our choices of how to spend taxpayer money, this shift to a high and rising level of mandatory spending takes money away from the kinds of useful investments in our nation and its future that we once made. For instance, it has been estimated that the combined cost of providing universal preschool for all American children, better prenatal care, better-targeted educational programs for poor children, and programs to reduce teen pregnancy would be less than 1 percent of current federal spending.[1]

Wouldn't we all be better off if we could "just" pare off half of that trillion-plus dollars that we spend on entitlements and devote it instead to rebuilding our transportation system and cities, research and seed money for new technologies and industries that would create high-paying jobs, better and more-equal access to all levels of education, developing the energy sources and policies to leave our children with a healthier environment, helping Americans to save, maintaining a "rainy day" fund to deal with natural disasters or public health emergencies, and, generally, fostering the economic conditions that can keep the American Dream alive during the twenty-first century?

In some ways, it's a silly question. Almost everyone supports these goals. But these and other "good" policy goals require money. If we are pouring our national treasure into wrong-headed, debt-financed, current consumption, we cannot fund these goals, and we will not have such a future. So reducing our national debt is also about shifting our national priorities and realigning what our government spends its money on. This also may entail shifting some spending and taxing responsibilities from the federal government to the states, and vice versa. Just as the potential policies to reduce our deficits and debt may be about as easy to realize as turning a battleship on a dime, rethinking our government, its goals, and its spending will be a formidable challenge.

But it is essential. And it is as much of a reason to reduce our debt and fiscal imbalances as the threats that they pose to our economy, our national strength, and our citizens' living standards. The United States always has been a future-oriented country. Debt and financing current consumption make us neglect our future. So in this sense, bringing our national finances back into whack is also about bringing America back to what has made it a great, forward-looking country with its historic faith in progress.

Many talk about creating a "new social contract," presumably to replace the dying, unsustainable public-private social contract that lasted from FDR until recent years. This is a multipronged task, but one that has much to do with debt reduction and reconfiguring our public finances. As we have seen, our public and private pension and health care systems are breaking and need—for the strength of our economy, the survival of our government, and the security of our people—to be radically revamped into a system of risk insurance that changes the roles of government and employers, while requiring individuals to take greater financial responsibility for their lives. A rich, civilized democracy like ours needs to care for all its people, which means providing a safety net when bad things happen to good people. Catastrophic medical conditions, very old age, loss of a job and income, and natural or other disasters fall into this category. But these can be covered by an insurance model in which we actuarially pool risks and provide for fellow Americans when such unfortunate events occur.

But there is the other side of the equation, too. Individuals should take greater responsibility and save money. However, at least three basic conditions need to be met. One, they need to know that a basic safety net will protect all of them in times of true emergencies—and this does not mean pensions for healthy, middle-aged Americans or health care coverage that pays most costs for almost any care that they want.

Two, we once again need to foster a vibrant middle class, a society in which a "rising tide lifts all boats" rather than providing opulence for a large but elite fleet of yachts while leaving most Americans barely afloat on dinghies, or clutching to driftwood in a sea of economic uncertainty. When incomes were rising for virtually all Americans, as they were from the 1940s to the early 1970s, the economy boomed, Americans felt secure and optimistic, businesses profited handsomely, and government was able to spend its money on future-oriented investments. Economic growth averaged an unprecedented 4 percent a year from World War II to the Johnson administration, corporate profits were high, living standards rose more rapidly than at any time in U.S. history, and poverty rates fell faster and farther than ever before or since.[2] When individual real incomes are stagnant or falling for many Americans and government is straitjacketed by debt, as is true today, economic growth is uneven, only cutting-edge, globally oriented businesses succeed, and our people are uneasy and worried about their families' futures. Thus any new social contract needs to make broadly shared economic growth and security a guiding principle for public policy.

Finally, if the second of these items should appeal at least to liberals, the third particularly should appeal to conservatives. America needs to move away from the *culture* of entitlement fostered not just by the Great Society or the "me decade," but also by a business, political, and popular culture that has led us to believe we can have almost anything we want without much effort or cost. Whether it's consuming health care without really paying for it or running up credit card debt for the baubles of our consumer culture, Americans must be weaned from the narcissistic mentality that they can get everything they desire, at least not without earning and saving for it. Individuals do need to take responsibility—for savings, retirement, and their finances more generally, and also need to return to an ethic of educational (and not just psychological) self-improvement and hard work that were once cornerstones of the American credo.

If we can reform our fiscal failings; reinvest economically, politically, and psychologically in our nation's future; and build a new social contract that embraces these principles, America's future is bright. If we do not, Ronald Reagan's famous phrase about "morning in America" may undergo a time-zone shift of historical proportions: if it's night time in America, isn't it morning in China? As the social scientist John Gardner once said, "What we have before us are breathtaking opportunities disguised as insoluble problems."[3]

Notes

1. WHAT ARE DEFICITS AND DEBT, AND WHY ARE THEY GROWING?

Epigraphs. T. David Zukerman, "Are We Redeeming Our National Debt Too Hastily?" *Political Science Quarterly* 40, no. 2 (1925); Joseph White and Aaron Wildavsky, *The Deficit and the Public Interest: The Search for Responsible Budgeting in the 1980s* (Berkeley: University of California Press, 1989), 331.

1. http://thinkexist.com/quotes/publilius_syrus/.

2. White and Wildavsky, *The Deficit and the Public Interest*, xv–xvi, 69; John Steele Gordon, *Hamilton's Blessing: The Extraordinary Life and Times of Our National Debt* (New York: Walker, 1997), 131–33; interview with Robert Samuelson, Sept. 27, 2006.

3. Interview with David Walker, Dec. 13, 2006; interview with Rep. Jim Cooper, Jan. 5, 2007; Alison Acosta Fraser, "Federal Budget Should Include Long-Term Obligations from Entitlement Programs," Heritage Foundation, Executive Memorandum no. 1004, June 22, 2006. The $50 trillion number is based on the accrual accounting methodology employed by U.S. businesses, but not by government, which uses cash accounting. If one used accrual accounting, which would count liabilities at the time that benefits are earned— as the Federal Accounting Standards Advisory Board (FASAB) has urged and the Government Accountability Office (GAO) has suggested might be useful for federal insurance programs such as Social Security—the official 2005 cash deficit of $319 billion would have been $760 billion. Although there are prob-

lems with both accrual and cash accounting, businesses, as well as state and local governments, are required to report their long-term unfunded liabilities. The $319 billion also excludes the $174 billion in borrowed Social Security Trust Fund surpluses. See FASAB, "Accounting for Social Insurance," Oct. 23, 2006; GAO, "Understanding Similarities and Differences Between Accrual and Cash Deficits," December 2006; and Susan Irving, "Budgeting for Federal Insurance Programs," GAO, Apr. 23, 1998.

4. U.S. Census Bureau, "State and Local Government Finances by Level of Government and by State: 2003–04," http://www.census.gov/govs/estimate/0400ussl_1.html; David Walker, "Fiscally, U.S. Wrenching: D.C. Overdue to Join Clamor Over Soaring Federal Debt," *Atlanta Journal-Constitution,* Feb. 15, 2006; "Rules 'Hiding' Trillions in Debt," *USA Today,* May 29, 2007; Christian Weller, "Consumer Fatigue Weakens Job Growth," Center for American Progress, Oct. 6, 2006; Center for American Progress, "Economic Snapshot for September 2006," http://www.americanprogress.org/issues/2006/09/econ_snapshot.html; "Retiree Benefits Grow into Monster'" *USA Today,* May 24, 2006; FASAB, "Accounting for Social Insurance," Oct. 23, 2006; "Public-Sector Pensions," *Economist,* Nov. 18, 2006; Concord Coalition, "A Fiscal Wake-Up Call" (2007), http://www.concordcoalition.org/events/fiscal-wake-up/fiscal-wake-up-call.htm; "Forestalling Foreclosures," *Washington Post,* Aug. 31, 2007; Jacob Hacker, *The Great Risk Shift: The Assault on American Jobs, Families, Health Care, and Retirement and How You Can Fight Back* (Oxford: Oxford University Press, 2006), 13, and "The Turning Point," *Economist,* Sept. 20, 2007. According to the Cato Institute and the *Economist,* state and local unfunded pension and health care liabilities totaled about $1.7 trillion in 2006. Average household credit card debt rose from about $2,700 in 1989 to $8,650 in 2004; Federal Reserve, *Consumer Credit Outstanding* (Washington, D.C., 2005).

5. See The View From Washington, pp. xi–xii.

6. Council of Economic Advisers, *Economic Report of the President 2005* (Washington, D.C.: Government Printing Office, 2005). By comparison, national debt as a percentage of GDP in the United States is about double what it is in Britain, about the same as in France and Germany, and considerably lower than in Italy and Japan, where it is about 100 percent and 170 percent, respectively; "Fit at 50," *Economist,* Mar. 17, 2007. National Income Product Accounting defines GDP both as total output and total income, which are equal. A strict macroeconomic definition would focus on production, including consumption, investment, net exports, and government spending.

7. David Broder, "Congress' Sorry Session," *Washington Post,* Oct. 8, 2006.

8. Urban Institute, *Annual Report,* 2005 (Washington, D.C.: Urban Institute, 2005); Sebastian Mallaby, "A Bad, Bipartisan Tax Plan," *Washington Post,* Jan. 8, 2007; Center on Budget and Policy Priorities, "Extending the President's Tax Cuts and AMT Relief Would Cost $3.5 Trillion Through 2017," Jan. 31, 2007; Center on Budget and Policy Priorities, "Background on the Federal Budget and the Return of Budget Deficits," 2006.

9. Diane Lim Rogers, "Good Reasons for Taxes," *Boston Globe,* Apr. 16, 2006; "IMF Says Rise in U.S. Debts Is Threat to World's Economy," *New York Times,* Jan. 8, 2004; Peterson quoted in Gerald J. Swanson, *America the Broke: How the Reckless Spending of the White House and Congress Are Bankrupting Our Country and Destroying Our Children's Future* (New York: Currency Doubleday, 2004), 54–55.

10. Concord Coalition, "Social Security Reform," Mar. 4, 2005; "Don't Know Much About History," *New York Times,* July 1, 2006; U.S. Comptroller General David Walker, quoted in "As Social Security Surges and Medicare Takes Off, the Deficit Will Soar," *USA Today,* Nov. 15, 2005; Peter Peterson, *Running on Empty: How the Democratic and Republican Parties Are Bankrupting Our Future and What Americans Can Do About It* (New York: Farrar, Straus and Giroux, 2004), 34; Alice M. Rivlin and Isabel Sawhill, eds., *Restoring Fiscal Sanity: How to Balance the Budget* (Washington, D.C.: Brookings Institution Press, 2004), 26; "Bush Plan Reins in Domestic Spending," *Washington Post,* Feb. 6, 2007; interview with Maya MacGuineas, Oct. 27, 2006.

11. Economic Policy Institute, "U.S. Current Account Deficit Breaks Record at 7 Percent of GDP," Mar. 14, 2006, http://www.epi.org/content.cfm/webfeat_econindicators_capict_20060314; Jonathan Shaw, "Debtor Nation," *Harvard Magazine,* July–August 2007; "Oil Prices, China Disparity Push Trade Gap to Record," *Washington Post,* Feb. 14, 2007. Although private borrowing is responsible for much of the current-account deficit, balancing the federal budget might reduce the current-account deficit from its present 6.5 percent of GDP to 5.5 percent, some economists believe.

12. David Walker, "The Four Deficits Confronting the United States," *Kansas City Star,* Apr. 16, 2006; and Government Accountability Office, "National Savings," June 2001.

13. Cited in Diane Lim Rogers and Andrew L. Yarrow, "Rising Debt Is Very Scary," *Baltimore Sun,* Apr. 2, 2006; George W. Bush, signing the Deficit Reduction Act of 2005, in February 2006.

14. Some of the more noted proponents of this viewpoint are Harvard's Robert Barro; Michael Boskin, chairman of President George H. W. Bush's Council of Economic Advisers; and Northwestern University's Robert Eisner; see Laurence J. Kotlikoff, "Federal Deficit," *The Concise Encyclopedia of Economics,* http://www.econlib.org/library/Enc/FederalDeficit.html.

15. Walker is quoted in "Official Likens Budget Deficit to Hurricane," *Richmond Times Dispatch,* Sept. 27, 2005.

16. Martin Feldstein, "Here Are the Facts," *Wall Street Journal,* Feb. 12, 2004.

17. Volcker and Rubin are quoted in Peterson, *Running on Empty,* xiii; Alan Greenspan, *The Age of Turbulence: Adventures in a New World,* cited in "Greenspan Is Critical of Bush in Memoir," *Washington Post,* Sept. 15, 2007; Feldstein, "Here Are the Facts." Reischauer is quoted in "Budget Wish Lists Come and Go, But Entitlements Outweigh All," *Wall Street Journal,* Feb. 3, 2006; Bergsten is quoted in "IMF Says Rise in U.S. Debts Is Threat to World's Economy," *New York Times,* Jan. 8, 2004.

18. Quoted in Peterson, *Running on Empty,* xxiv.

19. Benjamin Friedman, *Day of Reckoning* (New York: Random House, 1988), 13.

20. Brian M. Riedl, "Runaway Spending: Left Unchecked, Washington's Overspending Could Drown America in Taxes and Debt," Heritage Foundation, 2006.

21. Quoted in Robert Eisner, *How Real Is the Federal Deficit?* (New York: Free Press, 1986), [v].

22. "Bush Plan Reins In Domestic Spending," *Washington Post,* Feb. 6, 2007; U.S. Census Bureau, "State and Local Government Finances by Level of Government and by State: 2003–04," http://www.census.gov/govs/estimate/0400ussl_1.html.

23. Diane Rogers, "Why Worry About the Deficit," Brookings Institution, 2006, unpublished; Riedl, "Runaway Spending"; interview with Maya MacGuineas, Jan. 8, 2007; "Greenspan Is Critical."

24. *Business Week* editors cited in Robert Rubin, "Attention Deficit Disorder," *New York Times,* May 13, 2005.

25. Marc Friedman, *Encore: Finding Work That Matters in the Second Half of Life* (New York: Public Affairs, 2007), 37. In 1950, almost half of men were still working at age sixty-five; in 2000, fewer than one in five was.

26. Leonard Schaeffer, "Putting the Lid on Health Care Costs," presentation, Brookings Institution, Washington, D.C., Oct. 20, 2005; Concord Coalition, "Social Security Reform"; Walker interview; Peterson, *Running on Empty,* 37; United States Department of Health and Human Services, Centers for Medicare and Medicaid Services (CMS), *2006 Medicare Trustees Report* (Washington, D.C., 2006); "As Social Security Surges"; "Social Security, Medicare Panel Adjusts Forecast," *Washington Post,* Apr. 24, 2007; Alice M. Rivlin and Joseph Antos, eds., *Restoring Fiscal Sanity: The Health Spending Challenge* (Washington, D.C.: Brookings Institution Press, 2007), 21.

27. "Social Security, Medicare Panel Adjusts Forecast," *Washington Post,* Apr. 24, 2007; CMS, *2006 Medicare Trustees Report;* Rivlin and Antos, *Restoring Fiscal Sanity;* Stuart M. Butler, "Solutions to Our Long-Term Fiscal Challenges," testimony before the Senate Budget Committee, Jan. 31, 2007; Stuart M. Butler, "The Budget and Entitlements: Time to Take Action," Web Memo 1303, Jan. 9, 2007, www.heritage.org/Research/Budget/wm1303/cfn; Alison Acosta Fraser, "U.S. Spending Grows at Historic Rate," *Philadelphia Inquirer,* Apr. 30, 2006; Congressional Budget Office, "The Budget and Economic Outlook: Fiscal Years 2007–2016," January 2006; Joe Antos, "Medicare and the Prescription Drug Benefit," testimony to the Committee on Homeland Security and Government Affairs, Sept. 22, 2005, http://hsgac.senate.gov/_files/092205Antos.pdf; and Concord Coalition, "Social Security Reform."

28. United States Government Accountability Office, *21st Century Challenges: Reexamining the Bases of the Federal Government* (Washington, D.C.: GAO, 2006), 6, 8; Heritage Foundation, "Federal Revenue and Spending," 2006; Concord Coalition, "A Fiscal Wake-Up Call," 2007 http://www.concordcoalition.org/events/fiscal-wake-up/fiscal-wake-up-call.htm; Fraser, "U.S. Spending Grows."

29. "Congressional Agency Predicts War Costs Will Climb," *Washington Post,* July 11, 2007.

30. Congressional Research Service, "Earmarks in Appropriations Acts: FY 1994, FY 1996, FY 1998, FY 2000, FY 2002, FY 2004, FY 2005," Jan. 26, 2006, http://www.fas.org/sgp/crs/misc/m012606.pdf; "Bush to Request Billions for Wars," *Washington Post,* Feb. 3, 2007; George Will, "A Loss's Silver Lining," *Washington Post,* Nov. 9, 2006.

31. Maya MacGuineas, "New America's Tax Reform Plan," New America Foundation, Dec. 5, 2005.

32. Charles Kolb, "Statement on Earmarks," Committee for Economic Development, Dec. 19, 2006; White and Wildavsky, *The Deficit and the Public Interest,* 1–14; Congressional Research Service, "The Spending Pipeline," June 13, 2003; Paul Seam and Brad Schron, "Government Shutdowns," Harvard Law School, Federal Budget Policy Seminar, Briefing Paper 10, 2005; Cooper interview; Brian Riedl, "Still Spending," Heritage Founda-

tion, Sept. 26, 2006, http://www.heritage.org/Research/Budget/wm1222.cfm; "Demo-crats Plan to Restore Budget Discipline," *Washington Post,* Mar. 22, 2007.

33. Dennis S. Ippolito, *Why Budgets Matter: Budget Policy and American Politics* (University Park: Pennsylvania University Press, 2003), 238; Concord Coalition, "Facing Facts Quarterly," December 2006.

34. William Gale and Peter Orszag, "The Outlook for Fiscal Policy," *Tax Notes,* Feb. 14, 2005.

35. "DeLay Declares 'Victory' in War on Budget Fat," *Washington Times,* Sept. 14, 2005.

36. David M. Walker, "Saving Our Future Requires Tough Choices Today," presentation, Denver, Nov. 28, 2006.

37. Quoted in C. Eugene Steuerle, *Contemporary U.S. Tax Policy* (Washington, D.C.: Urban Institute Press, 2004), 1.

38. International Monetary Fund, "U.S. Fiscal Policies and Priorities for Long-Run Sustainability," Jan. 7, 2004; Urban Institute, *Annual Report,* 2005; E. Laumann, J. H. Gagnon, R. T. Michael, and S. Michaels, *The Social Organization of Sexuality: Sexual Practices in the United States* (Chicago: University of Chicago Press, 1994).

39. IMF, "U.S. Fiscal Policies and Priorities"; Peterson, *Running on Empty,* 144; Max Sawicky, "Do-it-Yourself Tax Cuts: The Crisis in US Tax Enforcement," Economic Policy Institute, Apr. 12, 2005; Citizens for Tax Justice study cited in "As Audits Decline, Fewer Taxpayers Balk at a Bit of Cheating," *New York Times,* Jan. 19, 2002; Chris Edwards, "Ten Outrageous Facts About the Income Tax," Cato Institute, Apr. 15, 2003; U.S. Bureau of Labor Statistics, *Occupational Outlook Handbook,* http://www.bls.gov/oco/home.htm; GAO, *21st Century Challenges,* 71. According to Sawicky, IRS resources have fallen since 1992, with a net loss of twenty thousand full-time employees, with the audit rate falling from 2.15 percent in 1978 to 0.58 percent in 2001.

40. Mankiw is quoted in Eric Leeper and Shu-Chun Susan Yang, "Dynamic Scoring," NBER Working Paper 12103, National Bureau of Economic Research, March 2006; Stein is quoted in George Hager and Eric Pianin, *Mirage: Why Neither Democrats Nor Republicans Can Balance the Budget, End the Deficit, and Satisfy the Public* (New York: Times Books, 1997), 93; William A. Niskanen, "'Starve the Beast' Just Does Not Work," Cato Institute, http://www.cato-at-liberty.org/2006/05/11/starve-the-beast-just-does-not-work/; Niskanen is quoted in Jonathan Rauch, "Stoking the Beast," *Atlantic,* February 2006.

41. U.S. Treasury Financial Management Service, *2005 Financial Report of the U.S. Government* (Washington, D.C.: Government Printing Office, 2006); "By the Numbers," *Washington Post,* Nov. 12, 2006; Diane Lim Rogers, "Reducing the Deficit Through Better Tax Policy," Brookings Institution, 2007; "Oregon Senator Wants to Take on the Burden of Fixing the Tax Code," *Washington Post,* July 24, 2006.

42. Sen. Kent Conrad (D-N.D.), Senate floor statement, May 11, 2006; Edmund L. Andrews, "Tax Cuts Offer Most for Very Rich, Study Finds," *New York Times,* Jan. 8, 2007.

43. Citizens for Tax Justice, "Bush Tax Policies Drive Surge in Corporate Freeloading," Sept. 22, 2004, http://www.ctj.org/corpfed04pr.pdf.

44. Gale and Orszag, "The Outlook for Fiscal Policy"; Peter A. Diamond and Peter R. Orszag, *Saving Social Security: A Balanced Approach* (Washington, D.C.: Brookings In-

stitution Press, 2004), 204; Joseph J. Minarik, *Making America's Budget Policy: From the 1980s to the 1990s* (Cambridge, Mass.: National Bureau of Economic Research, 1995), 22.

45. Social Security and Medicare Board of Trustees, *Status of the Social Security and Medicare Programs: A Summary of the 2006 Annual Reports* (Washington, 2006), 15.

46. "Health Care Already a Key Issue in 2008 Race," *Washington Post,* Mar. 7, 2007; Butler, "Solutions."

47. Henry Aaron, "Health Care Rationing: What It Means," Brookings Institution, December 2005, http://www.brookings.edu/comm/policybriefs/pb147.htm; Centers for Medicare and Medicaid Services, "The Nation's Health Dollar," 2006; U.S. Office of Management and Budget, "Mid-Session Review: Budget of the U.S. Government, Fiscal Year 2008," Government Printing Office, July 11, 2007; Rivlin and Antos, *Restoring Fiscal Sanity,* 22, 40–41, 106; Market Research.com, "Pet Care Services in the U.S.," 2d ed., 2006, http://www.packagedfacts.com/Trends-Pet-Care-935962/. As for the pet health care spending comparison, federal spending fifty years ago is in current, not inflation-adjusted constant dollars.

48. Cited in Leif Wellington Haase, *A New Deal for Health: How to Cover Everyone and Get Medical Costs Under Control* (New York: Century Foundation, 2005), 46; Centers for Disease Control, "NCHS Data on Health Care and Access to Care," 2007, http://www.cdc.gov/nchs/data/factsheets/healthinsurance.pdf; "U.S. Poverty Rate Drops; Ranks of Uninsured Grow," *Washington Post,* Aug. 29, 2007; Malcolm Gladwell, "The Moral-Hazard Myth," *New Yorker,* Aug. 29, 2005; Citizens Health Care Working Group, "Interim Recommendations: Health Care That Works for All Americans," June 1, 2006. This working group, established by the Medicare Modernization Act of 2003, which created the prescription drug plan, also found that ninety-eight thousand Americans die each year from medical errors, and that one in three families has experienced a medical error.

49. "Who Killed U.S. Medicine," *Washington Post,* July 25, 2007. Regina E. Herzlinger reports that doctors' inflation-adjusted incomes fell by 7 percent between 1995 and 2003.

50. Centers for Medicare and Medicaid Services, "The Nation's Health Dollar"; Gladwell, "The Moral-Hazard Myth."

51. "As Social Security Surges"; Leonard Schaeffer, "Putting the Lid on Health Care Costs," presentation, Brookings Institution, Washington, D.C., Oct. 20, 2005; interview with C. Eugene Steuerle, Sept. 15, 2006; Economic Policy Institute, "The Chronic Problem of Declining Health Coverage," Sept. 16, 2004; Concord Coalition, "Social Security Reform; Gladwell, "The Moral-Hazard Myth."

52. Congressional Budget Office, "Long-Term Budget Outlook," December 2005; Congressional Budget Office, "Budget Update," August 2006; James Capretta, "Articulating a Policy Framework for Long-Term Federal Entitlement Reform," Brookings Institution Working Paper, October 2005; GAO, *21st Century Challenges,* 33; and CMS, *2006 Medicare Trustees Report.* Mankiw has estimated that about one-sixth of the revenues lost from income tax cuts and about half of the revenues of capital tax cuts are recouped through higher growth; cited in "A Heckuva Claim," *Washington Post,* Jan. 6, 2007.

53. Center on Budget and Policy Priorities, *Social Security and Poverty Among the Elderly*

(Washington, D.C.: CBPP, 1999). This study found that Social Security reduced the incidence of poverty among the elderly from about 50 percent to 12 percent and raised more than one-third of elderly Americans above the poverty line.

54. Interview, Jared Bernstein, Economic Policy Institute, Sept. 14, 2006.

55. White and Wildavsky estimate that half of the American people receive benefits from at least one of eleven entitlement programs, averaging about $10,000 a year in 1990; *The Deficit and the Public Interest*, 187; Henry J. Kaiser Family Foundation, "Medicaid and SCHIP," www.kff.org/Medicaid/index.cfm; Rivlin and Antos, *Restoring Fiscal Sanity*, 131; Hillary Clinton, address, New America Foundation, Jan. 31, 2007, http://clinton.senate.gov/news/statements/details.cfm?id=272682&&.

56. David Walker, "The Mortgage You Didn't Know You Had," *San Francisco Chronicle*, May 25, 2006; Generations United, "The State of Children, Youth and Families in Social Security," 2005; Melissa Kearney, "Introduction to Medicaid," presentation, Brookings Institution, Washington, D.C., Oct. 4, 2005.

57. Jacob Hacker, "The Great Risk Shift," presentation, New America Foundation, Washington, D.C., Oct. 18, 2006.

58. Social Security Online, "Social Security: Basic Facts," Jan. 31, 2007, http://www.ssa.gov/pressoffice/basicfact.htm; Laura Beedon, "Social Security: Basic Data," AARP, Apr. 2005; Organization for Economic Cooperation and Development, *OECD Economic Survey: The United States* (Paris: OECD, 2005). For example, in 2006 and 2007, Social Security recipients received 4.1 percent and 3.3 percent cost-of-living adjustments; cited in "Government Benefits Rise," *Washington Post*, Oct. 19, 2006.

59. Congressional Budget Office, "Historical Budget Data," Jan. 26, 2006; Swanson, *America the Broke*, 68, 72.

60. Diamond and Orszag, *Saving Social Security*, 15, 24, 51.

61. Congressional Budget Office, "Historical Budget Data."

62. Sen. Jim DeMint (R-S.C.), Oct. 5, 2005, http://demint.senate.gov/public/index.cfm?FuseAction=PressReleases.Detail&PressRelease_id=8c78df39-04f2-47bf-a375-445bd0959717&Month=10&Year=2005&Type=Op-Ed.

63. Social Security and Medicare Board of Trustees, *Status of the Social Security and Medicare Programs: A Summary of the 2006 Annual Reports* (Washington, D.C., 2006), 4; Alison Acosta Fraser, "Heading Toward a Deficit Disaster," Heritage Foundation, Apr. 24, 2006, http://www.heritage.org/Press/Commentary/ed042406b.cfm; Butler, "Solutions"; Walker interview; Antos, "Medicare and the Prescription Drug Benefit,"http://hsgac.senate.gov/_files/092205Antos.pdf; CBO estimate reported in "Democrats Face Hurdles in Bid to Close Medicare Gap," *Washington Post*, Jan. 7, 2007; Robert Samuelson, "Benefit Disaster," *Washington Post*, Nov. 23, 2005. The monthly Part B premium was $88.50 and the Part D premium was about $32 in 2006. Samuelson estimated that three-quarters of Medicare recipients already had drug coverage. The so-called doughnut hole refers to the fact that under the original law, a $265 annual deductible applies to the first $2,400 in coverage, after which beneficiaries must pay for the full cost of medicines until they reach $3,850 in yearly drug expenses, at which point catastrophic coverage comes into play.

64. Cato Handbook for the 108th Congress, Cato Institute, 2005.

65. Interview with Rep. William Frenzel, July 21, 2006; Kearney, "Introduction to Medicaid."

66. Concord Coalition, "Social Security Reform."

67. Steuerle interview.

68. "Another Day Older and Deeper in Debt," *Minneapolis Star Tribune,* Oct. 16, 2005; Peterson, *Running on Empty,* p. 37; Diane Rogers, "How Did We Get Back to Big Deficits?" Brookings Institution, September 2006, unpublished.

2. BALANCING AND UNBALANCING OUR BUDGET

Epigraph. George Washington, Fifth Annual Address to Congress, Dec. 3, 1793, American Presidency Project, http://www.presidency.ucsb.edu/ws/index.php?pid=29435.

1. Thomas Jefferson, Letter to William Plumer, July 21, 1816, http://www.bartleby.com/73/383.html.

2. John Steele Gordon, *Hamilton's Blessing: The Extraordinary Life and Times of Our National Debt* (New York: Walker, 1997), 120; U.S. Bureau of the Public Debt, "Historical Debt Outstanding—Annual, 1791–1849," http://www.treasurydirect.gov/govt/reports/pd/histdebt/histdebt_histo1.htm; U.S. Bureau of the Public Debt, "Historical Debt Outstanding—Annual, 1850–1899," http://www.treasurydirect.gov/govt/reports/pd/histdebt/histdebt_histo2.htm; U.S. Bureau of the Public Debt, "Historical Debt Outstanding—Annual, 1900–1949," http://www.treasurydirect.gov/govt/reports/pd/histdebt/histdebt_histo3.htm; U.S. Office of Management and Budget, *Budget of the United States Government, Fiscal Year 2008: Historical Tables* (Washington, D.C.: Government Printing Office, 2007), 21–22; Center for Budget and Policy Priorities, "A 'Mere' $300 Billion," June 5, 2006.

3. U.S. Bureau of the Census, http://www.census.gov/popest/national/asrh/NC-EST2005/NC-EST2005-01.csv; U.S. Bureau of the Public Debt, "Historical Debt Outstanding—Annual, 1950–2005," http://www.treasurydirect.gov/govt/reports/pd/histdebt/histdebt_histo4.htm.

4. Bishop Berkeley, in the eighteenth century, called British debt for imperial investment "a mine of gold"; cited in T. David Zukerman, "Are We Redeeming Our Public Debt Too Hastily?" *Political Science Quarterly* 40, no. 2 (1925).

5. Gordon, *Hamilton's Blessing,* 11–15, 2–3; Kenneth W. Thompson, ed., *The Budget Deficit and the National Debt* (Lanham, Md.: University Press of America, 1997), 69.

6. Gordon S. Wood, *The Creation of the American Republic, 1776–1787* (Chapel Hill: University of North Carolina Press, 1998); Jack N. Rakove, *Original Meanings: Politics and Ideas in the Making of the Constitution* (New York: Vintage, 1997); Leonard Levy, ed., *Essays on the Making of the U.S. Constitution* (New York: Oxford University Press, 1969); and Herbert J. Storing, *What the Anti-Federalists Were For* (Chicago: University of Chicago Press, 1981).

7. Gordon, *Hamilton's Blessing,* 19–32, 38–41; Thompson, *The Budget Deficit,* 74; Harvey E. Fisk, *Our Public Debt: An Historical Sketch with a Description of U.S. Securities* (New

York: Bankers Trust Company, 1919), 1, 6; George Hager and Eric Pianin, *Mirage: Why Neither Democrats Nor Republicans Can Balance the Budget, End the Deficit, and Satisfy the Public* (New York: Times Books, 1997), 85.

8. Fisk, *Our Public Debt*, 3, 12; James M. Buchanan, Charles Kershaw Rowley, and Robert D. Tollison, eds., *Deficits* (New York: Basil Blackwell, 1987), 16; Thompson, *The Budget Deficit*, 77–78; Gordon, *Hamilton's Blessing*, 43; and U.S. Bureau of the Public Debt, "Historical Debt Outstanding—Annual, 1791–1849."

9. U.S. Bureau of the Public Debt, "Historical Debt Outstanding—Annual, 1791–1849"; U.S. Bureau of the Public Debt, "Historical Debt Outstanding—Annual, 1850–1899"; Fisk, *Our Public Debt*, 19, 20, 22, 27, 31.

10. Claudia Goldin and Frank D. Lewis, "The Economic Costs of the Civil War," *Journal of Economic History* 35, no. 2 (1975), 305, 308; Fisk, *Our Public Debt*, 36–37; Buchanan, Rowley, and Tollison, *Deficits*, 17; Hager and Pianin, *Mirage*, 89; Gordon, *Hamilton's Blessing*, 75; U.S. Department of the Treasury, "Taxes: History of the U.S Tax System," http://www.ustreas.gov/education/fact-sheets/taxes/ustax.shtml; U.S. Bureau of the Public Debt, "Historical Debt Outstanding—Annual, 1850–1899. Estimates of the Civil War's direct costs are slippery, given that they can include military costs, destruction of physical and human capital, and arguably postwar pension and medical costs; moreover, Confederate financial records after 1863 are incomplete. It is noteworthy that Lincoln's sentiment—that debt owed by a nation's government to its people—is not a problem had been presaged by an eighteenth-century British financial official, who said: "Debts owed by the right hand to the left, by which the body will be in no way weakened"; cited in Zukerman, "Are We Redeeming Our Public Debt Too Hastily?"

11. Dennis S. Ippolito, *Why Budgets Matter: Budget Policy and American Politics* (University Park: Pennsylvania University Press, 2003), 61, 80–81, 86; U.S. Office of Management and Budget, *Budget of the United States Government, Fiscal Year 2008: Historical Tables*, 21; U.S. Bureau of the Public Debt, "Historical Debt Outstanding—Annual, 1850–1899"; U.S. Bureau of the Public Debt, "Historical Debt Outstanding—Annual, 1900–1949."

12. U.S. Department of the Treasury, "Taxes"; Gordon, *Hamilton's Blessing*, 98.

13. Ippolito, *Why Budgets Matter*, 102–3; U.S. Department of the Treasury, "Taxes."

14. U.S. Office of Management and Budget, *Budget of the United States Government, Fiscal Year 2008: Historical Tables*, 21; and U.S. Bureau of the Public Debt, "Historical Debt Outstanding—Annual, 1900–1949."

15. U.S. Bureau of the Public Debt, "Historical Debt Outstanding—Annual, 1900–1949."

16. Congressional Research Service, "Introduction to the Federal Budget Process," Dec. 28, 2004; Joseph White and Aaron Wildavsky, *The Deficit and the Public Interest: The Search for Responsible Budgeting in the 1980s* (Berkeley: University of California Press, 1989), 1, 8; and Ippolito, *Why Budgets Matter*, 99.

17. Gordon, *Hamilton's Blessing*, 122; Ippolito, *Why Budgets Matter*, 128–29; Buchanan, Rowley, and Tollison, *Deficits*, 23; and Leonard J. Santow and Mark E. Santow, *Social Security and the Middle-Class Squeeze: Fact and Fiction About America's Entitlement Programs* (Westport, Conn.: Praeger, 2005), 17.

18. Ippolito, *Why Budgets Matter*, 130–42; U.S. Office of Management and Budget, *Budget*

of the U.S. Government, Fiscal Year 2007: Historical Tables (Washington, D.C.: Government Printing Office, 2006); and "Life Expectancy at Birth by Race and Sex, 1930–2004," http://www.infoplease.com/ipa/A0005148.html.

19. Peterson, *Running on Empty*, 110–15; William G. Gale, John B. Shoven, and Mark J. Warshawsky, eds. *The Evolving Pension System: Trends, Effects, and Proposals for Reform* (Washington, D.C.: Brookings Institution Press, 2005), 18–21.

20. U.S. Office of Management and Budget, *Budget of the United States Government, Fiscal Year 2008: Historical Tables,* 21; and U.S. Bureau of the Public Debt, "Historical Debt Outstanding—Annual, 1900–1949."

21. U.S. Office of Management and Budget, *Budget of the United States Government, Fiscal Year 2008: Historical Tables.*

22. U.S. Department of the Treasury, "Taxes."

23. U.S. Bureau of the Public Debt, "Historical Debt Outstanding—Annual, 1900–1949"; Hager and Pianin, *Mirage,* 87–88.

24. U.S. Office of Management and Budget, *Budget of the United States Government, Fiscal Year 2007: Historical Tables.*

25. Seymour Harris and Alvin Hansen, "Targets for Tomorrow's Economy," *New Republic,* Mar. 19, 1945; Treasury Secretary Fred Vinson, House, Full Employment Act of 1945: Hearings, 921–27.

26. U.S. Department of the Treasury, "Taxes."

27. In the famous prewar phrase of the Harvard economist and American Economic Association President Alvin Hansen, describing the United States as a "mature economy." Hansen quietly recanted the idea after the war.

28. The U.S. economy grew by an annual average of about 4 percent between 1947 and the late 1960s, with the fastest growth from 1947 to the mid-1950s and from 1961 to 1968. Per capita output rose three times as fast between 1950 and 1973 than the average of the previous 130 years. By comparison, annual per capita growth between 1790 and 1860 has been estimated to have been 1.3 percent. Robert L. Heilbroner and Aaron Singer, *The Economic Transformation of America* (New York: Harcourt Brace Jovanovich, 1977), 54; Godfrey Hodgson, *America in Our Time* (New York: Vintage, 1976), 83.

29. U.S. Office of Management and Budget, *Budget of the United States Government, Fiscal Year 2007: Historical Tables.*

30. C. Eugene Steuerle, *Contemporary U.S. Tax Policy* (Washington, D.C.: Urban Institute Press, 2004), 67; Peterson, *Running on Empty,* 114; Gale, Shoven, and Warshawsky, *The Evolving Pension System,* 21; Santow and Santow, *Social Security and the Middle-Class Squeeze,* 68; Godfrey Hodgson, *America in Our Time* (New York: Vintage, 1976); Alan Wolfe, *America's Impasse: The Rise and Fall of the Politics of Growth* (New York: Pantheon, 1981), 65; Robert M. Collins, *The Business Response to Keynes, 1929–1964* (New York: Columbia University Press, 1981), 153, 155; Richard Parker, *John Kenneth Galbraith: His Life, His Politics, His Economics* (New York: Farrar, Straus and Giroux, 2005), 319; interview with Charles Schultze, June 3, 2005; Eisenhower's November 12, 1956, letter to Arthur Burns, accepting his resignation as CEA chairman, Papers of Arthur S. Burns, box 103, Dwight D. Eisenhower Library, Abilene, Kan.; Social Security Administration, "Social Security Online: History," www.socialsecurity.gov/history.

31. U.S. Bureau of the Public Debt, "Historical Debt Outstanding—Annual, 1950–2005"; Gordon, *Hamilton's Blessing*, 139; and Steuerle, *Contemporary U.S. Tax Policy*, 47–48.

32. U.S. Bureau of the Public Debt, "Historical Debt Outstanding—Annual, 1950–2005"; U.S. Office of Management and Budget, *Budget of the United States Government, Fiscal Year 2007: Historical Tables.*

33. John F. Kennedy, June 11, 1962, President's Office Files: Speech Files, box 39, and C. Douglas Dillon Papers, box 60, John F. Kennedy Presidential Library, Boston; Hager and Pianin, *Mirage*, 92; and Ippolito, *Why Budgets Matter*, 4.

34. Gary R. Evans, *Red Ink: The Budget, Deficit, and Debt of the U.S. Government* (San Diego: Academic Press, 1997), 107; Santow and Santow, *Social Security and the Middle-Class Squeeze*, 69, 21; Peterson, *Running on Empty*, 115; U.S. Department of the Treasury, "Taxes."

35. Hager and Pianin, *Mirage*, 95; Gerald J. Swanson, *America the Broke: How the Reckless Spending of the White House and Congress Are Bankrupting Our Country and Destroying Our Children's Future* (New York: Currency Doubleday, 2004), 43; U.S. Bureau of the Public Debt, "Historical Debt Outstanding—Annual, 1950–2005"; U.S. Office of Management and Budget, *Budget of the United States Government, Fiscal Year 2007: Historical Tables.*

36. William Gale and Peter Orszag, "The Outlook for Fiscal Policy," *Tax Notes*, Feb. 14, 2005; Marvin H. Kosters, *Fiscal Policies and the Budget Enforcement Act* (Washington, D.C.: AEI Press, 1992), 48; Alice M. Rivlin and Joseph Antos, eds., *Restoring Fiscal Sanity: The Health Spending Challenge* (Washington, D.C.: Brookings Institution Press, 2007), 176; Diane Rogers, "Why Worry About the Deficit?" Brookings Institution, February 2006, unpublished.

37. Gordon, *Hamilton's Blessing*, 156.

38. Robert D. Reischauer, ed., *Setting National Priorities: Budget Choices for the Next Century* (Washington, D.C.: Brookings Institution Press, 1997), 4, 7.

39. Ronald Reagan, Inaugural Address, Jan. 20, 1981, http://www.reaganfoundation.org/reagan/speeches/first.asp.

40. White and Wildavsky, *The Deficit and the Public Interest*, 338–39; U.S. Bureau of the Public Debt, "Historical Debt Outstanding—Annual, 1950–2005"; U.S. Office of Management and Budget, *Budget of the United States Government, Fiscal Year 2007: Historical Tables.*

41. Ellen Frank, *Raw Deal: How Myths and Misinformation About Deficits, Inflation, and Wealth Impoverish America* (Boston: Beacon, 2004), 81–82; White and Wildavsky, *The Deficit and the Public Interest*, 227; Hager and Pianin, *Mirage*, 103–4.

42. Interview, Joe Antos, Mar. 8, 2007.

43. White and Wildavsky, *The Deficit and the Public Interest*, 310–31; OECD, *Aging and Employment Policies: United States* (Paris: OECD, 2005); Hager and Pianin, *Mirage*, 125–26.

44. Steuerle, *Contemporary U.S. Tax Policy*, 142; Joseph J. Minarik, *Making America's Budget Policy: From the 1980s to the 1990s* (Cambridge, Mass.: National Bureau of Economic Research, 1995), 14; Gordon, *Hamilton's Blessing*, 165; and White and Wildavsky, *The Deficit and the Public Interest*, 473–95.

45. Robert Eisner, *The Great Deficit Scares: The Federal Budget, Trade, and Social Security*

(New York: Century Foundation Press, 1997), 3; Hager and Pianin, *Mirage,* 57–58, 148, 275–76, 439, 454; Alan S. Blinder and Janet L. Yellen. *The Fabulous Decade: Macroeconomic Lessons from the 1990s* (New York: Century Foundation Press, 2001), 3–7; White and Wildavsky, *The Deficit and the Public Interest,* 126; and Reischauer, *Setting National Priorities,* 15.

46. Peterson, *Running on Empty,* 138; Reischauer, *Setting National Priorities,* 13–15; Steuerle, *Contemporary U.S. Tax Policy,* 4, 154–59; Ippolito, *Why Budgets Matter,* 242, 250–51.

47. Ross Perot, *United We Stand: How We Can Take Back Our Country, a Plan for the 21st Century* (New York: Hyperion, 1991), ix; Ellen Frank, *Raw Deal: How Myths and Misinformation About Deficits, Inflation, and Wealth Impoverish America* (Boston: Beacon, 2004), 66–67.

48. Congressional Budget Office, "Historical Budget Data," January 2007.

49. Ippolito, *Why Budgets Matter,* 12, 262–63; U.S. Department of the Treasury, "Taxes"; and Steuerle, *Contemporary U.S. Tax Policy,* 172–74.

50. Lee Price and B. Sawicky, "The Budget Arithmetic Test: Repairing Federal Fiscal Policy," Economic Policy Institute, Oct. 13, 2004; interview, Robert Samuelson, Sept. 27, 2006.

51. Ippolito, *Why Budgets Matter,* 242, 280–81; Council of Economic Advisers, *Economic Report of the President* (Washington, D.C.: Government Printing Office, 2001).

52. Rogers, "Why Worry About the Deficit?"

53. Blinder and Yellen. *The Fabulous Decade,* 75; Hager and Pianin, *Mirage,* 275–76; Samuelson interview; Steuerle, *Contemporary U.S. Tax Policy,* 202; and Peterson, *Running on Empty,* 123.

54. U.S. Bureau of the Public Debt, "Historical Debt Outstanding—Annual, 1950–2006"; U.S. Office of Management and Budget, *Budget of the United States Government, Fiscal Year 2008: Historical Tables;* Peterson, *Running on Empty,* 9; "Democrats' Budget Plan Narrowly Passes in House," *Washington Post,* Mar. 30, 2007.

3. HOW DEFICITS ARE FUNDED

1. Interview, Rep. Jim Cooper, Jan. 5, 2007.

2. Congressional Research Service, "The Spending Pipeline," June 13, 2003; U.S. Senate Committee on the Budget, *Committee on the Budget, 1974–2006* (Washington, D.C.: Government Printing Office, 2006); Center for Budget and Policy Priorities, "Background on the Federal Budget Process and the Return of Budget Deficits, 2006; Joseph White and Aaron Wildavsky. *The Deficit and the Public Interest: The Search for Responsible Budgeting in the 1980s* (Berkeley: University of California Press, 1989), 3, 4, 12–14; Aaron Wildavsky and Naomi Caiden, *The New Politics of the Budgetary Process,* 3rd ed. (New York: Longman, 1997), 10–15.

3. Government Accountability Office, "Federal Trust and Other Earmarked Funds," January 2001; Social Security and Medicare Board of Trustees, *Status of the Social Security and Medicare Programs: A Summary of the 2007 Annual Reports* (Washington, D.C.: Social Security Administration, 2006), http://www.ssa.gov/OACT/TRSUM/trsummary.html.

4. "Repo Men," *Economist,* Nov. 4, 2006; interviews with David Walker and Susan Irving, Dec. 13, 2006.

5. U.S. Bureau of the Public Debt, "Frequently Asked Questions About the Public Debt," n.d.; U.S. Bureau of the Public Debt, "Debt to the Penny and Who Holds It," n.d.; Financial Management Service, *Treasury Bulletin,* Sept. 2007, http://www.fms.treas.gov/bulletin/index.html; U.S. Treasury, "Ownership of Federal Securities," March 2006.

6. Financial Management Service, *Treasury Bulletin,* Sept. 2007; "The Looming Dangers of U.S. Debt," *China Forum,* Sept. 7, 2006; "Just Who Owns the U.S. National Debt?" MSNBC, Mar. 4, 2007, http://www.msnbc.msn.com/id/17424874/.

7. Stephen Roach, "Global Collision Course," *Investment Perspectives,* Sept. 27, 2004, and Stephen Roach, "Global Economy Coming Apart," *Business Times Singapore,* Oct. 4, 2004, http://www.lexisnexis.com.proxyau.wrlc.org/us/lnacademic/search/homesubmitForm.do.

8. Congressional Joint Economic Committee, Democratic Caucus, "Economic Policy Brief," June 2006.

9. Congressional Research Service, "Foreign Holdings of Federal Debt," Nov. 23, 2005.

10. Ibid.; Sen. Evan Bayh, quoted in the *Chesterton Tribune,* Mar. 18, 2005, http://www.freerepublic.com/focus/fr/1365473/posts.

4. HOW DEFICITS AND DEBT AFFECT AMERICA AND YOU

Epigraphs. Laurence Ball and N. Gregory Mankiw, "What Do Budget Deficits Do?" in *Budget Deficits and Debt: Issues and Opinions,* symposium proceedings (Kansas City, Mo.: Federal Reserve Bank of Kansas City), 116; Bonhoeffer quoted in Peter G. Peterson, *Running on Empty: How the Democratic and Republican Parties Are Bankrupting Our Future and What Americans Can Do About It* (New York: Farrar, Straus and Giroux, 2004), 27.

1. Cheney's quotation was cited by former Treasury Secretary Paul O'Neill. O'Neill's recollection of the comment was reported in Ron Suskind, *The Price of Loyalty* (New York: Simon and Schuster, 2004).

2. "Comment: Taxing," *New Yorker,* Jan. 26, 2004; see also Suskind, *The Price of Loyalty.* Cheney's infamous comment reflected his Reaganesque belief that reducing the size of government and spending is more important than the level of deficits.

3. Kemp quoted in "The International Economy," *LookSmart,* Summer 2003. Many have made the short- vs. long-term distinction: interview with Stan Collender, Nov. 22, 2006; interview with Charles Kolb, July 31, 2006.

4. Robert Eisner, *The Great Deficit Scares: The Federal Budget, Trade, and Social Security* (New York: Century Foundation, 1997), 8, 26, 57–58; Francis Warnock and Veronica Warnock, "International Capital Flows and U.S. Interest Rates," NBER Working Paper 12560, National Bureau of Economic Research, 2006; Paul N. Courant and Edward M. Gramlich, *Federal Budget Deficits: America's Great Consumption Binge* (Englewood Cliffs, N.J.: Prentice Hall, 1986); Gary Evans, *Red Ink: The Budget, Deficit and Debt of the U.S. Government* (San Diego: Academic Press, 1997), 200–206.

5. Ball and Mankiw, "What Do Budget Deficits Do?" 97.

6. General Accounting Office, "Federal Debt: Answers to Frequently Asked Questions," November 1996; Evans, *Red Ink,* 189–91.

7. Eric Leeper and Shu-Chun Susan Yang, "Dynamic Scoring," NBER Working Paper 12103, March 2006; Center on Budget and Policy Priorities, "Background on the Federal Budget and the Return of Budget Deficits," Feb. 28, 2006, http://72.14.209.104/search?q=cache:BFACvPPT3_EJ:www.gistfunders.org/documents/greenstein.ppt+Center+on+Budget+and+Policy+Priorities,+%E2%80%9CBackground+on+the+Federal+Budget+and+the+Return+of+Budget+Deficits%E2%80%9D&hl=en&gl=us&ct=clnk&cd=2; and "The Return of Voodoo Economics," *Washington Post,* May 15, 2006.

8. Franco Modigliani, "Long Run Implications of Alternative Fiscal Policies and the Burden of Debt," *National Economic Journal* 71 (December 1961); Martin Feldstein, "Here Are the Facts," *Wall Street Journal,* Feb. 12, 2004; Peterson, *Running on Empty,* 97–98; William Gale and Peter Orszag, "The Outlook for Fiscal Policy," *Tax Notes,* Feb. 14, 2005; Douglas B. Bernheim, *The Vanishing Nest Egg: Reflections on Savings in America* (New York: Priority, 1991), 38; David P. Calleo, *The Bankrupting of America: How the Federal Budget is Impoverishing the Nation* (New York: W. Morrow, 1992), 11–12, 156; General Accounting Office, "Federal Debt: Answers to Frequently Asked Questions."

9. Peterson, *Running on Empty,* 46.

10. William Niskanen of the Cato Institute has argued that, since 1981, tax cuts actually have been associated with increased government spending, and tax increases have been associated with less government spending. He says that demand for spending declines as taxes increase, and vice versa. See William Niskanen, " 'Starve the Beast' Does Not Work," *Cato Policy Report* (Washington, D.C.: Cato Institute, 2004).

11. Ball and Mankiw, "What Do Budget Deficits Do?" 96–98. Stein is quoted in Joseph White and Aaron Wildavsky, *The Deficit and the Public Interest: The Search for Responsible Budgeting in the 1980s* (Berkeley: University of California Press, 1989), 352; Feldstein is quoted in Daniel N. Shaviro, *Do Deficits Matter?* (Chicago: University of Chicago Press, 1997), 84.

12. Alan Greenspan, July 15, 2003, quoted in "U.S. Economy: Budget Deficits Force Record Government Borrowing," Bloomberg, July 28, 2003; Robert Rubin, Peter R. Orszag, and Allen Sinai, "Sustained Budget Deficits: Longer-Run U.S. Economic Performance and the Risk of Financial and Fiscal Disarray," presented at AEA-NAEFA joint session, San Diego, Jan. 4, 2004, http://www.brookings.edu/dybdocroot/views/papers/orszag/20040105.pdf.

13. Ball and Mankiw, "What Do Budget Deficits Do?"; Peterson, *Running on Empty,* 40–41; Rubin, Orszag, and Sinai, "Sustained Budget Deficits."

14. "Red Ink Rising," *AARP Bulletin,* February 2006; Rubin, Orszag, and Sinai, "Sustained Budget Deficits"; interview with Alice Rivlin, Oct. 11, 2006; Thomas Laubach, "New Evidence on the Interest Rate Effects of Budget Deficits and Debt," Federal Reserve Board, 2003, http://www.federalreserve.gov/pubs/feds/2003/200312/200312pap.pdf; Third Way, "Why Deficits Matter," Aug. 28, 2006.

15. Shaviro, *Do Deficits Matter?* 198; Evans, *Red Ink,* 208; Rubin, Orszag, and Sinai, "Sustained Budget Deficits"; and James M. Buchanan, Charles Kershaw Rowley, and Robert D. Tollison, eds., *Deficits* (New York: Basil Blackwell, 1987), 37.

16. Feldstein, "Here Are the Facts."

17. Cited in Robert Eisner, *The Great Deficit Scares: The Federal Budget, Trade, and Social Security* (New York: Century Foundation Press, 1997), 68; Shaviro, *Do Deficits Matter?* 123, 125, 151; Jim Saxton, "Payroll Taxes and the Redistribution of Income," Joint Economic Committee Study, July 1997; Peter A. Diamond and Peter R. Orszag, *Saving Social Security: A Balanced Approach* (Washington, D.C.: Brookings Institution Press, 2004), 69–72.

18. Ball and Mankiw, "What Do Budget Deficits Do?" 101–2.

19. Committee on Budget and Policy Priorities, "Contrary to the President's Claim, Large Majority of Americans Ultimately Are Likely to Lose from the Tax Reconciliation Bill," press release, May 17, 2006; interview with Diane Rogers, Sept. 8, 2006.

20. Ron Haskins and Isabel Sawhill, eds., *Restoring Fiscal Sanity: Meeting the Long-Run Challenge* (Washington, D.C.: Brookings Institution Press, 2005), 8; Joe Antos, "Medicare and the Prescription Drug Benefit," testimony to the Committee on Homeland Security and Government Affairs, Sept. 22, 2005, http://hsgac.senate.gov/_files/092205 Antos.pdf; Peterson, *Running on Empty,* xiv; Cato Institute, *Cato Handbook for Congress* (Washington, D.C.: Cato Institute, 2005); Committee for Economic Development, "Fixing Social Security: A CED Policy Update," 2005.

21. While some sort of private accounts may be beneficial in the long run, the costs of transition under the plan proposed by President Bush could add $4.9 trillion to the debt over twenty years, according to the Center for American Progress; http://socialsecurity.our future.org/constituencies/young-people/.

22. Economic Policy Institute, "Social Security Price Indexing Proposal Means Benefit Cuts for Workers," June 1, 2005; James Capretta, "Building Automatic Solvency into U.S. Social Security: Insights from Sweden and Germany," Brookings Institution Policy Brief 151, March 2006; Diamond and Orszag, *Saving Social Security,* 8.

23. Employee Benefit Research Institute, "Income of the Elderly Population Age 65 and Older," *EBRI Notes* 27, no. 1 (January 2006); Century Foundation, *Social Security Reform: Revised Report* (New York: Century Foundation, 2005); Jeff Sessions, "A Bipartisan Fix for Retirees," *Washington Post,* Dec. 16, 2006.

24. U.S. Census Bureau, *Statistical Abstract of the United States 2003* (Washington, D.C.: Government Printing Office, 2003), 455; Federal Reserve Board, *Consumer Credit Outstanding* (Washington, D.C.: DEC, 2005).

25. Peterson, *Running on Empty,* xvi, 51, 53; Sessions, "A Bipartisan Fix for Retirees"; Josh Bivens, "The Chronic Problem of Declining Health-Care Coverage," Economic Policy Institute, Sept. 16, 2004.

5. THE POTENTIAL DANGERS OF DOING NOTHING, OR FIDDLING
WHILE OUR ECONOMY GOES UP IN SMOKE

Epigraph. "Fed Chief Sends Warning on Budget," Associated Press, Jan. 18, 2007.

1. Stein's often-quoted wisdom can be found, among other places, in IMF Director Stanley Fischer's 2001 eulogy at the American Economic Association: Stanley Fischer, "Remembering Herb Stein," Prepared for delivery to the American Economic Association, New Orleans, Jan. 6, 2001, http://www.imf.org/external/np/speeches/2001/010601.htm.

2. Quoted in Peter Peterson, *Running on Empty: How the Democratic and Republican Parties*

Are Bankrupting Our Future and What Americans Can Do About It (New York: Farrar, Straus and Giroux, 2004), xxiv.

3. L. Josh Blivens, "Debt and the Dollar," Economic Policy Institute, Dec. 14, 2004.

4. Interview with David Walker, Dec. 13, 2006.

5. Concord Coalition, "A Fiscal Wake-Up Call," 2007, http://www.concordcoalition.org/events/fiscal-wake-up/fiscal-wake-up-call.htm; Ron Haskins and Isabel Sawhill, eds., *Restoring Fiscal Sanity: Meeting the Long-Run Challenge* (Washington, D.C.: Brookings Institution Press, 2005), 4, 106; Congressional Budget Office, "The Budget and Economic Outlook: Fiscal Years 2007 to 2016," January 2006; Congressional Budget Office, *Budget and Health Reforms* (Washington, D.C.: CBO, 2005); "As Social Security Surges"; interview with Douglas Holtz-Eakin, Sept. 28, 2006; Blivens, "Debt and the Dollar"; interview with Diane Lim Rogers, Sept. 8, 2006; Concord Coalition, "Social Security Reform," Mar. 4, 2005; "Medicare Costs Will Rise with Private Care Plans," *Washington Post,* Dec. 3, 2006; GAO's Long-Term Budget Scenario, cited in Concord Coalition, "Facing Facts Quarterly," December 2006.

6. http://www.treasurydirect.gov/NP/BPDLogin?application=np.

7. Quoted in Center on Budget and Policy Priorities, "Contrary to President's Claim, Large Majority of Americans Ultimately are Likely to Lose from Tax Reconciliation Bill," CBPP, May 17, 2006.

8. Interview with Robert Samuelson, Sept. 27, 2006; Haskins and Sawhill, *Restoring Fiscal Sanity,* 87; Brian Riedl, "Another Day Older and Deeper in Debt," *Minneapolis Star Tribune,* Oct. 16, 2005; Lee Price and Max Sawicky, "The Budget Arithmetic Test: Repairing Federal Fiscal Policy," Economic Policy Institute, 2005.

9. C. Eugene Steuerle, "The Incredible Shrinking Budget for Working Families and Children," Urban Institute, December 2003; interview with Jared Bernstein, Sept. 14, 2006; "A Bridge Gone Too Far," *Economist,* Aug. 11, 2007.

10. Joseph Antos, "Medicare and the Prescription Drug Benefit," testimony to the Committee on Homeland Security and Government Affairs, Sept. 22, 2005, http://hsgac.senate.gov/_files/092205Antos.pdf; Concord Coalition, "Social Security Reform," Mar. 4, 2005.

11. Robert Samuelson, "The Big Economic Worry," *Washington Post,* Jan. 3, 2007.

12. "Cost of Iraq War Could Surpass $1 Trillion," MSNBC, Mar. 17, 2006, http://www.msnbc.msn.com/id/11880954/; "What $1.2 Trillion Can Buy," *New York Times,* Jan. 17, 2007, http://www.nytimes.com/2007/01/17/business/17leonhardt.html?ex=1326690000&en=7f221bfce7a6408c&ei=5090; "Bush to Request Billions for Wars," *Washington Post,* Feb. 3, 2007; CBO Letter to Senate Budget Committee on Iraq War Costs, Feb. 7, 2007.

13. "Katrina May Cost as Much as Four Years of War," MSNBC, Sept. 10, 2005, http://www.msnbc.msn.com/id/9281409; "Potential Southern California Tsunami Could Cost Up to $42 Billion," Live Science, Mar. 31, 2005, http://www.livescience.com/environment/050331_tsunami_california.html.

14. James R. Hoffa, "Retirement Insecurity," *Global Report on Aging* (Washington, D.C.: AARP, 2006), http://www.aarp.org/research/international/gra/spring2006/policyForum.html.

15. Peterson, *Running on Empty,* 51, 53; Robert Rubin, Peter R. Orszag, and Allen Sinai, "Sustained Budget Deficits: Longer-Run U.S. Economic Performance and the Risk of

Financial and Fiscal Disarray," presented at AEA-NAEFA joint session, San Diego, Jan. 4, 2004; interview with Bob Bixby, Dec. 6, 2006; "Inequality and Health Care," *Washington Post,* Dec. 13, 2006.

16. Lawrence Kotlikoff and Scott Burns, *The Coming Generational Storm: What You Need to Know About America's Economic Future* (Cambridge: MIT Press, 2004).

17. Quoted in Rubin, Orszag, and Sinai, "Sustained Budget Deficits."

18. Laurence Ball and N. Gregory Mankiw, "What Do Budget Deficits Do?" in *Budget Deficits and Debt: Issues and Opinions,* symposium proceedings (Kansas City, Mo.: Federal Reserve Bank of Kansas City), 117.

19. Ibid., 112–13; Walker interview; interview with Rep. Jim Cooper, Jan. 5, 2007; Saul H. Hymans, "United States," *Asia Pacific Business,* http://www.asiapacificbusiness.ca/peo/outlook2005/unitedstates_05.pdf; "Warren Buffett's View of the U.S. Dollar," *Gold Money Alert,* Nov. 18, 2003, http://goldmoney.com/en/commentary/2003-11-18.html. In August 2006 Italy's central bank announced that it would sell off a significant amount of its dollar holdings, shifting them into British pounds, and Russia, Sweden, and the United Arab Emirates earlier had announced modest reductions of their dollar holdings, citing their fears of U.S. deficits and expectations of a consequent fall in the dollar. Other big U.S. investors such as George Soros also have said that they were moving money out of dollars to currencies they perceived to be less risky.

20. Ball and Mankiw, "What Do Budget Deficits Do?" 113–16; Rubin, Orszag, and Sinai, "Sustained Budget Deficits."

21. "IMF Says Rise in U.S. Debt Is Threat to World Economy," *New York Times,* Jan. 8, 2004. Fred Bergsten, who heads the Peter G. Peterson Institute for International Economics, commented, "If the IMF is right, . . . you are increasing the risk of a day of reckoning when things can get pretty nasty."

22. Quoted in Public Agenda, "Facing Up to Our National Finances," May 23, 2006, unpublished; Public Agenda, "It's Time to Pay Our Bills," 2007, http://www.publicagenda.org/research/pdfs/facingup_leaders_report.pdf.

23. David Walker, "The Four Deficits Confronting the United States," *Kansas City Star,* Apr. 16, 2006.

24. Interview with Alice Rivlin, Oct. 11, 2006; interview with Douglas Holtz-Eakin, Sept. 28, 2006; interview with William Frenzel, July 21, 2006; interviews with Stuart Butler, July 27 and Sept. 20, 2006.

25. Brian Riedl, "Runaway Spending: Left Unchecked, Washington's Overspending Could Drown America in Taxes and Debt," Heritage Foundation, 2006.

6. THE POLITICS OF DEFICITS AND DEBT

Epigraphs. Marx quoted in Leonard J. Santow and Mark E. Santow, *Social Security and the Middle-Class Squeeze: Fact and Fiction About America's Entitlement Programs* (Westport, Conn.: Praeger, 2005), 109; Sen. Chuck Hagel (R-Neb.), May 4, 2006, http://hagel2008.blogspot.com/2006_08_01_archive.html.

1. Concord Coalition, "Understanding the Federal Debt Limit," 2006.

2. Peter Peterson, *Running on Empty: How the Democratic and Republican Parties Are Bank-*

rupting Our Future and What Americans Can Do About It (New York: Farrar, Straus and Giroux, 2004), 12, xiv.

3. "Federal Page," *Washington Post,* Dec. 7, 2006.

4. Douglas Holtz-Eakin, "Out on a Limb," *Washington Post,* Feb. 5, 2006; Brookings Institution–Heritage Foundation Federal Fiscal Seminar, May 17, 2005; interview with Stan Collender, Nov. 22, 2006.

5. Interview with Rep. William Frenzel, July 21, 2006.

6. "California, Ohio to Vote on Redistricting Changes," *Washington Post,* Nov. 2, 2005.

7. National Taxpayers Union, press release, June 22, 2006.

8. Quoted in Peterson, *Running on Empty,* xxvi.

9. Cato Institute, *Cato Handbook for Congress* (Washington, DC: Cato, 2005); Cato Institute, "On Spending, Bush Is No Reagan," August 2003.

10. Interview with Alice Rivlin, Oct. 11, 2006. Similar sentiments have been expressed by a number of Hill staff and other Washington insiders: interview with Lee Price and Sarah Kline, Sept. 6, 2006; interview with Joe Antos, Oct. 18, 2006; interview with Mike Franc, Oct. 25, 2006.

11. Interview with Robert Samuelson, Sept. 27, 2006.

12. C. Eugene Steuerle, *Contemporary U.S. Tax Policy* (Washington, D.C.: Urban Institute Press, 2004), 250.

13. Interview with Stuart Butler, Sept. 20, 2006.

14. Sen. Dick Durbin, Mar. 21, 2007, http://www.commoncause.org/atf/cf/%7BFB3C17 E2-CDD1-4DF6-92BE-BD4429893665%7D/SENATOR%20DURBIN'S%20 FLOOR%20SPEECH.PDF; Center for Responsive Politics, "2006 Election Analysis," http://www.opensecrets.org/pressreleases/2006/PostElection.11.8.asp; Shaw quoted in Steuerle, *Contemporary U.S. Tax Policy,* 67.

15. Sen. George Voinovich speech, Jan. 1, 2006, http://voinovich.senate.gov/annual_report/ 2005_annual_report.pdf.

16. David Walker, "Fiscally, U.S. Wrenching: D.C. Overdue to Join Clamor Over Soaring Federal Debt," *Atlanta Journal-Constitution,* Feb. 15, 2006.

17. *Washington Post* and *New York Times* polls in 2006, for example, found that about 70 percent of Americans worried about rising deficits, but a Fox/Opinion Dynamics poll found only 2 percent ready to say that balancing the budget was the nation's top problem. *Washington Post*/ABC, Jan. 30, 2006; *New York Times,* Jan. 27, 2006; Fox/Opinion Dynamics, Sept. 14, 2006.

18. Quoted in Edward Miller, "Management Advice: Getting Others to Do What You Want . . . and Like It," 2001, http://www.asne.org/kiosk/editor/01.march/miller1.htm.

19. Quoted in "Bush Sees 'Opportunities' on Social Security, Immigration," *Washington Post,* Dec. 20, 2006.

20. Seminar, Brookings Institution, Feb. 6, 2006.

21. Viewpoint Learning, Inc., "Americans Deliberate Our Nation's Finances and Future: It's Not About Taxes—It's About Trust," 2006, http://www.viewpointlearning.com/ publications/reports/finances_future_1206.pdf; Mar. 9, 2005, poll by the Program on International Policy Attitudes, cited in "Bush's Spending Priorities Not in Line with Americans'—Poll," http://www.commondreams.org/headlines05/0309-03.htm.

22. Viewpoint Learning, Inc., "Americans Deliberate Our Nation's Finances and Future;" Public Agenda, *It's Time to Pay Our Bills* (New York, 2007).

23. Ibid.

24. The focus group comments are from a Viewpoint Learning/Public Agenda "Choice Dialogue" in Philadelphia, July 15, 2006. The college students' comments are from communications with the author by students at American University in Washington, D.C.

25. Interview with Stuart Butler, Sept. 20, 2006; Viewpoint Learning, Inc., "Americans Deliberate Our Nation's Finances and Future"; Alice Rivlin and Joe Antos, eds., *Restoring Fiscal Sanity: The Health Spending Challenge* (Washington, D.C.: Brookings Institution Press, 2007), 194, 216.

26. Interview with Charles Kolb, Apr. 8, 2007.

7. WHAT CAN AND SHOULD BE DONE TO REDUCE AMERICA'S DEFICITS AND DEBT?

Epigraphs. Sen. Ken Salazar (D-Colo.), Mar. 16, 2006,http://salazar.senate.gov/news/releases/060316debt.htm; Sen. John McCain (R-Ariz.), Sept. 23, 2004, http://mccain.senate.gov/press_office/view_article.cfm?id=229.

1. Jared Bernstein, *All Together Now: Common Sense for a Fair Economy* (San Francisco: Berrett-Koehler, 2006).

2. Hillary Clinton, address to New America Foundation, Jan. 31, 2007, http://clinton.senate.gov/news/statements/details.cfm?id=272682&&.

3. Joe Antos, "Medicare and the Prescription Drug Benefit," testimony to the Committee on Homeland Security and Government Affairs, Sept. 22, 2005, http://hsgac.senate.gov/_files/092205Antos.pdf.

4. William A. Galston and Elaine Kamarck, "The Politics of Polarization," *Third Way,* October 2005; Morris P. Fiorina, Samuel J. Abrams, and Jeremy C. Pope, *Culture War? The Myth of a Polarized America* (New York: Pearson, 2005); Martin Kettle, "Americans Are Less Polarized Than Their Politicians Would Have Us Believe," *Guardian,* Aug. 3, 2004.

5. Quoted in Thomas E. Mann and Bruce E. Cain, eds., *Party Lines: Competition, Partisanship and Congressional Redistricting* (Washington, D.C.: Brookings Institution Press, 2005), 1.

6. Ibid., 95–106; Michael P. McDonald and John Samples, eds., *The Marketplace of Democracy* (Washington, D.C.: Brookings Institution Press, 2006), 27–29, 228, 236–41; Congressional Research Service, "Congressional Redistricting: The Constitutionality of Creating an At-Large District," Mar. 20, 2007.

7. McDonald and Samples, *Marketplace of Democracy,* 199–200, 245; Chris Edwards, *Downsizing the Federal Government* (Washington, D.C.: Cato Institute, 2005), 133.

8. Rep. Steve Israel, http://www.house.gov/israel/biography/index.htm; Henry Aaron and Stuart Butler, "A Bipartisan Attempt to Break the Health-Reform Stalemate," *Salt Lake Tribune,* Jan. 1, 2007; "A New Consensus on Universal Health Care," *Washington Post,* Jan. 17, 2007; David Broder, "'Common Ground' Caucus," *Washington Post,* Mar. 8, 2007; Unity08 Web site, http://www.unity08.com/.

9. Sen. Mike Crapo (R-Idaho), June 21, 2006, http://crapo.senate.gov/media/newsreleases/release_full.cfm?id=257585.

10. The ways in which budget rules can be made to force action are discussed by Rudolph G. Penner and C. Eugene Steuerle, "Budget Rules," Urban Institute, 2004.

11. Sen. Russell Feingold (D-Wis.), http://feingold.senate.gov/issues_budget.html.

12. Maya MacGuineas, testimony to the Senate Homeland Security and Governmental Affairs Subcommittee, May 25, 2006, http://crfb.org/documents/TestimonyMacGuineas ProcessMay2006.pdf; interview with David Walker, Dec. 13, 2006; interview with Bob Bixby, Dec. 6, 2006; interview with Rep. Jim Cooper, Jan. 5, 2007; interview with Maya MacGuineas, Jan. 8, 2007; David Walker, "U.S. Financial Condition and Fiscal Future Briefing," Aug. 7, 2007, http://www.gao.gov/cghome/d071189cg.pdf; C. Eugene Steuerle, *Contemporary U.S. Tax Policy* (Washington, D.C.: Urban Institute Press, 2004), 254–55; interview with Alison Acosta Fraser, Sept. 20, 2006; Center on Budget and Policy Priorities, "TABOR," http://www.cbpp.org/ssl-series.htm; Brian Riedl, "Runaway Spending: Left Unchecked, Washington's Overspending Could Drown America in Taxes and Debt," Heritage Foundation, 2006; Brian Riedl and Alison Acosta Fraser, "Four Principles of Budget Process Reform," Heritage Foundation, 2006; "House Adopts Pay-as-You-Go Rules," *Washington Post*, Jan. 6, 2007.

13. United States Government Accountability Office, *21st Century Challenges: Reexamining the Bases of the Federal Government* (Washington, D.C.: GAO, 2006), 81–86; Walker, "U.S. Financial Condition and Fiscal Future Briefing"; Edwards, *Downsizing the Federal Government,* 133–40; Concord Coalition, "Understanding the Federal Debt Limit," Feb. 17, 2006; Steuerle, *Contemporary U.S. Tax Policy,* 254–55; Democratic Policy Committee, "The Fresh Fifty," Nov. 1, 2005; MacGuineas testimony to the Senate Homeland Security and Governmental Affairs Subcommittee; MacGuineas interview; New America Foundation, *Ten Big Ideas for a New America* (Washington, D.C.: New America, 2007); interviews with Stuart Butler, July 27, Sept. 20, and Oct. 25, 2006.

14. As David Walker says, Social Security accounts for "just" $6–7 trillion of the $50 trillion or so of the federal government's unfunded liabilities; Walker interview.

15. On the precariousness of private retirement funds see James R. Hoffa, "Retirement Insecurity," *Global Report on Aging* (Washington: AARP, 2006), http://www.aarp.org/research/international/gra/spring2006/policyForum.html. The employees of Enron and WorldCom lost $1 billion in 401(k) funds, and even IBM announced it was freezing its pension in 2006.

16. Interview with C. Eugene Steuerle, Sept. 15, 2006; Walker interview.

17. Interview with Alison Acosta Fraser, Apr. 3, 2007; Centers for Disease Control and Prevention, *Health United States 2005* (Washington, D.C.: Government Printing Office, 2005), table 27, "Life expectancy at birth, at 65 years of age, and at 75 years of age, according to race and sex: United States, selected years 1900–2003," ftp://ftp.cdc.gov/pub/Health_Statistics/NCHS/Publications/Health_US/hus05tables/.

18. Marc Friedman, *Encore: Finding Work That Matters in the Second Half of Life* (New York: Public Affairs, 2007). Friedman estimates that the number of workers ages 34 to 54 will grow by only 3 million between 2000 and 2020, compared to growth of 30 million be-

tween 1980 and 2000, resulting in labor shortages of up to 18 million workers by 2020; p. 77.

19. Committee for Economic Development, "Fixing Social Security: A CED Policy Update," CED, May 2005; Peter A. Diamond and Peter R. Orszag, *Saving Social Security: A Balanced Approach* (Washington, D.C.: Brookings Institution Press, 2004), 85–86; Bixby interview; OECD, "Aging and Employment Policies," 2005; OECD, *Economic Survey: The United States,* 2005; Jeffrey Liebman, Maya MacGuineas, and Andrew Samwick, "Nonpartisan Social Security Reform Plan," New America Foundation, Dec. 14, 2005, http://www.newamerica.net/publications/policy/nonpartisan_social_security _reform_plan; Brookings Institution, Heritage Foundation, and Concord Coalition, "Does It Take a Commission?" public forum, May 15, 2006; Peter G. Peterson, *Will America Grow Up Before It Grows Old? How the Coming Social Security Crisis Threatens You, Your Family, and Your Country* (New York: Random House, 1996); interview with Charles Kolb, July 31, 2006; Collender interview; James Capretta, "Articulating a Policy Framework for Long-Term Federal Entitlement Reform," Brookings Institution, October 2005, unpublished.

20. Peter Orszag, "Social Security Reform," testimony to the Senate Finance Committee, Apr. 25, 2005; Liebman, MacGuineas, and Samwick, "Nonpartisan Social Security Reform."

21. Diamond and Orszag, *Saving Social Security,* 87; Peter L. Edelman, Dallas L. Salisbury, and Pamela J. Larson, eds., *The Future of Social Insurance: Incremental Action or Fundamental Reform?* (Washington, D.C.: National Academy of Social Insurance, 2002); Josh Blivens, "Social Security's Fixable Financial Issues," Economic Policy Institute, Apr. 26, 2005. The only progressive, work-enhancing aspect of current Social Security taxes is the provision not to fully tax the first $12,900 in income of workers sixty-five and older.

22. OECD, *OECD Economic Survey,* 2005.

23. Diamond and Orszag, *Saving Social Security,* 86; interview with Rep. William Frenzel, July 21, 2006; Peter Peterson, *Running on Empty: How the Democratic and Republican Parties Are Bankrupting Our Future and What Americans Can Do About It* (New York: Farrar, Straus and Giroux, 2004), 21, 150–51.

24. Peterson, *Running on Empty,* 200; Ron Haskins and Isabel Sawhill, eds., *Restoring Fiscal Sanity: Meeting the Long-Run Challenge* (Washington, D.C.: Brookings Institution Press, 2005), 64–65; OECD, *Economic Survey,* 2005; Economic Policy Institute, "Social Security Price Indexing Means Benefit Cuts for Workers," June 1, 2005.

25. Orszag, "Social Security Reform"; Bush cited in Bixby interview.

26. Capretta, "Articulating a Policy Framework."

27. Liebman, MacGuineas, and Samwick, "Nonpartisan Social Security Reform,"

28. Business Roundtable, "Issue: Federal Budget 2006,"; Peterson, *Running on Empty,* 202–4; John Podesta, "A Tax Plan for Progressives," Center for American Progress, June 24, 2005, http://www.americanprogress.org/issues/2005/06/taxplanprogressives.html; Barry Bosworth and Gary Burtless, eds., *Aging Societies* (Washington: Brookings Institution Press, 1998).

29. Some estimate that fully privatizing Social Security could cost U.S. taxpayers nearly $5

trillion in transition costs, whereas others expect that even a partial privatization would increase deficits for about forty years before starting to reduce them; Jeffrey Tebbs, "Summary of Major Budget Reform Proposals," Brookings Institution, Aug. 10, 2005, unpublished; Capretta, "Articulating a Policy Framework."

30. Bixby interview.

31. "Financial Futures," *Wall Street Journal,* Sept. 24, 2006; J, Mark Iwry and David C. John, "Pursuing Individual Retirement Security Through Automatic IRAs," Heritage Foundation white 02122006, http://www.heritage.org/Research/SocialSecurity/wp20060212.cfm.

32. OECD, *Economic Survey,* 2005; Podesta, "A Tax Plan for Progressives."

33. Liebman, MacGuineas, and Samwick, "Nonpartisan Social Security Reform"; CED, "Fixing Social Security."

34. Peter R. Orszag, J. Mark Iwry, and William Gale, eds., *Aging Gracefully: Ideas to Improve Retirement Security in America* (New York: Century Foundation Press, 2006), 5–11; Jacob S. Hacker, *The Great Risk Shift* (New York: Oxford University Press, 2006), 171, 186; New America Foundation, *Ten Big Ideas.*

35. William G. Gale, John B. Shoven, and Mark J. Warshawsky, eds., *The Evolving Pension System: Trends, Effects, and Proposals for Reform* (Washington, D.C.: Brookings Institution Press, 2005), 8–9, 186–87; New America Foundation, *Ten Big Ideas;* Jeff Sessions, "A Bipartisan Fix for Retirees," *Washington Post,* Dec. 26, 2006; Gene Sperling quoted in Sebastian Mallaby, "A Fix for Social Security," *Washington Post,* Nov. 27, 2006.

36. Diamond and Orszag, *Saving Social Security,* 214–15.

37. Robert J. Samuelson, "Welfare State Stasis," *Washington Post,* Feb. 14, 2007.

38. U.S. defense spending was $305 billion in 2001, or 3.0 percent of GDP. The government's 2008 estimate is $607 billion, or 4.2 percent of GDP, although President Bush's fiscal year 2008 budget request included $482 billion for the Pentagon, plus a supplemental appropriation for $142 billion in military spending (and $3 billion in State Department spending) for the wars in Iraq and Afghanistan, bringing total military spending to about $624 billion. U.S. Office of Management and Budget, *Budget of the United States Government, Fiscal Year 2008: Historical Tables* (Washington, D.C.: Government Printing Office, 2007), 53-54; Congressional Budget Office, "Historical Budget Data Tables," 2007; "Bush Plan Reins in Domestic Spending," *Washington Post,* Feb. 6, 2007; "Bush's Defense Budget Biggest Since Reagan Era," *Washington Post,* Feb. 6, 2007; Jeffrey M. Tebbs, "Pruning the Defense Budget," Brookings Institution, 2007.

39. Citizens Against Government Waste, *2006 Pig Book* (Washington, D.C.: CAGW, 2006); "Problems Stall Pentagon's New Fighting Vehicle," *Washington Post,* Feb. 7, 2007.

40. Tebbs, "Pruning the Defense Budget"; "Audit Confirms Boat Design Flaws," *Washington Post,* Feb. 15, 2007.

41. "Military Waste Under Fire: $1 Trillion Missing—Bush Plan Targets Pentagon Accounting," *San Francisco Chronicle,* May 18, 2003; Rumsfeld quoted in "The War on Waste," CBS News, Jan. 29, 2002; Scott Garrett, "Defense Spending Accountability," Dec. 15, 2006, http://www.townhall.com/columnists/ScottGarrett/2006/12/15/defense_spending_accountability__smarter_for_taxpayers,_safer_for_troops.

42. Katherine V. Schinasi, "Contract Management: DOD Vulnerabilities to Contracting

Fraud, Waste, and Abuse," letter to Senators John Warner and Carl Levin and Representatives Duncan Hunter and Ike Skelton, GAO, July 7, 2006; Shanahan quoted in "The War on Waste."

43. Peterson, *Running on Empty,* 195; "Red Ink Rising," *AARP Bulletin,* February 2006; Lee Price and Max B. Sawicky, "The Budget Arithmetic Test: Repairing Federal Fiscal Policy," Economic Policy Institute.

44. Program on International Policy Attitudes, "U.S. Budget: The Public's Priorities," Mar. 7, 2005, http://www.worldpublicopinion.org/pipa/articles/brunitedstatescanadara/85. php?nid=&id=&pnt=85&lb=btot. This poll found that 61–65 percent of Americans want to cut the defense budget, on average, by a remarkable 31 percent. The Defense Spending Report Card Act, defeated in 2006, would have required an accounting of at least the Defense Department's countless earmarks.

45. Jared Bernstein, "Ballad of the Beast-Starvers," *American Prospect,* March 2005.

46. Public Citizen, "Corporate Welfare," June 16, 2003, http://www.citizen.org/congress/welfare/index.cfm; Ralph Nader, *Cutting Corporate Welfare* (New York: Seven Stories, 2001); Citizens for Tax Justice, "Surge in Corporate Welfare Drives Corporate Tax Payments Down to Near Record Low," Apr. 17, 2002, http://www.ctj.org/html/corpo402. htm; Edward H. Crane, ed., *Cato Handbook on Policy 2005* (Washington, D.C.: Cato Institute, 2005).

47. Citizens Against Government Waste, "Prime Cuts," 2007, http://www.cagw.org/site/PageServer?pagename=reports_primecuts; *Cato Handbook for the 105th Congress* (Washington, D.C.: Cato Institute, 1996); James Capretta, "Restraining Federal Domestic Spending," Brookings Institution, 2007.

48. Charles Kolb, "Statement on Earmarks," Committee for Economic Development, Dec. 19, 2006; Citizens Against Government Waste, *2006 Pig Book.* Because "pork" and "earmarks" are variously defined, estimates of their total cost vary from about $30 billion to more than $60 billion in 2006.

49. Isabel V. Sawhill and Andrew L. Yarrow, "Chump-Change Budget Cuts," *Los Angeles Times,* Nov. 12, 2005; interview with Alison Acosta Fraser, Oct. 25, 2006.

50. Capretta, "Restraining Federal Domestic Spending"; Edwards, *Downsizing the Federal Government,* 122, 125, 130; Fraser interview, Oct. 25, 2006.

51. "In Washington, Contractors Take on Biggest Role Ever," *New York Times,* Feb. 4, 2007.

52. "The Progress Report: Taxpayers Deserve to Know How Their Money Is Squandered" (2006), www.progress.org/2006/corpw41.htm.

53. Edwards, *Downsizing the Federal Government;* Butler interview, Oct. 25, 2006; Capretta, "Restraining Federal Domestic Spending"; interview with Alice Rivlin, Oct. 11, 2006.

54. Robert Samuelson, "Hiding Health Care's Costs," *Washington Post,* Jan. 31, 2007.

55. The very fact that President Bush addressed health care in his 2007 state of the union address is one sign of this change, as is the fact that many Republicans—as well as Democrats—are taking the lead on health care issues. Another is the agreement among the Business Roundtable, the AARP, and the Service Employees International Union—normally not cozy companions—that universal health care's time has come; "New Consensus."

56. Alice M. Rivlin and Joseph Antos, eds., *Restoring Fiscal Sanity: The Health Spending*

Challenge (Washington, D.C.: Brookings Institution Press, 2007), 87; Bernstein, *All To-gether Now,* 6, 47. Medicare spending growth has been about 1 percentage point less than private-sector spending increases. According to Bernstein, private insurance companies consume about 20 percent of payers' premiums with advertising, administration, and profits, whereas Medicare "spends" about 2 percent of its costs on administration.

57. Henry Aaron, *Can We Say No?* (Washington, D.C.: Brookings Institution Press, 2005); interview with Jared Bernstein, Sept. 14, 2006; "Single-Payer Advocates Push Cause in States; Challenges Likely," Oct. 24–31, 2005, http://www.ama-assn.org/amednews/2005/10/24/gvsb1024.htm; "Labor's Rx for Health Care—AFL-CIO Touts Single-Payer System," California Nurses' Association, Jan. 13, 2007, http://www.calnurse.org/media-center/in-the-news/2007/january/page.jsp?itemID=29295682.

58. "House Passes Medicare Drug Bill," *Washington Post,* Jan. 13, 2007; "After Aggressive AMA-Led Campaign, Medicare Physician Payment Cut Averted," *AMA Agenda,* December 2006, http://www.ama-assn.org/ama/pub/category/17127.html; "President Strays into Democrats' Turf," *Washington Post,* Jan. 24, 2007; "Bush Seeks Shift in Health Coverage," Washington Post, Jan. 21, 2007; Edwards, *Downsizing the Federal Government,* 38–47; Joe Antos, "Medicare and the Prescription Drug Benefit," testimony to the Committee on Homeland Security and Government Affairs, Sept. 22, 2005, http://hsgac.senate.gov/_files/092205Antos.pdf; "America's Economy," *Economist,* Feb. 9, 2006; Rivlin and Antos, *Restoring Fiscal Sanity,* 90.

59. U.S. Targets Health-Care Fraud, Abuse," *Washington Post,* July 19, 2007; Antos, "Medicare and the Prescription Drug Benefit"; "America's Economy," *Economist,* Feb. 9, 2006; Rivlin and Antos, *Restoring Fiscal Sanity,* 90.

60. Haskins and Sawhill, *Restoring Fiscal Sanity,* 83–84; Steuerle interview; "States' Changes Reshape Medicaid," *Washington Post,* June 12, 2006; Fraser interview, Oct. 25, 2006; Edwards, *Downsizing the Federal Government,* 38, 47; Capretta, "Restraining Federal Domestic Spending"; "Rivlin and Antos, *Restoring Fiscal Sanity,* 6, 47, 56, 124.

61. Haskins and Sawhill, *Restoring Fiscal Sanity,* 82; Leif Wellington Haase, *A New Deal for Health: How to Cover Everyone and Get Medical Costs Under Control* (New York: Century Foundation, 2005); Stan Dorn, "A Vision for Health System Change," presentation, Heritage Foundation, Washington, D.C., Aug. 12, 2004.

62. New America Foundation, *Ten Big Ideas.*

63. Haase, *A New Deal for Health,* 34, 39; Peterson, *Running on Empty,* 208–9; Kolb interview; Butler interview, Oct. 25, 2006; Rivlin and Antos, *Restoring Fiscal Sanity,* 234; Gov Exec.Com, "Open Season Guide," http://www.govexec.com/health/plantypes2007.htm.

64. Leonard Schaeffer, "Putting the Lid on Health Care Costs," presentation, Brookings Institution, Washington, D.C., Oct. 20, 2005; Bernstein interview; Rivlin and Antos, *Restoring Fiscal Sanity,* 40–41; Cooper interview.

65. Schaeffer, "Putting the Lid on Health Care Costs"; Rivlin and Antos, *Restoring Fiscal Sanity,* 214, 62; Henry J. Aaron and Robert D. Reischauer, eds., *Setting National Priorities: The 2000 Election and Beyond* (Washington, D.C.: Brookings Institution Press, 1999), 195–96; Haase, *A New Deal for Health;* Samuelson, "Hiding Health Care's Costs"; Butler interview, Oct. 25, 2006.

66. Peterson, *Running on Empty,* 208–9; Aaron, *Can We Say No?* 3, 57; Rivlin and Antos,

Restoring Fiscal Sanity, 3, 64, 40–41; Fred Gluck, "Providing Affordable and Effective Health Care to the U.S. Population," presentation, Brookings Institution, Washington, D.C., June 15, 2006; Jared interview.

67. "Massachusetts Bill Requires Health Coverage: State Set to Use Auto Insurance as a Model," *Washington Post,* Apr. 5, 2006; Tebbs, "Summary of Major Budget Reform Proposals"; "Arnold Care," *Washington Post,* Jan. 15, 2007; "Tax the Wicked, Cure the Sick," *Economist,* Mar. 10, 2007; "Eyes on California as Lawmakers Pursue a Health-Care Deal," *Washington Post,* Aug. 26, 2007.

68. Capretta, "Restraining Federal Domestic Spending"; Len Nichols, "Enable a Moderate Health Care Solution," presentation, Brookings Institution, Sept. 29, 2006; Rivlin and Antos, *Restoring Fiscal Sanity,* 113, 121; Fraser interview, Oct. 25, 2006; Frenzel interview.

69. Rivlin and Antos, *Restoring Fiscal Sanity,* 160; Congressional Budget Office, *Budget and Health Reforms* (Washington, D.C.: CBO, 2005).

70. Rivlin and Antos, *Restoring Fiscal Sanity,* 210–11; Butler interview, July 27, 2006; Schaeffer, "Putting the Lid on Health Care Costs"; Aaron, *Can We Say No?;* Henry Aaron, "Health-Care Rationing: What It Means," Brookings Institution Policy Brief 147, December 2005; "A Health-Care Prescription That's Hard to Swallow," *Los Angeles Times,* Jan. 30, 2006; Frenzel interview; Collender interview; Bixby interview.

71. Butler interview, July 27, 2006.

72. Peterson, *Running on Empty,* 209–10; Haskins and Sawhill, *Restoring Fiscal Sanity,* 76; Butler interview, July 27, 2006; Citizens Health Care Working Group, "Interim Recommendations: Health Care That Works for All Americans," June 1, 2006; Haase, *A New Deal for Health;* Cooper interview; Rivlin and Antos, *Restoring Fiscal Sanity,* 3, 35–36, 46, 94; "In-Hospital Deaths from Medical Errors at 195,000 per Year USA," *Medical News Today,* Aug. 9, 2004; Institute of Medicine, "To Err Is Human: Building a Safer Health System," IOM, 2000, http://www.nap.edu/books/0309068371/html/.

73. For example, surgeons pay about $175,000 in malpractice premiums, and the image of the greedy, grubby malpractice lawyer has considerable truth, as only about 40 percent of settlements go to the aggrieved plaintiffs. Peterson, *Running on Empty,* 210; United States Government Accountability Office, *21st Century Challenges,* 37; National Conference of State Legislatures, "Medical Malpractice Tort Reform," May 2006, http://www.ncsl.org/standcomm/sclaw/medmaloverview.htm; Rivlin and Antos, *Restoring Fiscal Sanity,* 68–69, 211; Bixby interview.

74. Rivlin and Antos, *Restoring Fiscal Sanity,* 59; "Obesity Costs $9 Billion for Every 4 Million Born," *Clinical Psychiatry News,* December 2006.

75. United States Government Accountability Office, "Summary of Estimates of the Costs of the Federal Tax System," GAO, 2005.

76. Robert Rubin, "Attention Deficit Disorder," *New York Times,* May 13, 2005; International Monetary Fund, "Fiscal Policies and Priorities for Long-Run Sustainability," IMF, Jan. 7, 2004; Diane Lim Rogers, "Reducing the Deficit Through Better Tax Policy," Brookings Institution, 2007; Bixby interview; Bernstein interview.

77. John Podesta, testimony for the President's Tax Reform Panel, May 11, 2005, http://www.americanprogress.org/issues/kfiles/b681323.html.

78. Cooper interview.

79. Peterson, *Running on Empty,* 207; David Walker, quoted in Concord Coalition forum "Does It Take a Commission?" Washington, D.C., May 15, 2006; International Monetary Fund, "U.S. Fiscal Policies," IMF, Jan. 7, 2004; Fraser interview, Oct. 25, 2006; Bixby interview; Cooper interview; "Big Ideas Amid Big Deficits," *National Tax Journal,* May 19–20, 2005, 471; Maya MacGuineas, "The $800 Billion Tax Loophole," *Washington Post,* Jan. 18, 2007.

80. Michael J. Graetz, *The U.S. Income Tax: What It Is, How It Got That Way, and Where We Go from Here* (New York: Norton, 1999), 304; MacGuineas, "The $800 Billion Tax Loophole"; Ross Perot, *United We Stand: How We Can Take Back Our Country, A Plan for the 21st Century* (New York: Hyperion, 1991), 46; Paul N. Courant and Edward M. Gramlich, *Federal Budget Deficits: America's Great Consumption Binge* (Englewood Cliffs, N.J.: Prentice-Hall, 1986), p. 55; and OECD, *OECD Economic Survey,* 2005.

81. Scott A. Hodge, "Countdown to Tax Reform, Part II: Taypayers and Non-Payers," Tax Foundation, Oct. 13, 2005; "New Social Contract Revisited," *Growth Strategies,* February 2002; Butler interview, Oct. 25, 2006; Fraser interview, Apr. 3, 2007. Butler estimates that forty-four million adult Americans pay no income taxes.

82. Haskins and Sawhill, *Restoring Fiscal Sanity,* 103, 113; Frenzel interview; Aaron and Reischauer, *Setting National Priorities,* 250–51, 258; Committee for Economic Development, "A New Tax Framework"; Graetz, *The U.S. Income Tax,* 303–14, 413; William G. Gale, "Tax Reform Options in the Real World," Brookings Institution, October 2005; Butler interview, Oct. 25, 2006; "Big Ideas Amid Big Deficits" Rivlin interview; Diane Lim Rogers, "Reducing the Deficit Through Better Tax Policy," Brookings Institution, 2007.

83. Rogers, "Reducing the Deficit"; Ian W. H. Parry, "Are All Market-Based Environmental Regulations Equal?" *Issues in Science and Technology* 19, fall 2002; Steven R. Eastaugh, *Facing Tough Choices: Balancing Fiscal and Social Deficits* (Westport, Conn.: Praeger, 1994), 231–34; Maya MacGuineas, "New America Tax Reform Plan," New America Foundation, December 2005; Collender interview.

84. Republicans and Democrats were largely united in calling for the repeal of the luxury tax, as New England boat builders, for example, experienced a 70 percent drop in large yacht sales.

85. Viewpoint Learning Inc., "Americans Deliberate Our Nation's Finances and Future: It's Not About Taxes—It's About Trust," 2006. http://www.viewpointlearning.com/publications/reports/finances_future_1206.pdf.

86. MacGuineas, "New America Tax Reform Plan"; "Red Ink Rising," *AARP Bulletin,* February 2006; Graetz, *The U.S. Income Tax,* 312.

87. United States Government Accountability Office, *21st Century Challenges,* 74; "Senators Set Sights on Overseas Tax Havens," *Washington Post,* Feb. 18, 2007; "You Paid Your Taxes? Sucker," *Washington Post,* Apr. 15, 2007. The IRS estimated that Americans had $1.34 trillion parked in overseas tax havens in 2006, up from $796 billion in 2003, costing the Treasury $100 billion a year.

88. Rogers, "Reducing the Deficit Through Better Tax Policy"; "IRS Was Underpaid $345 Billion in 2001," *Washington Post,* Feb. 15, 2006; "Do You Cheat on Your Taxes?" *CNN Money,* Apr. 9, 2004. The CNN survey found that a quarter of Americans admitted to cheating on their taxes.

89. Rogers, "Reducing the Deficit Through Better Tax Policy"; Joint Committee on Taxa-

tion, "Additional Options to Improve Tax Compliance," Aug. 3, 2006; Henry J. Aaron and Joel Slemrod, *The Crisis in Tax Administration* (Washington, D.C.: Brookings Institution Press, 2004), 347–79.

90. Hours spent filing estimated in "Big Ideas Amid Big Deficits," 441.

91. Butler interview, Oct. 25, 2006; Tebbs, "Summary of Major Budget Reform Proposals"; Daniel J. Mitchell, "A Brief Guide to the Flat Tax," Heritage Foundation, July 7, 2005; Leonard Burman, "The Tax Reform Proposals," *Economists Voice,* December 2005; Gale, "Tax Reform Options in the Real World"; Grover Norquist, "Implementing a 'Return-Free' Tax Filing System," presentation, President's Advisory Panel on Tax Reform, May 17, 2005, http://72.14.209.104/search?q=cache:leqTtHM01GoJ:www.taxreformpanel.gov/meetings/docs/norquist_05172005.ppt+return-free+tax&hl=en&ct=clnk&cd=2&gl=us; Fraser interview, Oct. 25, 2006.

92. Burman, "The Tax Reform Proposals"; Peterson, *Running on Empty,* 111–12; Max Sawicky, "Do-it-Yourself Tax Cuts: The Crisis in US Tax Enforcement," Economic Policy Institute, Apr. 12, 2005; Graetz, *The U.S. Income Tax,* 105; Rogers, "Reducing the Deficit Through Better Tax Policy."

93. Concord Coalition, "Understanding the Federal Debt Limit."

94. Gale, "Tax Reform Options in the Real World"; *Urban Institute 2005 Annual Report* (Washington, D.C.: Urban Institute, 2006); Burman, "The Tax Reform Proposals"; "Tax Options; OECD, *OECD Economic Survey,* 2005; Jared Bernstein, "Ballad of the Beast Starvers," *American Prospect,* March 2005.

95. Butler interview, Oct. 25, 2006; Leonard E. Burman, Elaine Maag, and Jeffrey Rohaly, "Tax Credits to Help Low-Income Families Pay for Child Care," Urban Institute, 2005, http://209.85.165.104/search?q=cache:6sp9ljoodeIJ:www.urban.org/UploadedPDF/311199_IssuesOptions_14.pdf+expand+EITC&hl=en&ct=clnk&cd=11&gl=us; Thomas Z. Freedman, "How to Really Help Low-Wage Workers," *Washington Post,* Feb. 2, 2007; Tax Policy Center, "Historical EITC Recipients," http://www.taxpolicycenter.org/TaxFacts/Tfdb/TFTemplate.cfm?DocID=37&Topic2id=40&Topic3id=42.

96. Interview with Maya MacGuineas, Oct. 20, 2006; Butler interview, Oct. 25, 2006; Bernstein interview; Bixby interview.

8. CONCLUDING THOUGHTS

Epigraphs. Sen. Arlen Specter (R-Pa.), Feb. 8, 2005, http://specter.senate.gov/public/index.cfm?FuseAction=NewsRoom.Articles&ContentRecord_id=3729c3c7-dd58-4001-81ef-70db843cea03&Region_id=&Issue_id=; Sen. Maria Cantwell (D-Wash.), Jan. 28, 2003, http://cantwell.senate.gov/news/record.cfm?id=243005&.

1. Julia Isaacs, "Cost-Effective Investments in Children," Brookings Institution, 2007.

2. Robert L. Heilbroner and Aaron Singer, *The Economic Transformation of America* (New York: Harcourt Brace Jovanovich, 1977), 54; Godfrey Hodgson, *America in Our Time* (New York: Vintage, 1976), 83; U.S. Department of Commerce, *Historical Statistics of the United States,* Part I (Washington, D.C.: GPO, 1975); Stanley Lebergott, *The Americans: An Economic Record* (New York: Norton, 1984), 396.

3. Quoted in Marc Friedman, *Encore: Finding Work That Matters in the Second Half of Life* (New York: Public Affairs, 2007), 69–70.

Index

Steuerle, Eugene, ix, 27, 86, 101
Stockman, David, 43, 59
Supplemental spending bills, 52
Supplementary Medical Insurance, 26
Supreme Court, 32, 46, 52, 100
Surpluses, 5, 28, 29, 31–33, 46, 47, 60, 61, 63, 131

TABOR, 99
Tariff Act, 30
Tax base, 20, 44, 124, 125
Tax cheating, 19, 129
Tax collection, 11, 20, 127
Tax credits, 44, 60, 106, 117, 125, 126
Tax cuts, 4–7, 10–11, 19–20, 33, 40–44, 47, 62, 66, 72–73, 82–90, 93, 98
Tax deductions, 125–27, 131
Taxes: alternative minimum, 5, 124, 131; consumption, 126–28, 130; energy, 128; estate, 5, 19, 33, 54, 102, 129; excise, 19, 30–32; flat, 130–32; income, 18–20, 32, 33, 37, 38, 102, 124, 125–31; Hall-Rabushka, 130; luxury, 128–29; payroll, 19, 20, 24–26, 38, 74, 101–4, 115, 124–27, 130; sales, 73, 124, 126–28; sin, 128–29; value-added, 126; X, 130
Tax havens, 129
Tax enforcement, 19, 20, 124, 128, 129
Tax expenditures, 10, 125
Taxpayers, xii, 5, 6, 18, 40, 49, 56, 62, 66, 74, 75, 84, 87, 89, 93, 99, 106, 108, 110, 123–24, 129, 131, 134
Tax preparation, costs and time, 18, 123
Tax reform, 123–32
Tax Reform Act of 1986, 43
1040 form, 33
Third-party payers, 23, 113, 117
Three Stooges, 22
Trade deficits, 6, 8, 49, 55, 90,
Transportation spending, 60, 62, 73, 74, 87, 111, 128, 134–35
Treasury, U.S. Department of the, 4, 6, 8, 30, 31, 48, 53–57, 72, 73, 78, 11, 124, 126, 131

Treasury securities, 49, 53–55, 56, 57, 78, 105, 131
TRICARE, 116–17
Truman, Harry, 13, 26, 35, 39, 41, 58, 63, 88, 95, 101, 136
Trust funds of the federal government, 25, 26, 44, 50, 52, 53, 56, 66, 72, 99, 100, 101, 105, 131
Tsongas, Paul, 45

Unemployment insurance, 53
Unfunded liabilities, 2, 3, 23, 50, 56, 58, 61, 63, 123
Unfunded mandates, 63
User fees, 111, 124, 128

Value-added tax (VAT), 126
Veterans' benefits, 14, 21, 24, 114, 121
Veterans' Health System, 24, 62, 114,
Vietnam War, 16, 17, 29, 38, 40–42, 106
Viewpoint Learning, 90
Voinovich, George, 87, 97, 119
Volcker, Paul, 8, 42
Volunteer corps, 17, 62

Walker, David, x, 7, 18, 49, 55, 79, 88, 102
War of 1812, 32
Wars in Iraq and Afghanistan, 13, 16, 47, 52, 75, 83, 95, 106, 107
Washington, George, 2, 28, 30, 64, 83
Ways and Means Committee, House, 15, 52
Whiskey Rebellion, 31, 79
Wilson, Woodrow, 33
Witte, Edwin, 37
Workforce, size of U.S, 74, 75, 77, 101, 134
World power, U.S, 8, 72, 77, 113
World War I, 30, 33
World War II, 2, 19, 25, 26, 32, 35, 38, 40, 42, 65, 69, 78, 86, 93, 106

X tax, 130

Yankelovich, Daniel, 91
Young, Don, 110

About the Author

Andrew L. Yarrow is a writer, historian, and longtime journalist. He is vice president and Washington director of Public Agenda, teaches U.S. history at American University, and is a consultant to several organizations. A former reporter for the *New York Times,* Dr. Yarrow has published extensively during the past twenty-five years. He is completing his next book, on the rise of modern America as an "economy."